IT IS WHAT IT IS

Grace through Acceptance

IT IS WHAT IT IS

Thomas W E Budge

Published by
Namasté Trust
Johannesburg, South Africa

IT IS WHAT IT IS

Published by: Namasté Trust

Postal Address: Box 72229, Parkview, 2122, South Africa

Website: www.iiwii.co.za

Email address: info@iiwii.co.za

First published 2013

ISBN: 978-0-620-55500-5 – eBook
ISBN: 978-0-620-55501-2 – Print

Editor: Dr. Peter Merrington, affiliated professor extraordinaire in the English Department, University of the Western Cape

Cover design by: Turnbuckle (Pty) Ltd, Box 412485, Craighall, South Africa, 2024

Cover photographs: David Ross, http://www.davidross.co.za/

This book is dedicated to **Ram Dass**
my spiritual teacher and mentor.

It was written for Justin Lovell, my nephew,
to fulfil a promise I once made to him.

Acknowledgements

Many people deserve and have my appreciation for their aid in making this book possible. A large group of people provided direct and tangential suggestions. Ram Dass inspired me greatly. Maharaj-ji, Neem Karoli Baba, via his portrait hanging on Ram Dass's wall, encouraged the writing of this book. My late father's meticulous record keeping allowed me to create a precise timeline of historic events. Yvonne's patience and prompting pushed me through my times of inner darkness and self-doubt when I had to face the monsters of my past. I also thank my editor, Dr Peter Merrington, for his coaching and mentorship. His efforts and suggestions transformed a manuscript of ideas into a story I'm proud to tell. I'm also thankful for the collaboration of two friends, Martin Meerholz and David Ross, whose extraordinary artistic talents created the cover that wraps this book. Lastly, my thanks to Pamela Quin, former headmistress of Parktown Girls High, for proofreading this text.

Table of Contents

Foreword

This is a story of a very ordinary person who had a few unique experiences. Anyone could have made the choices I did, which have culminated in a wonderful life of grace. What happened to me could happen to you too. I share my story optimistically that it might inspire you, but I wish for more: I'm hoping that you're encouraged to make braver and better choices, to pave the way to a better and more meaningful life. You don't have to be special in the eyes of the world to benefit richly from life; that would make it exclusive and only for the elite. We're all special and I hope to show you a way to a rich and fulfilled life no matter who you are. *A Course in Miracles* says '[Seek] not to change the world, but choose to change your mind about the world.' It continues: 'What you see reflects your thinking. And your thinking but reflects your choice of what you want to see.'

My story is about change. Change that brings release and healing is indeed miraculous. Part of my story is about injustice, the ways in which the state, society, and creed systems often suppress the life of individuals like you and me. But, through and out of this, I also speak of the release and deeper transformation that comes from wise and courageous choices – aided by the friends and mentors that led me, in my own life, along that path.

In retrospect my story seems outrageous. I wonder at how things came to pass, and how as a young man of eighteen I found the resources to make a stand. With regard to the first chapter in particular, there are grave implications, social, spiritual, and legal – and I have chosen to document my narrative with detailed evidence from that past. 'If way to the Better there be, it exacts a full look at the Worst,' wrote the poet Thomas Hardy. This, at times, requires substantiation and the reader may wish to follow up the references in my footnotes, or not. I present them as a reminder of how serious, how very real, these things were – how at the time it was important that we should have kept a close and written record of events. Now, looking back, I write for the present and the times to come, taking hold of new truths, and the joy of release.

The Army

One of my most profound but difficult experiences is a saga that I buried deep inside and shared with very few. It unfolded when I was eighteen. Decades have passed, during which I held back from disclosure. The passage of time allows me to describe personalities and situations that, in past years, required discretion, although the retelling has opened up deep emotions of my own. Among other things the saga led to my rejecting an influential organisation, and this choice had many implications for myself, my family, and others. Writing now about that season in my life is painful, but it is also a cathartic and therapeutic action.

This book is about the path towards liberty and personal enlightenment, and I begin, in the first part, with South Africa and its history of the exact opposite – social injustice, oppression, prejudice: and in my case as a white South African, the truth that prejudice damages the oppressors as well as the oppressed.

In the early 1990s, as the old apartheid regime cracked and crumbled, there was uncertainty in the hearts of many white South Africans. Nelson Mandela's release was an opening up of long-suppressed collective emotion. Many whites along with the black majority rejoiced. But the rise to power of the African National Congress also led to an exodus, called the 'brain drain' or (more bluntly) the 'chicken run'. Those who feared social change and had the necessary resources packed and emigrated to Australia, New Zealand, Britain and Canada. Every conversation revolved around change, and the celebration or fear of change.

In conservative quarters there were even predictions of civil war and the mass slaughter of whites. The Afrikaans Voortrekker narrative of bloody conflict between white settlers and black frontier tribes was retold in a new context, with a mindset that relived the history of the battle of Blood River.

This battle, a foundational event in white Afrikaner history, held iconic status within the apartheid regime's identity and propaganda. On 16 December 1838 on the banks of the Ncome River in the old colony of Natal the Voortrekkers, led by Andries Pretorius, massacred three thousand Zulus. This was to avenge the murder of their leader Piet Retief and his men. God, proclaimed the Voortrekkers, gave them the victory in a covenant of protection for his people. It stood, writ large, as a formula for the sanctioning of armed conflict through faith and group identity. Would this pattern be renewed? Such was the dire mindset that had been instilled into a racially programmed and aggressive apartheid society for whom even the Christian faith was entangled in questions of national identity and survival.

If the imagining of civil war didn't strike fear in the hearts of many whites, the idea of redistribution of wealth did. Many feared that the ANC government would legitimise the plundering of white minority wealth (amassed through generations of economic privilege) and distribute it to the impoverished. Fear was tangibly present within many – fear of reprisal, fear of change and loss.

Born years earlier into the abnormality of apartheid society I balked, growing up, at the injustice of racial segregation; and yet I'm ashamed that I did nothing about it. I wonder with sadness at how good men fail to stand up for their beliefs and speak out boldly. Nazi Germany is a clear example: intelligent, moral men and women stifled their conscience, allowed Hitler's rise to power, and ignored the subsequent atrocities. For many of us in South Africa it was similar. I don't know why I remained silent. I was young. Maybe I was timid. Maybe I knew they wouldn't listen. A conservative Christian upbringing taught me to accept authority, to observe a demure detachment from the ways of the world, to seek solace in the future hope of a kingdom yet to come. I don't think I ever lacked the courage to speak out, but where would one begin?

Perhaps, moreover, I was silent because South Africa had marginalised and persecuted me too, not for racial reasons but because in various ways I had grown up as part of an outcast minority. A sexually bigoted Calvinistic world discriminated against me as a gay man; mainstream Christian society distrusted me as a Jehovah's Witness; and, whenever I was abroad, people condemned white South Africans because of the country's separate development policies. I come from Scottish roots, and as a teenager I disliked my ginger hair, freckles and almost translucent white skin, which also set me apart from others; and I found various coping mechanisms (mainly withdrawal) to carry me.

Forty years ago, around the time of my matriculation in 1970, the South African Defence Force conscripted every *white* male into the army after he left school. Many fought in the South African border war or bush war, which developed into full scale conflict in Angola where many died fighting what the Nationalist regime described as *die Swart Gevaar* [the Black Peril]. Others, including Jehovah's Witnesses, opposed conscription, objecting to warfare and refusing military duties due to personal conscience. Despite my deep conflict with the Jehovah's Witnesses' teachings and their dogmatic rejection of homosexuality, I nevertheless believed in their creed of non-violent pacifism and I refused to go to war. I've repeatedly asked myself whether I would have done military training had I not, at the time, been associated with the Witnesses; and I believe that my personal conscience would, on the grounds of secular pacifism, have led to the same decision.

I know now that warfare is the futile and destructive way of a collective ego trying to defend the indefensible. National boundaries are invented or imaginary lines of separation. Migratory animals have no concept of our political structures that create false economic and social enclaves in which the impoverished are trapped and the greedy profit. But as a schoolboy born into the heavily indoctrinated white society of apartheid South Africa, and given my family's membership of the Witnesses, I had to make complex decisions that were influenced as much by family values as by my youthful instinct. Given these contrary demands, I am proud that I chose as I did. However, the consequences, as you shall see, were dire.

November is an interesting month in Johannesburg and Pretoria. These cities, although some sixty kilometres apart, are like slowly merging amoebae, their pseudopodia entangling into a continuous urban sprawl. At an altitude of some 5000 feet [approximately 1500 meters] above sea level this conurbation lies in the country's summer rainfall region. November marks the start of the Highveld thunderstorms, violent, magnificent outbursts of nature's might that leave ozone freshness in stark contrast to the dry and cold winter. Thunderstorms occur almost every afternoon between four and six o'clock, washing away streams of lilac jacaranda flowers that carpet the city pavements. November, springtime in the southern hemisphere, also marks the start of year-end exams.

One evening in November 1968 I was in my room studying for a Standard 8 (Grade 10) exam when my father showed me a newspaper cutting. 'What,' he asked, 'are we going to do about this?' It was a notice placed by the South African Defence Force.[1] I was expected, as a white male, to register at the age of sixteen for a year's national service in the military. This call-up would begin immediately on my leaving high school two years later. National service was

---

[1] 'Persons who are compelled to apply for registration', newspaper (source unknown) [#1].

restricted to white South African males – the military was an intimate part of the apartheid regime.

'I'm not going to the army,' I replied, 'if that's what this means.'

But I hid my anxiety and it grew and gnawed at me, interrupting my thoughts and dreams. I had nightmares of war – bombs, men blown apart, corpses and death – lots of death. My father, as an eighteen-year-old volunteer, had served with the South African forces in North Africa and Italy during the Second World War. He spoke little about it and the only traces of him having been there were his army beret, a cigarette tin of medals, and a single brass button cut from a naval jacket.

January and February 1969 came and went. I turned sixteen and I refused to register, notifying the army by letter of my decision.[2] They wrote back: 'a person who refuses or fails to apply for registration for national service, shall be guilty of an offence.'[3] I ignored this. Then came a summons to appear before a court, in July, in the middle of mid-year preparatory matric exams.[4]

The presiding officer of the court had what seemed to be a compelling argument:

'All that I require is registration. I'm not requesting you to report for duty. I'm only asking you to comply with the law, and register. Registration couldn't possibly offend your conscience, so wouldn't it be reasonable for you, as a law-abiding citizen, to fill in the form?'

I looked at my parents, seeking their guidance, but they did as the Witnesses instructed and left the decision entirely up to me. I chose to register.[5]

The Witnesses had a strange way of dealing with us. I felt that they gained a lot of publicity from our stand against the government, and yet they did little to assist us in any material, legal or emotional sense. A reporter from a Johannesburg daily, the *Star*, interviewed a spokesman for the sect at its Elandsfontein headquarters:

---

[2] My letter to the South African Defence Force, 16 February 1969 [#5].
[3] South African Defence Force letter of reply, 10 March 1969 [#6].
[4] Summons D19382, 4 July 1969 [#7].
[5] Acknowledgement of Receipt of Registration, 22 July 1969 [#8].

'Obviously, not all Jehovah's Witnesses refuse service. Does any opprobrium attach to them, within the organisation, if they serve?'

The answer was bland and unhelpful:

'They cannot serve [as national servicemen] and remain Witnesses. If they decide to serve, it means that they have voluntarily withdrawn from the organisation. It is a wholly personal decision.'[6]

At sixteen I needed affirmation that I was doing the right thing, but nobody sat with me and helped. In hindsight, it's evident that the Witnesses protected themselves by not telling us outright to refuse military service. There would have been legal repercussions if they were seen to influence us directly. That's probably why they sidestepped the issue, declaring that it was 'wholly a personal decision'. And yet we all knew what was expected of us within the organisation and we felt compelled to obey their rulings.

In the same article, the organisation claimed that they 'do not disfellowship people [Witness jargon for excommunication] for joining the army'. However, we knew full well that a coercive *voluntary withdrawal* and *excommunication* were the same thing regardless of the evasive phrasing. Within close-knit Witness families the implications of this dilemma were severe: obey the state and be disfellowshipped obey the organisation and go to prison. Loss of membership had extreme consequences within the totalising universe of the Jehovah's Witnesses. Families could be forced apart. Those parents who had the resources escaped the problem by sending their sons abroad to study or live with relatives.

In June 1970, at the height of the Vietnam War, it was announced that the United States Supreme Court had resolved to exempt from military service 'all young men who have strong moral or ethical objections to military duty – so long as their beliefs are deeply held and are not based on expediency.'[7] This gave rise to hope that South Africa might follow suit and that I might escape conscription but, by February 1971, at least fifty young Jehovah's Witnesses had lost their liberty for refusing national service. The military incarcerated them in their Pretoria detention barracks and my fate seemed sealed.[8]

[6] 'Case against serving in the army', Jean Le May, the *Star*, Johannesburg, 6 November 1971 [#15].
[7] 'Religion not needed now to escape the draft', the *Star*, Johannesburg, 16 June 1970 [#10].
[8] '50 Witnesses in jail in deadlock over conscience', *Sunday Times*, 7 February 1971 [#11].

Army propaganda sought to turn white youths into national heroes. Under the heading 'Why is National Service Necessary?' an army guide for young national servicemen avowed that it was 'the indisputable privilege and duty of every citizen to be available and able to defend his country in time of need'.[9] National service, it claimed, was an opportunity 'to make that sacrifice which constitutes such an essential element of the concept "LOVE" – love of that which is our own, love of the fatherland, love of peace, love of freedom'.

What the propaganda did not say is that this kind of 'love for the fatherland' fostered racial hatred and instilled prejudice and fear. Instead of promoting unity, peace and freedom, it resulted in a paranoid and suspicious nation. The brochure added that national service was 'an opportunity [for the serviceman] to be spiritually, physically and militarily formed and polished at that stage of his life where he can derive the maximum benefit under the beneficial influence of military training'. It was laid on thick: 'an opportunity to praise his Creator in full awareness of his virile youth, by attending divine services and other religious gatherings with his comrades'. State-affiliated churches had enormous influence over all aspects of white South African society, and the Government exploited this in order to reconcile matters of law and conscience.

The same publication quoted from a radio interview with the Commandant General of the South African Defence Force:

> In my view [the national service system] has to be regarded to an important extent as a positive educational process in citizenship. In many different ways, most of these subconsciously, the young national serviceman is instilled with pride in himself as citizen of the country, a pride in his Defence Force as instrument for maintaining his nationhood and a pride in and love for his country which can be created in no other way. Our aim is to hand back to the nation a young citizen who is more mature and more positively formed, possessing skills and know-how he did not previously possess.

Did he not mean brainwashing?

---

[9] Form DD1806E, 'A Guide for National Servicemen who are required to commence National Service during 1973' [#95].

Many white South Africans, particularly the Afrikaners, were deeply patriotic to South Africa under the apartheid regime; but it was a feeling I cannot say I shared. Like many other English-speaking South Africans I felt an affinity with a global Englishness and with Britain under whom South Africa was once a dominion, rather than to a highly partisan and nationalistic Afrikaans government. Even now, under a new democracy, I still don't feel entirely secure as a white person under ANC rule because there's a subtext of reverse racism, commonly seeing us as a colonially invasive species. And yet none of this bothers me at root because I view myself as a temporary resident or citizen of a far wider world and I have no urge to display national affiliation or fervour. Back then, as a young adult, it was a matter that I could not so easily dismiss.

Refusal to perform national service was more than a refusal to fight. It was defiance at a fundamental level and it verged on treason. Blunt challenges were thrown at me: 'Why should I fight for your safety?' and 'If some black *kaffir* [the ugly racial slur] came into your house and raped your wife and daughter, would you do nothing?' Someone, quoted in a newspaper article, said 'They're yellow, the lot of them. They're just trying to get out of their military service. My son is doing his – why shouldn't they? They should be locked up for keeps, if necessary.'[10]

Emotions ran high, and Colin Eglin, the parliamentary Leader of the Opposition (the Progressive Party), warned that South African society was developing a 'war psychosis'.[11]

The political scientist Margaret Levi writes as follows on the topic of conscientious objection:

> Conscientious objection is a weapon of protest. It is not, however, a collective protest. It is an individual, but socially informed, act of resistance. It requires no organisation, no mobilisation of others, no group process. It is an action undertaken by single individuals albeit, generally, individuals who are part of self-conscious groups of war protesters.[12]

This description indicates the difficulties that I incurred. The liberal principle of personal conscience effectively meant a lone stand against an illiberal regime and partisan collective

---

[10] 'Case against serving in the army', the *Star*, Johannesburg, 6 November 1971 [#15].
[11] *Rand Daily Mail*, 16 August 1974 [#90].
[12] *Consent, Dissent, and Patriotism*, M. Levi, Cambridge University Press, 1997, p.165.

sentiment. Other than such cautions as were raised by the parliamentary opposition, there were no organised 'groups of war protesters'. What was lacking in South Africa back then was a clear common lobby against conscription, with legal counsel, resources, and a shared strategy, such as the End Conscription Campaign of the 1980s.

By August 1970, the army knew me by Force Number 69546711. I was duly issued with call-up papers and expected to report for duty when ordered.

On the fateful date, in the morning of 6 July 1971, I failed to show up. Eight o'clock at the Milner Park Show Grounds in Johannesburg, and I was absent. National service intake was a common sight in those days when young white men from all over South Africa gathered at urban centres. The army transported them to basic training camps across the country, by troop train and in convoys of brown Bedford trucks. Radio adverts persuaded civilians to give lifts to soldiers who stood in uniform at demarcated stops along major routes. Such was the national mindset, gauged at broad mobilisation in the cause of the white regime, against which I made my gesture of defiance.

There'd be no sympathy with my objection to national service. The military were known to take quick and decisive action against dissident behaviour.

The weeks that followed the July intake were strange and stressful. I lived in suspense: the military police might call at any time to arrest me. I couldn't plan ahead. I came to feel immense gratitude for every moment of freedom and comfort. The simplest activity seemed precious, and I indulged it fully. I didn't know about the concept of living in the Now, but circumstances gave me an instinctive sense of this.

You might know of the spiritual exercise in which you contemplate the possibility that death might come this very day. As morbid as it seems, the meditation helps to focus the mind and separate the essential from the inessential. If I knew that I would die before midnight (and let's face it, I could – for any number of accidental reasons), I'd certainly change my priorities and drop everything of no real consequence. Living according to this teaching, changes the old proverb: 'Never put off until tomorrow what you can do today.' My preferred version is, 'Never do today what you could possibly put off until tomorrow.' I live by the latter version of this adage because it has a nice way of self-prioritising events of the day. Vitally important tasks fall easily into the capacity of the day. I don't obsess about those that are postponed. It creates pockets of time for pleasurable things like 'smelling the roses' instead of frenetically pursuing life as though time was running out.

During this period of limbo, waiting for the military police, each day stood out separate from the next. I did only what seemed important. Eating every meal as though it were my last, sleeping in a comfortable bed, were certainly precious – but not as precious as relationships. Being with those I loved became my top priority. I felt as though I was about to lose them, for a time or for ever.

I remained certain that I was correct, was doing the right thing. Despite the daily anticipation of arrest I kept my focus and, in that, there was a kind of peace. It might have been said that I was in a state of mild shock and denial, but nothing could have persuaded me to change my mind – not even the threat of life in jail, or death. The *Sunday Times* reported that 'in theory [imprisonment] could continue for the rest of their lives, or at least until they are 65 and beyond the age of military service.'[13] I clung to my belief in what I'd resolved.

Most young men of eighteen were dreaming of independence, university and a career, after their army training, but I had no such long-term future. Looking back now, I realise that I'd come to let go. I jettisoned a huge layer of self-projection that is largely based on anxiety and social convention. Worry is an unhelpful state in which a person, concerned with future events, overestimates or exaggerates their possible outcomes. Where others found refuge in the conventional dreams of material acquisition, houses, cars, families, I had to realise that my future was totally unknown. I acquired skills to embrace uncertainty, living only for today, a technique that dissipated most of the socially-constructed desires by which our fear-based or anxiety-driven identities are governed.

The military police duly arrived. I was ordered to present myself in the early morning of Thursday 28 October 1971, in front of one Magistrate Strydom. I dressed in my suit, a white shirt and carefully knotted tie, and my best shoes. My parents went with me to Pretoria. We had breakfast together at a café across the road and then took our seats in the public gallery of Courtroom F. I was nervous. I sat on the edge of the wooden bench looking at the ground, rehearsing my defence. I put on an air of strength but I felt numb with the sense that I would soon enter prison for an undetermined period. Months, years, or even decades.

---

[13] Sampie Nel, quoted in '50 Witnesses in jail in deadlock over conscience', *Sunday Times*, 7 February 1971 [#11].

We had to sit through other cases before they asked me to take the stand. They called my name. My heart raced and my mouth went dry. I stood up and squeezed my mother's hand as she whispered her encouragement, but I was too nervous to hear what she said. My father seldom showed his feelings but his eyes were pools of sadness, and I knew he would readily have swapped places with me. We were united and consoled in our belief that we were doing God's will and had his blessing. And yet I'm sure the magistrate thought that God was equally on his side –about to favour his own efforts in protecting the fatherland from dissidence.

I entered the wooden dock, stood erect while the orderly adjusted the microphone, then swore the oath ('nothing but the truth') with my hand on the Bible, balking at the irony: a coercive means of insisting on courtroom truths. Way beyond that moment I had always upheld the Bible's principles. Love and compassion for others prevented me from doing harm; and yet the authorities ordained a racially motivated bush war on the Angolan border, using the same Bible to justify it. I still can't understand how people can be in such conflict over one set of scriptures, and how they interpret them so differently. It seems absurd.

The magistrate spoke in Afrikaans. It was a compulsory language taught to us at school, and I could have answered him in Afrikaans, but I chose to ask for an interpreter. I'm sure he could have spoken English too, but racial hatred was only one of South Africa's many problems during those apartheid times. I'm sure he had no great pity for the young *rooinek* [redneck, an Afrikaans term for the English] who defied government ordinances and refused to fight for the fatherland. Unpleasant cultural rivalry abounded. Afrikaners and English generally distrusted each other; we went to separate schools; and for the most part we lived separately. Where, for example, the suburbs of Johannesburg were predominantly English-speaking, Pretoria was mainly an Afrikaans domain.

The government believed it had to act decisively to stem the growing wave of conscientious objectors and my father's lawyer warned us that the magistrate could take a tough stance, placing us in military custody instead of civilian jail, since martial law allowed harsher punishment. In military detention, the army might try us for desertion or even treason. Nelson Mandela and his comrades had received life sentences for their acts of treason against the state. The *Star* reported that 'PW Botha, Minister of Defence, said in Natal that he was 'losing his patience' [...] and was considering asking for legislation to increase the penalties for refusing military service'.[14] Government had no sympathy with us.

As a family, we agreed beforehand that legal counsel was pointless because I argued a moral and spiritual principle and had no chance of defending myself against the law. I knew I stood no hope of winning, but when the moment came for me to speak in my own defence I presented my case with confidence and clarity. I read to the court a lengthy essay explaining my beliefs and the reasons for refusing to fight. The magistrate, fussing with papers on his desk, listened half-heartedly to the interpreter's rendition while the court stenographer recorded both versions.

I completed my argument. Then the public prosecutor summed up his case for the state and pointed out that I had not presented any evidence in law. He asked the magistrate to find me guilty and to sentence me with the harshest penalty. The verdict came:

'Guilty as charged.'

In Afrikaans, with scarcely a pause, the magistrate passed judgment, and I knew what he'd said long before the interpreter echoed it to me in English. The magistrate spoke again:

'I sentence you to ninety days in military custody.'

He wrapped up the case, struck his gavel, and ordered a court official to escort me to the holding cells below.

I had barely enough time to nod a tearful goodbye to my parents before I was jostled down the steep flight of stairs into the basement below.

The magistrate later commented that 'the men [fourteen of us whom he sentenced that week] showed no remorse for their deeds and had an appalling disregard for the country's laws'; but I'm certain he slept well, believing he had done his best to protect the beloved country from young men who held the system in such contempt.[15]

---

[14] 'Case against serving in the army', the *Star*, Johannesburg, 6 November 1971 [#15].
[15] 'Witnesses won't fight, but they can work', the *Star*, Johannesburg, 18 November 1971 [#19].

There was a striking contrast between the courtroom and the holding cells. The wood panelling ended abruptly inside the stairwell. Dingy grey walls led down a narrow flight of stairs to a steel gate that separated the cells from the courtroom above. They bundled me into a cell with flaking paint and the stench of urine, stale sweat and alcohol. Here I waited for the court to complete its paperwork and place me into the army's custody.

An elderly MP (a military policeman) led me – with an unexpected air of sympathy – to the parking area at the back of the courtroom. I caught a last glimpse of my parents at the gate and waved to them as he showed me into the back of his van. The door clanged and he drove across the city to the detention barracks[16] at Voortrekkerhoogte. This, the headquarters of the South African Army, is a vast military base close to the Voortrekker Monument west of Pretoria.

The van drove along a tidy gravel road past neat redbrick houses. Then came a high corrugated iron fence. A new universe; and all my senses were alert, recording every detail as if on film. I guessed that this fence was the prison's outer perimeter – there were loops of barbed wire spanning the reinforced corrugation. The van rounded a small island of aloes and pulled up alongside the iron fence, at the main entrance to the barracks.

The MP unlocked my door and told me to wait. The afternoon sun was warm and disarming, and he knew that I posed no threat. Carrying a manila file, he rang the bell outside the main gate in the fence. The bell jangled, there was a rattling of keys, warders opened up and my escort disappeared inside.

These detention barracks occupied a portion of land some two hundred metres wide by about one hundred deep. The front section of the great iron perimeter fence had three entrances: two on either side for vehicles, and the main pedestrian gate. The fence was high enough to obscure all interior buildings and dampen sounds, giving the place an air of mystery.

My MP and two other soldiers emerged. The MP regarded me with a look of concern, shook my hand, wished me luck and handed over custody. With a clank a young guard closed and locked the heavy door behind us, effectively sealing my fate and banishing me from the outside world for a long, long time to come. I was still too numb to react other than to register

---

[16] S25°47'44.99", E28° 8'2.57" – *Google Earth* keeps historical images as far back as 17 July 2001, showing the buildings before the Defence Force demolished them around 2003-4.

every unfamiliar and life-changing detail. I did what they asked with suspicion and caution. A bizarre rite of passage into adulthood; initiation by means of unknown trials.

'Sit and wait,' said one of the two soldiers, pointing to a wooden bench against the wall.

I obeyed. My best shoes were dusty and I tried to wipe them, but the static drew the dust straight back. I unbuttoned my jacket and straightened my tie, brushed aside the fringe of my schoolboy haircut. I riffled through my Bible and glanced at my defence speech which I'd folded and tucked into the book's cover. I was nervous but I tried to hide it. I felt overwhelmed, abandoned, small, but I suppressed the tears and grasped at small familiar things. I didn't realise how reliant I had been on my parents. This was, in fact, the first time I had been away from home without them. Despite these feelings, I should add that I was fortified by a well-rehearsed defiance, a youthful streak of rebellion, and part of me was ready to take on the challenge.

Built during the Second World War, the meticulously-kept redbrick detention barracks, capped with rust-red corrugated iron roofing, were a good example of British colonial architecture. The open-sided lobby where I sat formed part of a narrow L-shaped administration block. The long part of the 'L' ran parallel with the front perimeter fence while the short part protruded back into the barracks precinct. All rooms and offices opened to the inside, onto a broad highly polished cement *stoep* or veranda that ran the length of the wide overhanging eaves. Several wooden benches against the walls along the *stoep* offered seating out of the harsh sun. Each office had wide cottage-pane windows back and front, and the architectural character was more like an old African colonial homestead than a prison.

The lobby formed an open corridor between adjacent offices under the continuous roof of this deceptively agreeable administration block. The room on my right was the doctor's surgery and on my left was reception. A footpath inside the perimeter fence, along which guards made regular patrols, surrounded the entire precinct.

Coming through the main gate and crossing the open lobby and veranda, a short flight of steps then led down to a long narrow concrete quadrangle. The administration block bounded the front and left sides of the quadrangle and a building about eighty metres in length, running almost from front to back of the property, enclosed it on the right. I could see, at the far end of the quadrangle, the tall corrugated iron fence with its barbed wire, enclosing the back of the complex.

The long redbrick building to the right of the quadrangle had no significant features other than a row of small windows some two metres from the ground, hinged at the top. Vertical steel bars secured the windows, and the block-like building had no visible roof so I imagined that to prevent escape it was capped by a solid concrete slab. It was obviously a cellblock and I stared at it obsessively, guessing that somewhere, behind one of those high small windows, there'd be a cell that would be my home for the next ninety days.

Large trees shaded the far side of the quadrangle but the cellblock took the full brunt of the hot afternoon sun. There wasn't a leaf out of place within the precinct. In retrospect, a strange affinity: the neatness, the orderly precision, appealed to my fastidious Aquarian traits, my instinct for straight edges and the rationalism of geometry. Perhaps this instinct for clear-cut form is what, in the first instance, drove me in my refusal to compromise with the state?

Sitting as instructed I watched people go about briskly, with purpose. This was no place for slouches. The orderly at reception fussed in the back where I could see rows of wooden shelves stacked high with brown leather boots, clothing, helmets, towels and buckets. He sized me up as he assembled my kit on a wooden counter. I watched him tick off items on his inventory. A pair of socks, a khaki overall, a pair of brown Y-front briefs, a brown singlet vest, a brown tee shirt, a pair of black rugby shorts, one green plastic combat inner-helmet, two grey cotton-waste blankets, a brown towel, a white enamel bucket, a roll of toilet paper, a toothbrush and some toothpaste. Then he called me up to the counter and spoke:

'Take off your clothes. Place them in this carton and put on your kit.'

Others had forewarned me about dressing in army issue. This was a tactic, the thin edge of the wedge, and if I complied with that first instruction there'd be no end to their requests until they finally converted me into a soldier. The courts had sentenced me for not wanting to become a soldier, and I wasn't about to capitulate at the outset. A line had to be drawn, and I drew it.

'No,' I said. I found myself, vulnerable as I was, speaking boldly. Clarity of purpose, clarity of reasoning was all that I had left. 'The magistrate sent me here,' I said, 'because I refuse national service. I won't put on this uniform. It's the first step towards becoming a soldier.'

He seemed used to this. He tried to persuade me, but he'd heard it so many times before (I suspected) that his reply was routine:

'It's captain's orders. All prisoners have to wear uniform.'

'I'm not afraid of the captain. I won't obey his orders if they conflict with my conscience.'

'In any case you've got to get undressed because I can't let you in wearing civvies.'

'Where shall I do that?' I asked. I looked around for a changing booth or a toilet.

'What's *fokken* wrong with you? Just get undressed and put your things in the box.'

'Here, in reception?'

'Yes, idiot! "Here, in reception",' he mimicked me.

A first lesson in military life: no genteel manners and no privacy. I was always shy to undress in public. School gymnastics and swimming practice freaked me out because we had to undress together. I was embarrassed, in full view outside reception, but I stripped down to my underpants, folded my clothes and put them with my shoes into the carton.

'What's that book?' he asked.

'My Bible.'

'Put it in the box and take off everything.'

'My underpants too?'

'Yes, idiot! Your underpants.'

'But...'

'Just do it!'

I thought of the towel, but it was only a hand towel and wouldn't go around my body.

While I stood naked he made a comprehensive list of all my personal belongings. I shivered, although the day was warm.

'Bring your things and follow me,' he said.

I shoved most of the stuff in the white bucket, put some clothing into the upturned green plastic combat helmet, and carried it in front to preserve my dignity.

We didn't go more than a few paces to the doctor's consulting room that led off the lobby. The doctor had to check my fitness. He asked a barrage of questions and examined me from head to toe before scribbling his findings on a form. He concluded that there were no medical grounds to prevent my imprisonment. I was declared fit enough to serve my term.

'Come!' snapped the orderly again, leading me farther down the *stoep*. My bare feet squeaked on the cool polished cement as I nervously followed him.

There turned out to be three more enormous cellblocks lying parallel to the first. Covered walkways connected the first three to the *stoep*; the last one stood separate. Each block had a heavy steel door fitted with a large lever lock. Stretches of well-kept green lawn and simple flowerbeds of yellow marigolds separated them.

We entered a small barber's shop, sparsely furnished with an upright chair and a tiny table. On the table were an electric clipper, a bottle of Singer sewing machine oil, and a glass jar of blue sterilising water with a metal comb.

'Put down your stuff and sit,' said the barber.

He gestured at the chair and flicked the clipper into life, filling the room with its buzz. I sat butt-naked on his chair. I had no shoes to dust, no tie to straighten. I flicked back the hair from my eyes. Five seconds later and my fringe lay limply in my lap; and during the next minute or two my ginger hair rolled from my head in teased-out bundles that fell softly to rest on my shoulders.

'Get your things and come with me.'

I stood and ran my hands across my shaven head, feeling the strange brush of whiskers under my palms as I flicked away the loose hair. Thus far everything had been invasive. I felt intimately abused as their casual eyes scanned my body in ways that straight blokes do in changing rooms. I picked up the bucket and helmet and backtracked behind the orderly, along the *stoep*, to the entrance to Cellblock 1.

He inserted the key and pushed the heavy lever over, swinging the reluctant vault-like door outwards on its heavy hinges. He gestured that I should go inside ahead of him and locked the door behind us.

The cellblock interior wasn't nearly as dingy as I had imagined. Two rows of thirty-six cells on each side, facing onto a long central passageway about five metres in width and some eighty metres long. The passageway was surfaced with highly polished concrete slabs interrupted by a central furrow that ran down the building's length.

The interior walls were of the same redbrick as all the other buildings. Inwardly sloping corrugated iron roof sheets covered the rows of cells on both sides but they did not meet in the middle, leaving a gap to let in sunlight and fresh air. Rainwater flowed into gutters on both sides of the gap and from there into galvanised downpipes that marked off the cells into groups of six. There were identical doors at both ends of the block and next to each was a shiny brass water tap above a cement drain.

The great cellblock was silent. All the cells were open; there was nobody about. Looking in, I saw that each cell had a mattress on the floor on which was displayed the inmate's possessions. We walked halfway down to a vacant cell on the left.

'Here!' snapped the orderly in his economic way. 'Put your stuff down and bring the bucket and toilet paper.'

I followed him towards the door at the far end of the block.

'Leave the bucket there,' he instructed, pointing to the brass tap next to the door.

The perimeter fence at the far end was spanned by ablution blocks. A number of prisoners in khaki overalls tended the gardens there and they looked at me curiously as I followed, stark naked, behind the orderly.

'Shit, piss and shower,' he said bluntly, pointing to an exposed row of some twenty stainless steel toilets spaced along the back wall. Each had its wooden seat bolted to the rim and they were flushed by pulling on a wire chain attached to a cast iron cistern high up on the wall. The toilets faced a row of showerheads. Privacy was non-existent.

'You won't get another chance until tomorrow,' warned the orderly, noticing my hesitation.

I hadn't been to the loo all day and needed it badly but it was nearly impossible while he stood guard. Deeply embarrassed, I managed; and then took a cold shower and, using my hands to squeeze off the excess water as I'd left the towel in the cell, I let the hot air dry me and imagined how it would be when I had to do this in the middle of winter.

We returned to the block, where I filled the white bucket with clean water and took it back to my cell. It must have been after three o'clock by the time he swung the door closed, sealing my fate.

Cells were approximately one-and-a-half by two metres [five by seven feet]. A cheap foam mattress in an off-white canvas cover lay on the cement floor. It smelt stale. An empty galvanised latrine bucket without a cover stood in the corner.

I unfolded the blankets, laid them on the mattress and stacked the uniform in the far corner. The window I'd seen from outside was too high to look through but if I jumped up, grabbing the bars for support, I could peek outside. The window faced into the concrete quadrangle and if I pushed up against the bars I could just glimpse the main gate. The cell was relatively clean and the raw bricks were painted grey.

I turned and examined the door. It was clad in a sheet of thick steel and slightly recessed to make it flush with the wall. A covered peephole in the centre of the door funnelled inwards and a metal flap stopped me from looking through it. An open space above the door, secured with a grille of solid bars and steel mesh, provided ventilation. I hauled myself up by those bars but I couldn't hold my weight for long and dropped back to the floor to rest. I tried again. Again and again, obsessively, until I gave up and lay on the mattress, emotionally and physically exhausted. I lay there for some time, not knowing what else to do or to expect.

How, without a pen or calendar, was I going to remember the passing of the days? I thought of the time-honoured prisoner's method of counting the days in bundles of five – scratching four vertical lines on the wall to represent the first four days with the fifth scored horizontally through the others. Ninety days, that's eighteen bundles of five! At last I had something to do;

and I pondered it. How to mark off the bundles in my memory instead of scratching on the wall?

To succeed, I had to remember eighteen bundles. I tried grouping them into two lots of nine or three lots of six but I still didn't know how to find an easy way to keep mental track. Establishing six or nine loci on my body as a memory aid would help, as I could then associate each bundle with a different part of my anatomy.

I thought about it for a long time before I recalled a bit of childhood trivia that solved the puzzle:

'Did you know?' we challenged the adults: 'you've got nine holes in your body!'

They always pretended to be stupid: 'Never! I don't have nine holes in my body!'

'Oh yes you do! Two ears, two eyes, two nostrils, and a mouth!' we chirped, pointing at them in turn. 'That's seven!'

Then, convulsed, we demanded: 'Where are the other two?'

'Dunno...'

Giggling, we pointed below the belt, and squealed and ran away.

These nine loci could each host two bundles of five days. As my mind dwelt on the solution, it struck me just how long this sentence was. I held my head in my hands and sobbed as the tension of the long day ebbed. I later calculated that my release date would fall on my nineteenth birthday, 26 January 1972.

Around five o'clock the prisoners were marched into the concrete quadrangle for afternoon role call and inspection. Minutes later, they were hustled into the cellblock where they stripped, put on their black boxer shorts and disappeared outside again to wash their uniforms and shower. They moved in quick silence but, on their return and when the outer doors closed, whispered conversations rose across the block. I hauled myself up to look through the ventilation space above the door and was amazed to see that the others stayed locked in place hanging by their arms above their doors, whispering to one another.

'Hey, you're new here!' said a dark-haired soldier opposite me.

'I got in today.'

'How did *you* fuck up?'

'I refused to go to the army.'

'Oh, you're one of them. There's a lot of you guys in Block 2.'

'How do you stay up there so long? I can't do it.'

'Jump up and wedge your back against the wall and place your feet against the doorposts,' he explained.

It was easier than hoisting myself up but I tried a few times and still couldn't master it. Instead, I folded my blankets, placed them on top of the upturned latrine pail, and stood on that.

'I can't get it right.'

'You'll soon work it out,' he reassured me, and I did. An acquired technique. I had to pull myself up to the grille, put a foot on either side of the doorpost, and twist my body to the left to wedge my spine against the wall. I could then sit on my left heel and use the other to anchor myself on the opposite doorpost. It took weeks to develop the muscles to hold the position.

The other prisoners introduced themselves. Their sins were insubordination, absence without leave, disobedience.

'They send all the *moffies* [Afrikaans slang for gays] here too when they catch them,' said the dark-haired guy in a manner and tone that excluded him from those ranks.

'How many conscientious objectors are here?' I asked.

'Quite a lot,' he said. 'About fourteen came in just this week.'[17]

---

[17] 'Case against serving in the army', the *Star*, 6 November 1971 [#15].

The Army

'You say they're kept in Block 2, so why am I here?'

'You won't see them for a while. The captain doesn't want new prisoners bringing them outside news.'

'So what happens next? The rest of today? Tomorrow?' I asked, curious to know what lay in store. I got the full routine:

'We stop work and come back here at 16.50 for foot inspection, showering and washing clothes. Supper's at 17.40. Then we wash our dixies [steel serving trays] and come back to the cells by twenty-past. Lights-out at 20.30. Roll call on the parade ground every morning 4.45. Then we shower, clean the toilets, offices and corridors before breakfast. At 7.45 there's sick parade and time to prepare for inspection at 8.00.

'They inspect each cell and if it isn't perfect you *kak* off for the rest of the day. You can make personal requests during cell inspection but it's better to keep quiet. 8.15 is PT. 9.00, we drill on the parade ground. 10.00, we have tea for ten minutes then more drill until lunch at 12.30, and back to the parade ground until 14.00. We spend the rest of the afternoon gardening and suchlike. Same thing every day except for weekends which are free. On Sundays we go to the chapel next to the toilets and we're allowed visitors in the afternoon.'[18]

'I don't know how to prepare for Inspection,' I confided. The answer was a complex set of instructions regarding the layout of kit and how I had to dress. I wondered what would happen when they found me naked at inspection. What dire punishments lay in store?

At five-thirty a loud bell rang outside, close to my cell, and I jumped up to look through the back window. A group of prisoners carried large stainless steel bain-maries out of a Bedford truck to a concrete apron under a corrugated iron shelter where there were rows of steel trestle tables and benches. Within minutes, the outer cellblock doors were flung open and two prisoners ran down the rows of doors, unlatching them and yelling '*Tree aan!*' [fall in]. I opened my door and noticed that all the others were dressed in their black shorts and brown tee shirts and wearing their leather boots casually unlaced. Each man went out smartly and closed his door, standing to attention in front of it.

---

[18] Reconstructed from 'Rehabilitation is army detention centre's theme', *Sunday Express*, 16 April 1972 [#37].

What should I do? Stay inside or go out naked? I chose to stay.

They were marched out at the double for supper. I decided to forgo mine until I knew what was expected of me, but ten minutes later one of the prisoners brought me a steel plate of unappetising food and a mug of sickly tea, sweetened with condensed milk.

'Hey, thanks! Sorry you have to see me naked.'

'Ag no, it's *kief* [South African slang meaning wicked or cool]. Just watch out for the tea, man,' he added. 'They put in bluestone so that you won't get a hard-on.'

I never really knew whether the army added an anaphrodisiac to the tea, to subdue men's libido, or if it was only rumour; but I tried to drink as little of it as I could.

'Hey man, wash your dixie under the tap when you're finished, leave it at the door and I'll take it to the kitchen later.'

'Thanks,' I replied. 'That's good of you.'

The prisoners soon returned and the staff switched off the lights at eight-thirty, but the muffled conversations continued way into the night. I was too tired to join in so I wrapped a scratchy blanket around my bare body, covered the mattress with the other blanket, and slept.

--- oooOooo---

I awoke abruptly at quarter-to-five the following morning to the sound of doors opening and, for a moment, I had no idea where I was. The lights came on and two runners rapidly unlatched all the cell doors. A voice I hadn't heard before boomed from the end of the block:

'Goeie môre, Suid Afrika!' [Good morning South Africa].

The call, *'Vyf minute, mense!'* [Five minutes, people] caused a flurry of preparation as everyone dressed for morning roll call. The imprisoned soldiers emerged, leaving their cell doors open. Each stood slightly to the side, dressed in the same clothes they wore the evening before. Unnoticed, I peeped out through the grille above the door to see what was happening.

A corporal walked slowly, deliberately, down the row of cells on the opposite side going from one prisoner to the next. Each prisoner braced at attention as he came past. I dropped from the grille when he got near and, as I had done the previous evening, stood up against the back wall of the cell, my hands covering my groin. He looped around the far end and slowly approached from the left.

He flung my door open with force, ramming it up against the wall inside. In coarse Afrikaans, with violent oaths, he yelled at me to step outside - but I remained where I was, resolving in the heat of the moment that I wouldn't let this brute intimidate me.

He grabbed my neat pile of clothes from the corner and tossed them into the gully, boots and all. Out went the combat helmet which shot across the concrete slab, banging onto the opposite wall and scuttling to rest in front of my neighbour's feet. The corporal turned his attention to me and, grabbing my wrist and trying to wrench my hands apart, he hurled me outside.

Nobody flinched. Although they were defaulters, they were soldiers. They clearly understood the trouble that was brewing, but the tension was palpable.

'Get dressed!' he yelled.

'No.'

He backed me up against the wall and yelled at me at such close range that I felt the spray of saliva from his mouth. He pressed the flat of his hand against my chest, pinning me to the wall as he hurled unspeakable vulgarities at me.

I did nothing.

That infuriated him even more. After about fifteen minutes of trying to get me to dress, and failing, he stormed past the remaining cells and left via the door through which he'd entered.

Now I'd blown it. I'd dared to defy the system and its violent representative. I'd nailed my colours to the mast. My heart beat furiously and I could feel the pulse in my neck and in the blood vessels around my temples. They'd all seen me naked. I was now exposed in more ways than one. They'd witnessed my defiance. I'd stuck to my beliefs and I wasn't sure how those regular defaulters would respond; but my rebellion seemed to create a bond. They were impressed. They were gobsmacked. Was it reckless bravado? Was it real? The first shots had been fired in my pacifist struggle.

Someone yelled for the inmates to fall in outside and, once again, I chose to stay behind. In the quadrangle the orderlies called out names and each man answered and moved to the far side of the yard. I listened but they didn't call mine. The prisoners went for ablutions before breakfast and the same person again brought me my food.

The prisoners returned to their cells, changed into the khaki overalls they had washed the night before, and laid out their kit for morning inspection. I folded my belongings neatly and stacked them back in the corner.

Three shifts of barrack guards seemed to work eight-hour stretches and a new crew, probably having come on duty during breakfast, moved into the cellblock to conduct inspection. The Permanent Force lance corporal in charge was better-natured than the brute that opened up at daybreak. He was tall, well tanned and had a certain kindness in his eyes. He slowly pushed open my door with his baton and in a manner approaching politeness asked me to stand outside. It seemed a fair request and I complied.

'Don't you think you'd be more comfortable if you wore your tee shirt and shorts like the rest of the guys?'

'I prefer not to,' I replied. 'If I did, I wouldn't know where to draw the line. Forgive me if I have to set rules for myself.'

'Then put on just the shorts and leave off the tee shirt. That will separate you from the rest,' he suggested, seemingly genuine in his suggestion of a compromise.

'Not even that,' I said resolutely.

'Then bring your stuff after inspection and I will take you across to have a shower,' he said.

He commenced his inspection at Cell 1 without much fuss.

The two corporals were very different people, one decent and the other just plain brutish. What differentiates men like that? Fear, self-importance, hatred, and a sense of authority or ego? Why could they not all behave like reasonable men?

---oooOooo---

Military offenders served their time without seeking further trouble, by good drill and trained obedience, keeping below the radar to avoid further reprisal. But I stuck to my own rhythm. A fragment from a book I'd read made new sense:

> That drum has been our pulse, and often have I wondered what it is that starts the drum of a man's life to beating? For each of us walks to the beat of our own drum, an unheard rhythm to all our movements and thought.[19]

I was scared at first because I believed the guard might physically abuse me or that I might be sexually brutalised by other prisoners, but relief settled in as I realised that this wasn't any ordinary prison. It was vastly different from anything I had ever imagined. Here, for now, bullying and sexual assault seemed unlikely. The army had a strong grip on their soldiers and none of them appeared to be hardened criminals with ill intent.

They were a social cross-section of young men of eighteen, conscripted from across the country, who had already bucked the system in some way. All of us were in this together and nobody rejected or ridiculed me but, on the contrary, I felt an unspoken kinship between us, even considering our differences of belief.

I showered in company after morning inspection and returned to the cell when the others doubled off to the parade ground. There they were marched up and down on the open dusty ground. I heard them at drill for hours, obediently following a lone voice as it barked out commands.

The cellblock door opened around mid-morning, and I heard footsteps and muffled voices as a small group walked down the corridor towards my cell. I assumed my posture up against the wall and watched as they swung open the door.

_____

[19] *The Walking Drum*, Louis L'Amour.

Standing in the doorway was a short, squat soldier with a large brown handlebar moustache that almost completely hid his mouth. He wore a brown cap with a glossy black peak. It had a gilt cap band with a bright brass badge. His khaki shirt was open at the neck. His sleeves were rolled up above his elbows and his shirt was tucked into shorts of a slightly lighter shade. A leather belt hugged his paunch, and his calf-high polished brown boots were laced tightly over a pair of thick socks that reached just below his knees. He reminded me a lot of my father who was just as short and rotund and who wore a similar moustache.

He entered my cell and introduced himself, speaking good English with a heavy South African accent.

'I'm Sergeant Major. I hear you're not cooperating.'

This was Sergeant Major Delport. I didn't reply, for there was nothing much to say. He was riled and spoke again, this time with more force.

'I am your senior officer, Private Budge! And I am telling you to put on your uniform and report outside now.'

I kept my head, and took the plunge. Cleave to the truth!

'Sergeant Major Delport, you must understand that I am not *Private* Budge. I am a civilian who chooses not to be a soldier. Therefore, I shall not put on the army's uniform and I shall not report for duty. As a civilian, held here against my will, I am not under your command. But I will cooperate as fully as I can and I mean you no harm or disrespect ....'

I gulped. This was the acid test. An eighteen-year-old in open confrontation with a senior NCO in the presence of observers. One might consider my tenacity out of context for a teenager but I'd had years of training as a youth. We were well coached to overcome obstacles and to avoid flippant rebuffs from homeowners as we carried the Jehovah's Witness teachings from door-to-door. Standing up for myself in front of stern opposition came naturally and easily.

Delport growled and, raising his voice, cut over the top of my sentence:

'I am giving you a lawful command and you will obey me immediately!'

I remained resolute. 'Your command may be lawful in your eyes, but in view of greater universal laws I can't accept it. I therefore refuse to put on this uniform.'

He mumbled under his moustache and retreated from the cell to confer with the two men outside. Speaking in a near whisper, he gestured to one of them – a fatter, taller man. This ungainly soldier was dressed in brown overalls with the legs tucked into polished boots. The webbing belt around his waist peeked out between rolls of fat. He wore a cap similar to the sergeant major's. His legs folded inwards – knock-kneed, with collapsed ankles – propping up a barrel-shaped frame. He looked like a giraffe at a drinking hole. His thick thighs brushed against each other as he came into my cell.

'I am Sergeant Vermaak. *Ek is nie gebore nie, ek is gemaak!'* [I was not born, I was made] he said firmly, in a heavy Afrikaans accent. There was some irony in the laboured jest. Perhaps it was habit. Perhaps he meant to tell me he was special. But it tickled my wicked humour and I had to suppress the obvious retort – 'they could have done a better job of it'.

'First,' he said pointing at me, 'there is *you;* then this corporal,' he turned and gestured to the other man outside. 'Then there is *me'* he added, tapping his index finger on his sternum, 'and then Sergeant Major over and above us all. We are in that order. You are nothing! You are a private! Sergeant Major gave you an order and the corporal and I witnessed it. You disobeyed Sergeant Major's orders and I don't think you know what that means,' he said, pausing to inhale, which allowed the bloated face a moment's respite. 'You are going to get fucked up if the captain finds out. He's the commandant of this barracks and he doesn't take shit.'

Having drawn in air, he continued like a Chinese toy with fresh batteries. 'We are trying to help you here,' he said, softening his tone in an attempt to make rapport.

I thought I recognised what they were trying to do. Delport played the role of the bad cop, fomenting antipathy, while Vermaak, the good cop, acted with a semblance of support:

'Just put on the *fokken* uniform and I will talk to Sergeant Major and ask him to forget the whole *fokken* thing. Let's begin with the tee shirt and shorts, shall we? That will be enough for now.'

'Exactly, Mr Vermaak! Once I start wearing the shirt and shorts you will have got me, and I might as well wear the rest of the uniform. And when I've done that, I shall give up, become a soldier, pick up a gun, go to the border and fight the terrorists.'

His face reddened again and the rage rumbled up inside him like an afternoon thunderstorm.

'Firstly' (he seemed to start every statement with that word) 'I am not Mister! Mister is a name for a *fokken kaffir predikant!* [a black preacher referred to in the most demeaning way]. I am Sergeant. Do you hear that! From now on, you will call me Sergeant. And stand up *fokken* straight!' He swore a lot, which made me instantly dislike him. My parents raised me on a side of the fence where gutter language was unacceptable.

'I'll call you by the title of your choice, Sergeant,' I replied, calmly but with a strange feeling of disengagement. 'But I still don't recognise your authority over me and you won't tell me what to do.'

I didn't flinch. I felt that I had won. Stark naked, I seemed to find new depth to my personal resources. I remained standing at ease with my hands clasped together over my groin.

I'd now been given the army lecture on rank and the consequences of insubordination. I was about to be taught that civilian life ended at the gate outside the detention barracks.

'While you are here I am your *fokken* mother and father,' he said, 'and I will tell you what to do, when to do it and how to do it. When I say *jump*, the only thing you will ask is *how high*? Is that clear?'

'No sir,' I replied. 'You are neither my mother nor my father and since I have refused to become a soldier, I believe you have no authority over me at all.' I looked him in the eye. 'I obey my conscience and I don't care what threats you make – you can kill me if you like – but I will not do what you ask me to. If it conflicts with my conscience, I'll never do it – never!'

As I write this account, reflecting on the past, I realise the self-righteous prig that I must have been. Not to mention the outright impertinence, the recklessness of a boy out of school, naked, defying a sergeant in the army's detention barracks in Voortrekkerhoogte. I must tell a story to demonstrate what I mean.

In recent years I conducted many self-help training courses, but I remember one of the classes in particular. It was a mixed group of about thirty people. Like all the other classes, everyone was encouraged to open up by sharing views, talking of difficult experiences. This created kinship and group bonding. Everyone on the course shared freely, except for one woman in her mid-thirties. Her hair was in two plaits with ribbons. She wore a bright frock, bobby socks and white schoolgirl shoes that made her look like Dorothy Gale, the little Kansas farm girl played by Judy Garland in *The Wizard of Oz*.

The woman's voice [let's call her Mary] was immature and squeaky. She smiled continuously, and when it came to sharing, she simply said that there was nothing worth telling the class. Everything about Mary was deeply incongruent. Why did she attend a self-help group when there was nothing wrong? Why did she hang on so determinedly to a childlike identity? Why could she not smile with her eyes but only with her mouth? Later in the day when we were discussing elements of body language I engaged Mary with as much empathy as I could:

'I can read everyone here, Mary, except for you. There's something about you that I can't quite credit.'

She went on the defensive the moment I said the words 'can't credit', and she latched onto them. Her fake smile trembled, the corners of her mouth twitched and her eyes welled with tears. 'Can't credit?' she repeated. There was a tremor in her voice. 'What do you mean by that?'

I'd touched a nerve. I tried to feel my way:

'You present a picture of happiness, fresh youthfulness. But I'm reading something else. The picture's too perfect and I get a sense that it's not entirely believable. My gut feeling is, there're things you're trying to hide. It uses up a lot of energy to suppress them, Mary, and I grant that it's risky for you to acknowledge them. But that's not true here, is it?'

She burst into tears and unbundled, releasing volumes of suppressed emotion in a cathartic abreaction. The group supported her, and by the end of the year-long series she emerged a changed woman.

There's a similar look about Jehovah's Witnesses too, an incongruent body language, and one can pick them out a mile away. As 'God's chosen' there's a dash of arrogance, an unspoken sense that 'I'm better than you' – but in the way of the human psyche it's a facade masking a background of weakness, chinks in the armour, failings, shortcomings that we all face as people.

Witnesses carry a forced sense of joy because, on the one hand, they ought to be grateful for God's promise of a restored paradise and try to show it. But, on the other hand, they're temporary residents in a fallen world, working as hard as they can to avoid touching too much of it. Meanwhile, their organisation scrutinises every movement they make and is far too ready to chastise most of their worldly contact. The bar is set too high, the stress is enormous but insidious, and it shows up in their faces just as Mary's mask spoke of inner conflict.

There's a serenity and a sense of grace that reflect in the faces of the holy men and women who surrender to their humanity and embrace their spirituality. However, I don't recall having seen that look in any Witness face. The portrait is an incongruent mix of happiness and pain, righteousness and weakness, arrogance and yearning, and the result is a self-evident expression of inner turmoil.

I'm sure I wore that very mask as an eighteen-year-old as I tried to live a lifestyle I believed to be correct even while deep and murky waters swirled inside. I feared my vulnerability, my Achilles heel, my sexual orientation and its urge to connect with somebody in a place of love and happiness. My strength came partly from the intensity of the facade, and while it worked – for now – it was a brittle strength.

'Sergeant Vermaak, stand aside!' bellowed the Sergeant Major as he stormed back into my cell, and I thought he was about to punch me in the guts.

He might have, but he stopped short. I realised that there was a limit to their intimidation that didn't allow for physical violence. Their tactics were more insidious.

'*My boys*,' he said, talking of all conscripts as if they were his sons, 'they're at the border, fighting. Some lie in 1 Military Hospital down the road. They've lost arms and legs – blown off by landmines. They're the lucky ones. Others are in the morgue. Heroes who gave their lives to protect us. And for what?! You cowardly scum! You're a traitor and you know what we do to traitors – we hang them! You're just like those black bastards ... You're nothing!'

'Sergeant,' he ordered, 'come back in here!'

Sergeant Vermaak returned into my cell and stood behind Delport. The corporal remained outside observing silently.

'Hand Private Budge his uniform!'

Sergeant Vermaak lifted the neat bundle of clothes from the corner of the cell and held them in his upturned hands.

'Sergeant, you and this corporal are my witnesses.' He turned his attention to me, looked me in the eye, and demanded: 'Private Budge, I, as your senior officer, order you to put on your uniform and report outside for duty. You have five minutes in which to obey. Do you understand me?'

'I hear your threats, sir, but I don't need five minutes to decide. I say again, I will not put on the uniform.'

'And I say again, you will! That's a lawful command and if you disobey me I will charge you with insubordination. You will be punished if you refuse. Do you understand?'

'I don't care about punishment. I'm already being punished. And sir, no, I won't put it on!'

'So, you refuse to obey my orders?'

'Yes sir, I refuse.'

'Very well then. Corporal! Since he has no use for this uniform, return it to the storeroom.'

The corporal entered my cell and gathered the boots, helmet, and the pile of stuff in Vermaak's hands. They left some basic toiletries, the sanitation bucket, my foam mattress, two cotton waste blankets and a pail of water and locked me inside the now denuded cell.

Ram Dass (born Richard Alpert), a contemporary spiritual teacher, often told the story of a Chinese general sent to Tibet as part of China's relentless battle to annex that country. If China were to succeed, it would create a common border between itself and India, and hugely extend its influence. In his story, Ram Dass speaks of the general's arrogance and his ruthless terrorising of the Tibetan people. The Chinese ravaged the land, set villages ablaze, ordered monks from their temples or murdered them.

At some point during the vicious campaign the general asked his adjutant if they had dealt with all the monks.

'Yes, sir. Except for one who lives in the temple on this hill. He refuses to leave.'

Incensed by the blatant challenge, the general assembled a platoon of soldiers to accompany him at daybreak to the temple.

Arriving, he advanced with aggression upon the solitary figure who swept the courtyard – as he'd had done for many years. The general bellowed at the humble monk:

'Do you know who I am? In an instant, I could draw my sword and plunge it into your belly.'

The monk, still sweeping leaves, replied in a quiet voice:

'But you don't know who I am … for, in an instant, I would allow you to draw your sword and plunge it into my belly.'

What power does a bully have over someone who is unafraid? The general had nothing with which to trump the old monk. It dawned on him how empty he really was. As this truth sank in, the general slumped to his knees.

'Forgive me! Please forgive me,' he begged, looking up at the monk.

'I can't forgive you,' said the monk gently, 'for I have never taken offense.'

Sometime later that afternoon Vermaak and the corporal barged back into my cell.

'Follow me!' snapped the sergeant. 'You will now appear before the Captain.'

He led the way down the cellblock and the corporal fell in behind us. We proceeded in silence, broken only by the swish-swish of the sergeant's overalls rubbed by his thighs. The corporal unlocked the cellblock door, we passed through, and he secured it again. We turned onto the *stoep*, marched past the doctor's office, the reception and storeroom, and then rounding the corner tramped halfway down the verandah to the captain's office. Guarded by the corporal, I was ordered to wait. Sergeant Vermaak went in.

The office personnel and kitchen staff looked on curiously as I stood on the *stoep* in the nude. Their expressions varied between fear, concern and watchful curiosity.

'*Aandag!* [attention]' boomed Vermaak's voice.

The corporal braced and fixed his eyes on an invisible point in front of him. The explosive command startled me but I kept my usual stance.

Vermaak came up to us and yelled '*Voorwaarts mars!* [forward march] – *lic la, lic la,*' setting the pace. The corporal moved with parade-ground alacrity. I walked at my own pace.

Vermaak led the way as we took ten paces in the direction of the kitchen and then, at the captain's door, he shouted '*Links draai!* [left turn], *lic la, lic la. Halt!*' He steered us through the doorway to a spot in front of the captain's desk. The corporal faced the window but I'd already turned towards the captain when Vermaak barked his final order: '*Regtervoet, draai!* [right foot, turn].' The corporal swung around to face the captain, saluted, and was marched outside to wait on the *stoep*.

The captain remained seated behind his wooden desk. Made from saligna, all government furniture looked the same: desks, chairs, cabinets, cupboards, library shelves. The captain's desk was immaculate with a few manila files in trays. In front of him on the green leather inlay was my file, an executive notepad, and his fountain pen.

He opened the notepad and wrote down the date, 29 October 1971; and the time. He took longhand notes throughout the proceeding.

'Private Thomas William Erith Budge,' he said as he wrote, 'What is your date of birth?'

'26 January 1953.'

'And your force number?' He looked up at me for the first time, repeating his question. 'What is your force number?'

Army personnel are supposed to remember their force number. I received a card with my number soon after registering, but I hadn't the faintest idea what it was.

'Your force number, Private?' he demanded, staring at me with contempt.

I was terribly nervous, my hands were sweaty but I couldn't move them from my crotch. My mouth was dry and I shivered uncontrollably. The tension was far too much and I released it in an untimely, madly inappropriate jest.

'I haven't a clue what my force number is. We don't keep a pressure gauge on our toilet.'

This was not appreciated. Impudence and facetiousness had no place here. He omitted my outburst from the record and copied the number from the front cover of the manila file. I broke the tense silence:

'Firstly sir,' I began, sounding a little like Vermaak, 'I'm not a private and secondly....'

I was ready to give my speech about being a captive civilian, but he interjected:

'Sergeant, read the charges.'

Due process and discipline ruled these barracks. The captain had a neat, old-fashioned cursive style and I watched the nib of his pen glide smoothly across the paper as Vermaak began.

'On or about ten o'clock today, 29 October 1971, Private Budge disobeyed a lawful command given to him by Sergeant Major Delport, ordering him to wear the uniform as defined in Detention Barracks Regulations.'

He picked up a book of military law and opened it to a marked page, citing the legislation and reading its contents.

'In terms of these regulations, he is charged with Insubordination and wilful disobedience. Sergeant Major repeatedly warned Private Budge of the consequences of disobedience but twice he refused to obey.'

The captain addressed me without looking up. 'Private Budge, what do you have to say?'

'Captain, I first insist that the record reflects my unwillingness to be called private. I'm here in detention because I chose not to be a soldier. If I'm not a soldier, then I have no rank. Accepting the rank of private is the same as putting on the uniform – it identifies me as a soldier, which I am not.'

My much-rehearsed argument was aired again:

'I stand here naked in front of you because I will not put on the uniform nor will I allow the use of the term, private. Furthermore, since I'm not an enlisted member of the South African Defence Force, I believe that neither Sergeant Major Delport, Sergeant Vermaak, you nor any other officer has jurisdiction over me.

'I believe that it should first be proved that I am a soldier under your command before you can try me for insubordination. I think your assumption is incorrect: just because a civil magistrate placed me in the custody of this facility does not imply that I'm a soldier.'

The captain listened, noted my objections, shrugged, and called Delport to give his testimony. He, Vermaak and the corporal gave close accounts of what occurred that morning, corroborating each other's evidence. Having heard what he needed to hear, the captain made his ruling:

'I find you guilty of Insubordination and wilful disobedience. What comments do you wish to make in mitigation of your punishment?'

'I object to your verdict because you still haven't proven that you have jurisdiction over me. This trial is a farce and I think you know it. Regardless of that fact,' I continued, 'I would like to read a copy of the legislation, because I'm sure it has overriding clauses that make any order illegal if it doesn't have a valid military purpose and interferes with my private rights or personal affairs. May I please read the book before I conclude my arguments in mitigation?'

He wrote it all down without looking up and said to Vermaak, 'Make sure he has a copy in his cell for one week.'

'I have more to say, Captain.'

'Continue.'

'I also believe that the laws in this book are in conflict with higher universal principles of love, compassion and peacefulness as taught by Jesus. Imagine what he'd say if he sat in your chair right now. To whom should I give allegiance, to God or these laws? To make sure, I'd rather err in God's favour and be at odds with you. These laws are manmade and prone to error. God's laws are divine and flawless and I have no trouble deciding which to uphold. I believe that a time will come when we will see these manmade laws superseded. In the end, universal principles will honour our common brotherhood. I therefore see no unlawfulness in what I've refused to do and I will continue to follow my conscience.'

He replied: 'You will read the legislation for yourself, that the dictates of a person's conscience, religion, or personal philosophy cannot justify or excuse the disobedience of an otherwise lawful order. So, I have no choice in the matter and I find you guilty. Understand the seriousness of your offence. It leads to sedition and insurrection and our military takes a harsh stance against traitors and terrorists.'

He placed his pen on the leather inlay, cracked his knuckles to relieve his writing cramp, and continued:

'By the powers granted me, you have forfeited all your privileges in Detention Barracks for the period of your sentence for disobeying a lawful command this day Friday, 29th October 1971. You may not receive any visitors. You may not receive or write any letters. Further acts of disobedience will provoke much harsher punishment.'

'May I ask for my Bible?'

'Sergeant, make sure you give him his Bible.'

My parents were not to know for another eighteen days about this round of punishment and heard of it[20] only after my father wrote a letter to the captain, the commandant of the barracks, asking after me. [21]

I entered detention barracks on Thursday. Friday saw the forfeiture of all privileges, and on Monday they moved me to Block 2 to join the conscientious objectors. They kept us separate

---

[20] Commandant's letter, 16 November 1971 [#18].
[21] My father's letter to the commandant, detention barracks, 9 November 1971 [#17].

from other prisoners, perhaps because they feared we might convince them to rebel or because the others might help us to communicate with the outside world. Worse still, maybe they sought to keep their treatment of us secret. Negative publicity over the detention of conscientious objectors was emerging in the press.

My move to Block 2 was uneventful. Two orderlies arrived unannounced at about ten o'clock and told me to collect what little I had and bring it with me. I didn't know where they were taking me but I suspected that it was to join the others. Block 2's configuration was identical to Block 1 and they housed me in a cell near the far right of the block. The cell's interior was a little more dilapidated than the previous one, with paint flaking from the walls. The view from the exterior window looked onto Block 3 and I had a tiny glimpse of the ablution block behind a tree.

I arranged my room. The bed went into the corner to the right of the door. The mattress cover was dirtier than the last, with pungent odours and patches of dry sweat and semen. I covered it with a blanket and folded the other on top like a pillow on which I could sit. The latrine bucket was grubby and I put it in the opposite corner with the toilet roll, away from the bed. The water bucket went into a third corner at the foot of the mattress. I rolled the toothbrush and toothpaste into the towel and placed them next to the water pail. The two books, my Bible and the one on military law, stayed on the bed with me. That was it; I had nothing else.

The cellblock was deathily quiet when I came in, but the moment the orderlies left there arose a rustle of whispers. I climbed up to the customary position at the door and received an animated welcome. People shared their experiences and they elaborated, as they did so, on small personal distinctions that elevated them in some way or another. Soon enough I recognised around me the familiar pattern of Jehovah's Witness company.

There's always low-key competition among the Witnesses as each tries to outdo the other in terms of Bible knowledge, service quality, years of association and depth of persecution. It's a group that thrives on persecution. It binds them and gives them identity – it associates them with their interpretation of the suffering of Christ. Persecution is what they expect from Satan's world. In fact, the Witnesses can be amongst the most negative people on the planet: it's not credible to acknowledge beauty in a world allegedly controlled by the devil as that would be tantamount to ascribing virtue to evil.

The full sense of their untenable split psyche dawned on me. They eagerly anticipate (in some future time) the redemption of the world, and yet they rival one another in denunciation of it. My sexual orientation, a matter over which I had no choice, was for me a clear and present issue. If I didn't hide my sexuality, they would summarily condemn and shun me. How could they show such future hope for a fallen world, yet none for me? It was all mere abstract doctrine without substance or compassion.

In Block 2 mealtimes functioned otherwise. Inmates brought inside the cellblock a stack of dixies, knives, forks, steel cups, an urn of sweet tea and a bain-marie of food, which they arranged at the far end, close to where I was. The command was given for the orderlies to unlock the cell doors and everyone emerged and waited in the central passageway.

As I came out for my first lunch in Block 2, I realised that I was the only naked man in the company!

I was deeply embarrassed. I felt foolish. Why had the other objectors dressed in army shorts and tee shirts while I refused to wear them? Had someone been brainwashed and had the others followed suit? I shot back into my cell to hide and to think.

They filed past, collected trays, cutlery, mugs of tea, helpings of army food, and returned to their cells to eat. The orderlies removed the bain-marie and urn and locked the outer door again.

The whispered conversations resumed as each person finished eating. I had to ask my burning question:

'Why are you guys dressed and I'm not? Surely, there's no compromise on wearing the uniform. Either we do or we don't. There can't be shades of grey in such matters.'

'Nobody tells us what to do, brother. It's up to our conscience to make such decisions,' said one of them patronisingly from across the passage in his rehearsed and complacent voice. It made me want to vomit.

I hated that know-it-all, condescending, self-justifying crap and it certainly wasn't what I wanted to hear. I'd stood firm in my decision to distance myself from the army but clearly others had interpreted things to their own convenience. Once again, the organisation had failed us by not giving unambiguous guidelines on such matters – possibly out of fear of legal repercussions. I felt as though they dangled us in the wind in order to protect the organisation as a whole. I needed something concrete but all I got was pious rhetoric.

One of the guys farther down added a bit of useful information:

'Our parents are allowed to send us basics – soap, toothpaste, safety razors, shaving cream. They can also send two pairs of rugby shorts and two tee shirts. You just have to demand it when they come to your cell in the morning for medical inspection. They'll write to your folks and get them to send the stuff.'

Another voice added, 'I wear their underpants and that's as far as I'll go.'

I was sure my father didn't know of this arrangement. I sought a bit more clarity before despatching an order for supplies:

'I've forfeited all my privileges by not wearing uniform. Won't this prevent my parents from sending me supplies?'

'No, brother. We've all lost our privileges but we're still allowed to get some parcels. The army's happy to save money if we get stuff at our parents' expense. If our parents can't send goods they send cash, and the army buys our things with that.'

My father had written to the commandant of the detention barracks[22] and specifically asked if he could send personal toiletries and clothing, but the captain in his reply had ignored this request.[23]

I had been so dogmatic about not wearing the uniform that the army returned it all to storage; and I didn't want to backtrack and ask for this or that item of clothing as I would have weakened my case, so I decided to stay just as I was until another solution presented itself.

That afternoon, Delport and his entourage returned to give me the same 'lawful command' as before. The corporal carried a uniform which Vermaak held out to me while Delport tried again

---

[22] My father's letter to the commandant, detention barracks, 9 November 1971 [#17].
[23] Commandant's letter to my father, 16 November 1971 [#18].

to persuade me to wear it. This time I took the brown Y-front briefs and slipped them on. I refused the rest but I hated the glint of triumph in Vermaak's eyes. They had won a small victory and I resented giving them that honour.

This was clearly a cat-and-mouse game. They believed they could slowly whittle me down. But I remained resolute. I refused to capitulate any further. They took the uniform, one of the two blankets and the towel, and sent them back to storage. The captain sentenced me later that same day to spare rations and solitary confinement.

Where regular defaulters stayed outside for the bulk of the day, we remained locked inside. We initially took daily showers, but that soon stopped and the only time spent out of our cells was for meals, emptying our sanitary pails, and collecting buckets of fresh water. The pail of fresh water had to last an entire day, first for drinking and then for washing.[24] Under South Africa's new constitution this would probably be in breach of a basic human right, access to fresh food and water.

This cycle was repeated throughout my stay in detention barracks. Further, instead of the usual three meals a day, when we were on spare-rations they removed the white pail of fresh water and gave us each half a loaf of dry white bread and a hipflask of water per day for two consecutive days out of every nine.[25]

Detention barracks regulations permitted solitary confinement for a maximum continuous period of fourteen days but the captain seemed to override this by repeatedly charging us with insubordination and disobedience. Somehow, we stayed locked up indefinitely.[26] I had a lot of time to think. I liked my defiance and stubbornness, I liked my fearlessness, but I couldn't reconcile my sexuality. I knew that I was as committed as the other conscientious objectors and yet because of my secret I felt fraudulent and unworthy of their friendship and solidarity.

Had they discovered my secret, they would have had no compunction in shunning, disfellowshipping, me instantly. This was a strange situation that I could not come to terms with in my reasoning. The Witnesses preached love and compassion and yet, when it came to

---

[24] Letter from EG Budge to Prime Minister BJ Vorster, 20 March 1972 [#28].
[25] Letter from EG Budge to Prime Minister BJ Vorster, 20 March 1972 [#28].
[26] 'Witnesses won't fight, but they can work', the Star, Johannesburg, 18 November 1971 [#19].

dealing with human fragility (I viewed my sexual choices back then as fragility), they become tyrants of the law devoid of sympathy and understanding.

Amongst the many clippings and letters that my father deliberately kept, and which I've used extensively as research material, is a newspaper article written by an anonymous gay person (I assume a man) who lived in Hillbrow (strange that dad should have kept it!).

This unknown correspondent begins by contrasting the statements made by a conscientious objector who in one breath praises the Witnesses for their stance against army service and, in the next, 'in an effort to gain further sympathy for Jehovah's Witnesses and their convictions, sees fit to malign another minority group – namely homosexuals.' He points out to the Jehovah's Witness sympathiser that to 'urge condemnation of homosexuality while begging acceptance of the views of the Jehovah's Witnesses smells faintly of hypocrisy'. 'I challenge,' he writes, 'why tolerance, the greatest of all Christian principles, should be dished out to certain sections of the community while being denied to others'.[27]

Thankfully, my sentence spanned the summer months. But at a high altitude above sea level the night-time temperatures plummeted as soon as the sun went down. My cell faced east and caught the morning sun and half an hour of direct light in the afternoon through the interior gap in the roof. However, the bare concrete floor and the open ventilation above the door soon sucked out all heat and the only way to conserve my warmth was to mummify myself in the blanket.

As the three-month sentence progressed, I noticed a rapid loss of weight. I'm about 196cm [6' 4"] tall and should weigh between 85 and 90kg [187 and 198 lb] but I could clearly notice lost muscle tone across my body. My immune system weakened, and opportunistic respiratory and skin allergies began to plague me,[28] so I decided to maintain my fitness. I started an exercise regime, walking between opposite corners of the cell and using the bars at the window to pull myself up and strengthen my arms. I also tied my blanket to the bars by wrapping corners of the fabric around them and tucking it underneath itself, thus forming a hammock up against the wall where I could sit and do abdominal and leg exercises.

---

[27] 'A plea for acceptance', the *Star*, Johannesburg, 19 November 1971 [#20].
[28] My father's letter to the commandant, detention barracks, 21 December 1971 [#25].

Of all exercise, I most enjoyed walking. There was an endless and repetitive rhythm to it, 'One, two, three and turn. One, two, three and turn,' which soon induced a trance-like state. Time then became irrelevant and passed quickly. At first I thought I'd track the days, marking them off as I'd intended, in bundles of five, but that was too hurtful. It protracted my sense of time and I abandoned the idea and took each day as it came.

The army searched for ways to retain us in solitary confinement and on spare rations; but their regimented mindset made it easy to predict when they would launch their next raid and I soon learned how to relax in the quiet gaps between them. Coping with the Witnesses was much more complex.

Confine a group of young men over a prolonged period and a hierarchy will inevitably emerge: in the same way that dogs organise themselves into a pack, dominant ones in the lead and submissive ones following. A few tried to usurp leadership but that didn't catch on and their power quickly waned. We were mainly inexperienced boys fresh out of school and none at that tender age held any appointed rank inside the Witnesses' organisation. This meant that within our collective Witness identity we were technically leaderless, each fending for himself.

Perched above their doors at night, some zealous objectors, usually older ones of around twenty-one, tried to hold group prayers and Bible studies; but I joined the majority and largely kept to myself. The elders on the outside heard rumours and were concerned about the lack of leadership among us.

Although most of us had the resolve to stand firm (there was no doubt about what the organisation expected), one or two weakened and surrendered to the 'enemy'. I never heard of their fate but I'm sure it wasn't pleasant. They'd remain in poor esteem in the eyes of the military and lose all standing with the Witnesses, who would have purged them from their congregations without compunction.

Those who cracked did it quietly, the way some commit suicide. It shocked us to hear that they had suddenly gone, and I felt sad that they had come so far and couldn't continue. I understood their inability to reach out for help, in the same way that I couldn't reach out over my sexuality. The act of disclosing weakness somehow signed one's own warrant, placed the noose around one's own neck.

This dichotomy created strange behaviour in many Witnesses because they had to maintain an opaque veneer of righteousness to cover the real, feelingful and sexual person beneath; and this manifested as the incongruent body language that I spoke of earlier. The military took the ones who capitulated to army bases across the country where they served out their conscription, broken losers in an unequal struggle.

---oooOooo---

In mid-December, a batch of conscientious objectors was due for release. Anxious about my steadfastness over not wearing the uniform, my subsequent backtracking and wearing the army underwear, I asked Gerald to convey a message to my parents. I was concerned that the authorities had spread inaccurate rumours about me and I needed to set the record straight.

On his release, Gerald wrote to my father –

> If you heard a false message about [Tom] putting on the uniform don't believe it! He asks, if his grandfather is okay if you could post him two black pairs of shorts. If ill, two other colours, then he'll get the right message. Also please send him a sponge, facecloth and ask the military officials for a medical report. The doctor treated him for an allergy but without results.[29]

Dad posted two pairs of black rugby shorts, two white tee shirts and a few basic toiletries – soap, toothpaste, a safety razor and shaving foam.[30] At Christmas the barracks office sent one set of clothing to my cell while they kept the other in storage for later use. Having returned their brown underwear I dressed myself in a rudimentary civilian way and at last felt on top of the world.

It amazes me now how such simplicity brought such pleasure: a pair of black rugby shorts worn without underwear and a simple white tee shirt made me feel more content than the expensive Italian-styled clothing I wore in subsequent years.

Not long after my arrival, the army replaced the commandant of the detention barracks. Captain N J Nel was appointed the new CO. He was a tall, sinewy and ruthless man.

---

[29] Gerald Jordaan's letter to my father, 12 December 1971 [#21].
[30] Insured Parcel Receipt, 18 December 1971 [#23].

Within weeks, he issued 'lawful' commands to twenty-three objectors due for release and, when we disobeyed, he immediately referred the matter to the civilian courts for further sentencing.[31] An unsubstantiated rumour held that Nel and P W Botha, then Minister of Defence and later Prime Minister, were friends and that Botha tasked Nel with quashing the rise in conscientious objection. If there is truth in the rumour, Nel did so with ingenuity and gusto.

Other than by such high-up connivance, I find it hard to grasp how the judiciary and the army worked so closely. How did I come before a civilian magistrate when I had refused military service? Why did they not bring us before a summary trial or a court martial from the outset? How could Nel issue a military command requiring that we wear military uniforms and then refer the matter back to civilian courts for trial? None of it made sense to me except that it was abuse of the law.

Without telling my parents (although my father surmised that I'd be there), we appeared before Magistrate J J F Coetzer in Pretoria on Monday 24 January, two days before my sentence was to end.[32] Attorney I Swartzberg represented us and the court remanded the case to 4 February 1972. Seventeen young men went home on bail that day but six of us returned to detention barracks to complete our sentences. My release was imminent; after three long months I'd be returning home. I think that the court's remand ruling scuttled Nel's plans, as I'm sure he timed our trial, hoping to secure further convictions before our release, giving him reason to detain us beyond our release date.

I recall collecting my possessions at reception on my birthday, dressing in my suit and wearing shoes for the first time in three months. I remember walking out of the barracks and hesitating uncertainly, before seeing my parents parked down at the end of the road. Nel forbade them to come any closer. As I walked down to their car, two military policemen climbed out of their vehicle and approached me.

'Are you Mr. Budge?'

'Yes,' I answered warily.

---

[31] Newspaper clipping from an unknown source, 25 January 1972 [#39].
[32] My father's letter to I Swartzberg, Attorney, 21 December 1971 [#24].

'These are your call-up papers. You are required to report for duty on 6 July this year, here in Voortrekkerhoogte.' They handed me a sealed envelope, made me sign a receipt and let me continue.[33]

It cast a shadow on my day of release, my birthday. I knew I had no genuine freedom. I couldn't plan anything of real consequence in the six months following my release, because in July the whole cycle would repeat itself. Besides which, I would be in court within the next eight days and we didn't know how that judgement would unfold.

Refusing military training was always my choice, with or without my connection to the Witnesses. I took personal responsibility for my decisions and endured the harsh consequences as bravely as I could. And yet I had no real autonomy. I had a distinct feeling that the Witnesses took advantage of the situation and cajoled us, battered by the ruthless treatment meted out by the military, into serving their cause. Released detainees often went into full-time missionary work back then and I knew there would be a lot of pressure for me to conform.

Psychologist Robert Cialdini writes about decision-making in real-life contexts:

> You and I exist in an extraordinarily complicated stimulus environment, easily the most rapidly moving and complex that has ever existed on this planet. To deal with it, we *need* shortcuts. We can't be expected to recognise and analyze all the aspects in each person, event, and situation we encounter in even one day. We haven't the time, energy or capacity for it. Instead, we must very often use our stereotypes, our rules of thumb to satisfy things according to a few key features and then to respond mindlessly when one or another of these trigger features is present.[34]

And so it was. The Jehovah's Witnesses programmed and reinforced key trigger shortcuts in their follower's minds, and we responded without forethought when called to action. I felt like a puppet on a string and the Witnesses were my puppet master. The emotional pressure was overwhelming and my only coping mechanism was detachment and a consequent feeling of numbness. All I could do was go with the flow.

---

[33] Allotment for National Service, 16 November 1971 [#16].
[34] *Influence, the Psychology of Persuasion*, Robert B. Cialdini, Harper Collins, 2007.

I cannot remember the details of my week at home but I do recall how alarmed I was by the announcement P W Botha had made in Parliament the day before my release, that he 'intended introducing new legislation concerning the issue.'[35] The prevailing sentiment was that these changes meant further, harsher, punitive measures for conscientious objectors. P W Botha was Minister of Defence at the time. He was Head of the Afrikaner National Party for eleven years and became Prime Minister (later, executive State President) in 1978. Remembered for his finger-wagging, his fierce opposition to black majority rule and hatred of communism, his political tenacity and cunning, he earned the nickname *Die Groot Krokodil* [The Big Crocodile].

On Friday 4 February 1972 I was back in F Court in Pretoria with the other twenty-one in the group. This time, Attorney Swartzberg represented us and we had nothing personal to say. The magistrate sentenced us to one hundred and eighty days in military detention barracks, twice as long as the three-month period I had just completed, and we were now due for release only on 3 August 1972. Things had become a great deal tougher.

Back in our cells, our civilian clothing swapped for shorts and tee shirts, we waited anxiously to see what other treatment the army had in store.

After Nel's appointment as commandant we noticed a distinct reduction in our daily food rations, and rumours abounded from the other prisoners that he diverted most of it to feed his pigs. Nel soon used his discretionary powers to add further layers of punishment, not only in the form of reduced rations: prohibiting showers, keeping us on constant two-day spare rations out of every nine days, and permanent solitary confinement. Nel's intentions were clear. He wasn't about to soften. And within a fortnight he again commanded us to put on the uniform and when we refused, he again charged us and escalated the matter to a magistrate.

The night-time talks were tense and fearful. For not wearing the uniform we had forfeited privileges, regular rations, and freedom; but Nel's strategy sought stronger powers by referring the matter to a civilian court. We concluded that Nel had limited punitive measures at his disposal, which the magistrate didn't. One hundred and eighty days for not wearing the uniform was way out of proportion to the punishments handed down during the first three months. Now, less than two weeks into the six-month sentence, he charged us with the same

---

[35] 'New measures to deal with reluctant soldiers', the *Star*, Johannesburg, 25 January 1972 [#26].

offence again, to seek further sentencing from outside. Where was this going to end? If this was my punishment for not wearing a uniform, what would happen when I refused to attend my call-up later in July?

Nel allowed us to send a short telegram to our parents. I don't know the motivation behind this. Perhaps it was meant to threaten them in the same way we felt threatened, so I wrote: 'APPEARING IN F COURT MONDAY 21 FEBRUARY LOVE TOM.'[36] We were remanded in custody until Friday 17 March, when Magistrate Luyt sentenced twenty-one of us to an additional one-year sentence in detention barracks. This pushed my release date on to August 1973.

Led once again down to the holding cells after sentencing, we waited for the military police to escort us back to the barracks. This time, however, loading us in the military police van was different. Someone had left open the security gates at the back of the court and a number of parents met us briefly. I'm not sure whether my father had arranged this, whether it was a breach of security, or even a relaxation of protocol or act of compassion by the policemen who escorted us. Perhaps someone had his conscience pricked by the injustice and permitted a tender moment.

Dad asked, 'Are you okay, my boy?'

'I'm strong; but the captain's trying his best to break us down,' I told him in a faltering voice. 'He's going way further than before.'

I told him all I could in the little time we had. Following that brief chat, my father wrote to the then prime minister, B J Vorster, drawing his attention to the conditions of our incarceration and seeking his intervention:

> My son's condition, as well as that of his companions who were brought before the court on the same day, has deteriorated alarmingly and gives rise for concern as to their health.

He put his complaint fully before the Prime Minister:

---

[36] Post Office Telegram, 17 February 1971 [#27].

It is my contention which I respectfully place before you for consideration, that the superintendent of the Military Detention Barracks has far exceeded his authority in imposing such additional inhuman conditions of detention. It is my sincere conviction that he has developed an unwarranted dislike for our boys and that the issue has now become one of personal vindictiveness towards those conscientious objectors in detention.[37]

Dad described our repeated jail sentences, our forfeiture of all privileges, endless solitary confinement and continuous days of spare rations.

He sent a copy to the Parliamentary Select Committee for the Defence Amendment Bill, tasked to review the Minister of Defence's new proposals for tougher legislation.

I didn't know that my father had written to the Prime Minister, but one day in the middle of April the orderlies unexpectedly took us outside to exercise in the sun on the grassy patches between the cellblocks, encouraging us to remove our shirts. It happened for a few days and we tried to speculate why the situation had suddenly changed. We were allowed regular showers and, one morning, they instructed us to thoroughly clean our cells, pack out our possessions neatly, and report outside earlier than usual.

There was nervous anticipation amongst all the orderlies that day.

Lined up in rows on the quadrangle near the main door, we saw a contingent of military brass, journalists and press photographers, led by Captain Nel.

Vermaak and Delport took roll call and then Delport joined the others and Vermaak led us to the grassy patch between the cellblocks to exercise, where the press later photographed us.[38]

It was an obvious setup, a publicity stunt.

Captain Nel, Brigadier De Wet and Commandant Joe Keyter, of the army's public relations office, toured the premises showing the journalists and press photographers around. They found us with colour in our skin from the sunshine and photographed us exercising in the fresh

---

[37] My father's letter to the Prime Minister, B. J. Vorster, 20 March 1972 [#28].
[38] 'The penned in life of the objectors', A de V Marais, Defence Correspondent, *Rand Daily Mail*, 29 April 1972 [#40a].

outdoor air. The inmates had brought the barracks to a sparkle and we received a generous lunch that day.

However, despite Nel's efforts to obfuscate the truth, a Sunday newspaper wrote:

> Make no mistake, life in detention barracks is hard. You can see it in the cement floors that shine from non-stop polishing, the spotless courtyards where dirt is unknown and the brass handles of the doors and windows that are never allowed to become tarnished.[39]

The article corroborated Dad's allegations:

> Inmates are put into solitary confinement for offences within the barracks. Those who refuse to obey regulations for religious or other reasons will be tried and sentenced to a term of solitary confinement – with or without spare diet. With solitary confinement goes a loss of privileges where an offender may not write letters, receive post or see visitors. According to military regulations he cannot be kept in solitary confinement for more than fourteen days at a stretch. If he persists in disobeying the regulations, he will be retried and could be sent back to solitary.

When questioned in the same newspaper, Brigadier De Wet, defending the military, emphasised that the notorious 'dark cells' in which an inmate could neither read nor write had been done away with and that the solitary cell was the same size as those of other inmates.

The following Sunday, the newspaper published a follow-up article, probably in response to readers' queries:

> Solitary confinement in physical terms means four walls, a roof and a bolted door. In mental terms it means silence and solitude. A combination of the two could mean personality breakdown, psychosis and even suicide.

Various clergy and psychiatrists criticised the detention barracks, likening it to Nazi efforts to break people's minds and 'a very destructive process, a form of mental torture.'[40]

---

[39] 'Rehabilitation is army detention centre's theme', Tim O'Hagen, *Sunday Express*, 16 April 1972 [#37].
[40] 'Solitary detention in army barracks criticised', Tim O'Hagen, *Sunday Express*, 23 April 1972 [#39].

My father's letter to the Prime Minister obviously stirred up public sympathy and Nel needed a public relations exercise to discredit the accusations. However, from the press reports, it seems as though their efforts to put a different spin on our detention backfired and brought more criticism from many sectors, including opposition parties in Parliament.

My father founded a Parents' Legal Fund on 19 March 1972 to raise funds from anyone willing to donate money to defend us boys in detention. The Jehovah's Witness organisation never contributed a cent.

Advocate Israel (Issy) Aaron Maisels SC agreed to take on our case and soon sent a representative to interview us individually in Nel's office where we told our stories, corroborating what I had told my father outside the courthouse. Maisels was a Senior Counsel of distinction who had acted in high profile cases:

> Issy Maisels first emerged into prominence in 1932 as junior counsel to the great Harry Morris KC in the notorious case of Daisy de Melker who was charged with poisoning two husbands and her son. During his illustrious career Issy Maisels appeared in many high profile trials, the best known of which was probably the historic treason trial that commenced in 1958 before a Special Criminal Court in Pretoria. It was alleged by the Crown that the accused did attempt or actually did prepare to subvert or overthrow the state. The accused, all of whom were acquitted, included many prominent South Africans some of whom emerged as leaders in the post 1994 democracy.[41]

My mother told me that the Witnesses weren't too pleased with dad's handling of our case – they would have preferred silence on the matter. But it seems, from the correspondence, that my father pressed on. So, how much did the Witnesses' organisation care about us? The Johannesburg *Star* questioned one Seegers, a Jehovah's Witness spokesman, asking 'How many young men are now in detention barracks?' Seegers replied: 'Forty-six that we know of, but we don't keep a record. Usually we read about them in the newspaper.'[42] How feeble! Surely the organisation would have been expected to know of us and to track our individual cases, even if they failed to support our cause with any form of action.

---

[41] http://www.maiselsgroup.com/about_us.html [referenced 3 October 2012]
[42] 'Case against serving in the army', Jean Le May, the *Star*, Johannesburg, 6 November 1971 [#15].

Where the organisation lacked in active support, opposition parties leaned on the government to change the way they handled us. The *Sunday Express* reported that 'Mrs Helen Suzman, Progressive Party MP for Houghton, has demanded the immediate abolition of solitary confinement for religious objectors.'[43]

The *Rand Daily Mail*, a Johannesburg daily newspaper with a strong anti-apartheid bias, printed a full-page article in their Saturday edition a week after the *Sunday Express*'s criticism:[44]

> To find out what conditions are like for the unfortunates at DB I talked to officers at Voortrekkerhoogte and was taken on an 'open doors' tour of the barracks. I looked into the solitary confinement cells, examined the eating and washing facilities, saw the detainees at drill and at work, and was allowed to take photographs of all I wished. Two things only were prohibited: identifiable faces in the picture and talking to the inmates.

The article confronts the issue of solitary confinement:

> The most serious charges usually levelled at military detention are that some conscientious objectors, especially Jehovah's Witnesses, are held in continuous solitary confinement, against barracks regulations.

'Tripe!' replied Brigadier De Wet, military apologist. 'Solitary confinement, with or without spare diet, and forfeiture of privileges only result from offences committed inside the barracks [...]. If a soldier under sentence refuses to work or don the working dress of plastic helmet, overalls, socks and boots [...he] stays in his usual cell – and this is what happens to many Jehovah's Witnesses. But it is not solitary confinement.'

In an embedded article on the same page, the *Rand Daily Mail* quoted Mrs Helen Suzman in Parliamentary debate on the matter as having squarely laid the blame at Nel's feet when she said '[m]y point is not that they [conscientious objectors] have been sentenced unjustly or outside the terms of the regulations. My point is not that the man in charge [Nel] does not have the right to sentence them further in the detention barracks to solitary confinement and

---

[43] 'Solitary detention in army barracks criticised', Tim O'Hagan, *Sunday Express*, 23 April 1972 [#39].
[44] 'The penned-in life of the objectors', A de V Marais, Military Correspondent, *Rand Daily Mail*, 29 April 1972 [#40].

spare diet. My point is that he has been going outside the regulations.'[45] This was a crisp indictment of Nel's actions.

Nel seemed to follow a certain process. At the beginning of our incarceration, he kept us with regular enlisted offenders for a few days. Perhaps he hoped we'd feel isolated and surrender to peer pressure. Maybe it was aimed at a cooling-off period during which time we would lose track of outside events and current affairs and forget the messages that some parents asked us to deliver to their sons inside. In the presence of the regular offenders he sent in his heavies to frighten us with repeated summary trials, spare rations and intimidation.

He failed in his purpose. We were sent back to the other objectors. Under one roof, he could stop us influencing regular prisoners and could isolate us from outside news. On one occasion we were taken to work in somebody's garden near the Military Hospital but, otherwise, we stayed locked up in our cells. To further soften us, unscheduled brutal inspections occurred at all hours of the day and night. However, we formed close bonds and maintained our unity despite the pressure.

The Ministry of Defence sent my father a reply, an intended closure to the matter of his letter to the Prime Minister. They referred to their comprehensive enquiry into his complaints and asserted: 'it was established that your allegations are to a great extent exaggerated and unfounded. It is also obvious that you are not acquainted with the legal aspects of this case and the prescribed provisions and regulations governing a detention barracks.'[46]

Even so, as a friend once joked, mixing his metaphors, 'you've now stirred up a hornet's nest in a can of worms'. The issue of the treatment of conscientious objectors wouldn't go away. Within a month, the South African Council of Churches made a new call to 'create avenues of "peaceful and constructive" work for conscientious objectors to military service.'[47] In the same article, the United Party 'asked for the Bill to be changed so that conscientious objectors could not be sentenced more than once for refusing military training'. It was also reported that the Council of Churches passed a unanimous resolution calling upon 'religious and educational leaders to take the initiative in discussing, planning and experimenting with pilot programmes,

---

[45] 'Suzman charge: beyond the barrack rules', *Rand Daily Mail*, 29 April 1972 [#40].
[46] Letter from Major CE van den Berg, Military Secretary, Ministry of Defence, 5 May 1972 [#42].
[47] 'Conscientious objectors: a joint appeal', the *Star*, Johannesburg, 20 May 1972 [#43].

and to offer these to the Government as registered employment opportunities for conscientious objectors'.

While calls for reform echoed in Parliament and in the press, Chief Justice Ogilvie Thompson, sitting with Mr Justice Jansen and Mr Justice Kotze of the Appellate Division, overturned an appeal by a sect member in May 1972. Ogilvie Thompson said that 'it was obvious that recognition of claims such as those advanced [in seeking an appeal] would tend to both disrupt the smooth administration of the Act and cast an unfair burden upon the more patriotic of the country's citizens.'[48]

On the same day, another newspaper published an article, reporting on comments made during the committee stage of the Defence Amendment Bill:

> 'Jehovah's Witnesses were nothing but disciples of chaos,' the Minister of Defence, Mr P W Botha, said in the Assembly yesterday. 'They were merely a bunch of mischievous people not only as far as military service is concerned, but in other spheres as well.' He could not understand how people who were so religious could act in the way they did. They refused to accept responsibility. These people were a curse in any community and he had to reject them.[49]

I don't suppose that of itself my father's letter to the Prime Minister changed much, but I believe it brought matters into the public eye at a crucial time when Parliament considered amending the Defence Bill.

An unexpected downside to my father's letter was the way it provoked Nel to retaliate. I had spilt the beans during my brief encounter with dad in the court's parking area and it culminated in bad press for Nel. Although I never felt as though I had much power, Nel might have felt differently and I'm positive that he believed I was some kind of ringleader.

Outside news came via the occasional parcels, which the authorities permitted our parents to send us. They allowed essential toiletries, tee shirts and rugby shorts, and these parcels became ingenious hiding places for surreptitious communications from our families. We often found letters embedded in the centres of bars of soap and notes embossed in their waxy

---

[48] 'Appeal by sect member dismissed', the *Star*, Johannesburg, 25 May 1972 [#44].
[49] 'Jehovah's Witnesses "disciples of chaos"', *Rand Daily Mail*, 25 May 1972 [#45].

wrappings, but the officials soon discovered them, removed all wrappings, and from then on cut in half all the soap. The next obvious place to hide a note was inside a toothpaste tube. Tubes were, back then, made of aluminium, folded and crimped at the end. One could carefully unfold the end, insert a letter, reseal the tube and camouflage one's tampering with a daub of model aircraft enamel. Regrettably, they also cottoned onto this and banned all subsequent consignments of toothpaste.[50]

Within a few weeks of the press's visit to the barracks, Nel moved many of us out of Block 2 and into Block 1 where we shared cells with soldier detainees. I'm not sure what the army's rationale was because there were many open cells in Block 3 but I'm convinced they hoped that ordinary inmates would influence us, coerce us and perhaps bully us into becoming soldiers. The army's strategy of bundling us together in one cell had a devastating effect on my morale because I knew I was different in so many ways, sexually, religiously and politically. I hated the idea of sharing a cell with two soldiers who held extremely divergent views on life. I felt deeply out of place and vulnerable.

The commandant merged us late one afternoon. The conscientious objectors remained in their cells while the soldiers were marched out for supper and their end-of-day ablutions. They had full army kit while we possessed nothing but our blankets, shorts and tee shirts. The move happened on the first day of a two-day spare-rations sentence so we only had a half-loaf of bread to eat whereas our cellmates returned with bellies full of food. This was undoubtedly all part of Nel's carefully designed strategy to break us without leaving traces of his own handiwork.

I spoke with my two conscript cellmates after supper, sharing experiences and ideas as they folded their clothes for morning inspection. Exhausted, they soon lay down and slept. I sat in the corner, cocooned in my blanket, listening to their breathing and gentle snores; but I couldn't sleep. Hunger let in the bitter cold and I couldn't get warm. Evenings in May are chilly as winter begins to bite.

The pre-dawn wake-up boomed down the cellblock the next morning and my cellmates dressed quickly in shorts and tee shirts, ready for their morning shower, roll call and health inspection. I felt ill and could hardly stand up. The pair from my cell returned for morning

---

[50] Nel's letter to my father, 18 January 1973 [#78].

inspection after breakfast and arranged their items on their mattresses. Still cold, I remained wrapped in my blanket and watched them tweak their kit before they went out of the cell to wait for inspection.

We were third in line, very close to the cellblock's main entrance. The overnight guard stayed on to join the morning shift and so there were more people on duty than usual that morning.

Four NCOs barged into our cell and one approached me directly. 'What is this?' One yelled, ripping off my blanket and tossing it outside. 'You're supposed to fold your stuff like that!' he continued, red with anger, pointing at the two other beds. Then he grabbed me by the wrist and flung me outside.

They'd hatched some kind of plot and I stood by helplessly, frightened, not knowing what to expect. Induced by a rush of adrenalin and exacerbated by the icy concrete, which drew out the warmth through the soles of my bare feet, I shivered uncontrollably.

The inspectors grabbed the contents of the cell and threw them out into the gully where our things lay scattered and mixed with the disgorged items of the first two cells. The four moved systematically down the row, creating havoc, leaving a jumble of army kit, mattresses and crumpled blankets in puddles from upturned water buckets.

A fifth corporal followed, yelling: 'Get down, you fuckers – get down! Press-ups until I tell you to stop!'

My two enlisted roommates obeyed but I refused; and the more I refused, the more he brutalised them. The tactics were blatant. Detention barracks rules forbade corporal punishment, but they thought they could whip up resentment against conscientious objectors through abusing the regular national service prisoners, which would lead to a new kind of pressure against us.

The day was altogether hideous. The army targeted the soldiers for every refusal that I made, and resentment surely grew as they took the punishment I should have borne. I wished they'd punish me, but I was ignored. I hoped that the soldiers would stand up to the orderlies but it appeared that they lived by a different code. Their tough response was to 'take it', to 'handle it'. After a day of torture the NCOs locked us up and left. Perhaps they hoped for retaliation in the confines of the cell. But those two conscripts were a different breed with a kind of honour that ironically enough threatened my view of things and made me feel ashamed. On our own, the two of them merely grunted and closed ranks in stony silence.

I broke the ice. Where to begin? How to make amends?

'Guys, this is bad. I'm sorry. They punished you instead of me.'

I found myself babbling in the face of their grim silence. I felt the need to explain, to justify, to these men who took things with such pragmatism. It was important that I kept my overview, my own grasp of 'how' and 'why', but it came out as a mild hysteria, merely emphasising the vast difference in our reactions:

I've been in solitary confinement for nearly eight months. I have no visitors; they won't allow me to read anything other than my Bible. I can't write letters, I've been on spare-rations since the start. They don't know how to punish me anymore and they hope you'll do their dirty work. They hope you'll beat the crap out of me. Hit me if you wish! I'm ready.'

I plunged on recklessly:

'I'll understand you, I'll forgive you, if you do it! But you should realise that you're pawns in their hands. They're playing mind games with us. I've got nothing to wear other than this kit, I'm freezing cold, I'm hungry. I haven't eaten properly for ages. They're hoping to weaken me further by getting you to retaliate. They're hoping that I'll give up.'

I wrapped my blanket around my shoulders and slumped into the corner, squatting on my haunches on top of my mattress. The faces of the two young men were closed. The atmosphere was claustrophobic.

One of them broke the silence.

'*Ag* no, man! We're also pissed off with the army. Who the hell are they? We know it's not your fault,' he added, as the other nodded gravely. 'We don't take shit from anybody!'

'Be careful,' I prudishly replied. All I had in answer was my main theme. 'You guys might not eat tonight, you could lose your privileges. They might even extend your sentence if you don't do what they expect.'

'*Fok* man, we know that!' he said. I felt like a hapless prig.

The prisoners in the block went for supper as usual and these two smuggled back some food for me. When it came time to sleep, they pushed our mattresses together and we had three blankets instead of one. I slept between them. They offered to get news to my parents via theirs during the scheduled weekend visit. So much for retaliation. Nel's plans, as far as I suspected them, backfired in his face. Yet – it did have some effect: it worked, in that my self-assurance had been badly shaken. Here was a different kind of ethos, a tough camaraderie that, in its own way, resisted the authorities.

As suddenly as the army had put us together, they separated us and moved the objectors back to Block 2. Spurred by my father's letter to the Prime Minister and the press tour of the barracks, Nel watched me with growing suspicion. He thought I was a bad influence, inciting others to rebellion, and I suppose to some degree he was right. I had no qualms about speaking up and did so whenever I had the opportunity. After all, what more could he do to me? The life had toughened me in my own way, and I became progressively bolder.

After much debate, and criticism of the Jehovah's Witnesses, the Parliamentary Select Committee appointed to investigate changes to the Defence Bill approved the United Party's recommended changes and the State President signed the bill into law on 14 June 1972. This made specific provisions for those who refused military training. Young men would now be sentenced only once to a term of between twelve and eighteen months for their offence.[51] [52] Instead of acceding to Botha's call for harsher punishment, Parliament had promulgated laws that limited sentences.

Nel was humiliated. The press had exposed the vicious punishment meted out under his command and the Select Committee's approval of changes to the Bill ended his cunning use of civil judgements to hand down long sentences. Any additional punishment had to occur within the confines of the detention barracks where the army could keep it hidden from the public. But Nel had not yet done with me.

---

[51] 'Jehovah's Witnesses "disciples of chaos"', *Rand Daily Mail*, 25 May 1972 [#45].
[52] *Republic of South Africa Government Gazette*, 84.J, No. 3556, 14 June 1972 [#47a].

Soon after my return to Block 2, most likely near the end of May 1972, Delport and his entourage returned one morning with a new strategy. He usually targeted us as a group to find reason to extend solitary confinement and spare rations but, that morning, he singled me out.

'Private Budge,' he began, as Vermaak once again held out the uniform. I interrupted him in mid-sentence.

'Don't bother to continue, sir. There's no point in wasting your time and mine. We both know that Captain Nel's got another scheme up his sleeve for me. Why go through with the charade? Do what you have to do and skip the formalities.'

'I'm ordering you to put on this...'

'Yeah! I know. But, by now, you know how I'll respond – which gives the captain an excuse to punish me further. Besides which, I must tell you that I've enjoyed every one of his little summary trials because it gives me a chance to play a game with him, which he can't refuse. He's obliged to let me defend myself; and military rules require him to write down everything I say. My game is to see how long I can keep him busy writing.'

Nel knew what I was doing and it angered him, but I had him snookered.

Delport, once again to the letter, followed the prescribed steps of the process, ordering that I wear the uniform, and once again I interjected wherever I could. The event was a farce and we all knew it. They wanted the harshest continuous punishment but they had to find legal reasons to renew our sentences every fortnight. Delport needed evidence to secure conviction and he took his task seriously. I enjoyed teasing him and scuttling the process. The sterner he was, the more I played and the more furious he became. He, of course, won the game.

I was up in front of Nel that same afternoon and the proceedings followed their usual course; but his sentence flummoxed me:

'I sentence you to solitary confinement for the rest of your time in detention barracks,' he decreed. His face wore a look of cold triumph.

Technically, they had always kept us in solitary confinement even though the army tried to spin it otherwise. But, by the tone of Nel's voice, I realised that some new and deeper trouble lay ahead. Nel sought to quash my supposed influence over the others, and get even with my father, by silencing me. I had left the cellblock in a teasing mood. I returned solemnly.

---oooOooo---

Ordered to gather my sparse kit, I scooped up everything in my blanket and followed Vermaak and his Corporal to an undisclosed destination. There was a lot of whispering behind the ventilation grilles above the doors as my friends watched me leave. Vermaak thumped on the steel as he passed by, getting the guys to drop to the ground, but most disobeyed him.

They all asked much the same question: 'What's up, Tom? Where are they taking you?'

'Solitary confinement,' I called out for all to hear, defying the rules.

'What?'

I shouted louder: '*Solitary confinement, guys!*'

'When?'

'*Now!*'

'Where?'

'*I don't know!*'

'Quiet!' yelled Vermaak, but the questions ran on. 'Shut the fuck up!' he bellowed into the last cell before we left the block.

I followed them down the *stoep*, past the barber and the other offices, to the end of the administration block. The covered walkway to Block 3 led off to the left, directly opposite the last green door in this row. I'd never before been so deep into the precinct. This was new terrain. There were two vehicle entrances into the detention barracks, one behind the captain's office and this one here, rarely used, in the corner of the property. The gate opened up to a bay where a truck might park to despatch its cargo easily into Block 4.

This was a notorious and sinister part of the barracks and seldom frequented by anyone, including the staff. Block 4 had an aura of fear. Rumours abounded about its use. It never housed prisoners; it allegedly served as an ammunitions store. Many believed it to be haunted. The green door at the end of the office block led to Dark Cells, a section of the barracks with a disturbing reputation where tough recidivous prisoners spent time. Some emerged with their spirit broken, needing treatment in the psychiatric ward at 1 Military Hospital before they could function properly again.

I believed that we were going into Block 3 but at the entrance we turned right, down an exposed concrete walkway, to the main door of Block 4. I fretted over what lay ahead.

The latch opened with much effort. Then the heavy, reluctant hinges creaked as the door swung back. Prisoners kept the concrete floors polished to a high gloss throughout the barracks but the concrete here was raw and scarified from the dragging of heavy equipment. The dust confirmed that the block had been unoccupied for a very long time.

Vermaak walked halfway down the corridor towards an empty cell on the left. 'In here!' he snapped, as he pointed towards the open door.

I dumped my meagre bundle on the ground. A mattress stood propped up on its edge against the wall and someone had already filled a pail with water and placed it in the corner next to a galvanised latrine bucket. Vermaak locked the door without a word, and left.

It felt as though I'd been struck deaf. The other cell blocks seemed noisy by comparison. In the sudden stillness I heard the pulse of my own blood. I felt numb, helpless and abandoned. The chill of a midwinter afternoon on the still, mute, enclosed air.

I didn't have the emotional energy to unpack my kit. It was my habit, my ritual, in taking ownership of each cell I occupied, to arrange things the way I liked. This time I shook my stuff out of the blanket, pushed it into the corner, dropped the mattress to the floor, wrapped myself in the blanket and squatted, sitting motionless, as though unplugged from a power supply.

It was the first time in detention that I seriously thought I wouldn't make it. Life seemed empty of any kind of purpose. Not that I felt suicidal, not that I contemplated surrendering: it was a sense of sheer lack of purpose. I was struck fully by the contrast between their power and my helplessness. It seemed to me as though, for all this time, I'd been trying to puff away a thunderstorm. The closest I can compare those feelings is to the sense of failure when, in a sudden and lucid moment, we realise what we've done to this planet, the awful legacy we leave our children, our feebleness in changing it. Vain and pointless resistance. A wrong, wrong world and a futile endeavour to resist the wrong. Perhaps this is what the theologians mean by despair – the ultimate in fallen spirit.

I doubted my ability to continue. The military machine allied with the law and magistrates was far stronger than one young man of nineteen, isolated from the world. Would I have the emotional, physical and spiritual stamina to stand firm? Until, if needs be, I was sixty-five and my obligation to serve the state was over?

Cocooned in my blanket I squatted on the mattress with my back against the wall, my head resting on my knees, arms wrapped around my ankles. It was a seated foetal position in a womblike enclosure, and it comforted me. I remained shrouded there until way after the sun had set. The only light came from a naked globe in the corridor some distance off. Self-sabotaging thoughts wormed through my brain but my body remained numb, almost disconnected.

The distant and muted sound of the evening dinner bell and the muffled clang of doors in the neighbouring cellblock brought me back into the moment. The moment ran on. An hour later – and the latch on the main door squeaked and moaned. It opened with a clank and I heard purposeful footsteps. One person. He unlocked the cell door and swung it open. A visitor, an officer I hadn't seen before, dressed in shirt and tie. Pressed trousers, highly polished shoes, and a peaked cap. He had a rank that I didn't recognise.

'Thomas?' he enquired. This was the first time in my months of detention that anyone had called me by my first name. The intimacy of it was unexpected and I was instantly on guard. Here in Block 4, away from other eyes, from the testimony of others, what new horror could I now expect? I anticipated a new form of vicious abuse. Why else would they have placed me here?

'Yes sir,' I hesitantly replied.

'I'm Jacques Smit.' [I wish I could remember his real name but I simply can't.] 'I'm a Permanent Force lieutenant. I'm in charge here at night. They're all busy so I thought I'd open up for when they bring your food.'

Astonishing. A real human. A decent human! Afrikaans, in his thirties, and smartly turned out as becomes an officer. Unlike the slob Vermaak, whose elasticised waistband was always at full stretch, this tall and lean lieutenant was exact in dress and bearing.

I ate as usual from a dixie, sipped the tepid tea and waited silently in the semi-dark until an orderly came to collect the dishes. The lieutenant returned a little later and locked my cell. He said goodnight, turned off the light and secured the outside door. His minimal display of decency struck a deep connection at a human level. It lifted the lid off the place where I'd hidden my emotion and vulnerability, and some of this leaked out.

It had, up to now, been the most hideous night of my incarceration. His mild acknowledgement of *me* touched me deeply, and I wept. Yes, there are some men with conscience and the guts to show concern. The military policeman who let me talk with dad in the courtroom parking lot was one; Lieutenant Jacques was another. It knocked me. I felt physically done in, emotionally overwhelmed. With my vulnerability exposed, emotions re-engaged, I wept. And after this catharsis came fresh dejection and I slipped into a state of deep despondence.

Fatigued and overwrought, I nodded off to sleep for short spells; but most of the night I sat awake with self-berating thoughts that wouldn't go away. I mulled endlessly over the idea that perhaps I'd become too blasé, too cocksure. Had I kept a low profile, as many others did, Nel might not have segregated me and placed me in isolation. Perhaps I should have kept quiet about my games with him. Maybe it was a mistake to have challenged Delport with such flippant bravado.

These men were of a kind that I despised – ruthless, without conscience, self-serving bullies. But trying to draw them out, showing off my own self-styled superiority, was foolish. The science fiction author John Brunner said: 'If there is such a phenomenon as absolute evil, it consists in treating another human being as a thing'. My attempts to assert my independent self, to redefine myself in their eyes not as a thing but as a conscious individual, could not (for now) match that kind of evil.

I believed at the time that Nel separated me from the others because of my attitude, but I later understood that he had to isolate me to contain the damage caused by my father and me.

If the allegations were true that Nel and P W Botha were friends, and that Botha specifically tasked Nel with putting down our resistance, it then makes sense that Nel had gained government's sanction to turn to the civilian courts in seeking harsher punishment after he had reached the limits of his discretionary powers.

Nel had the authority to remove our privileges, to sentence us to spare-rations and to keep us in fortnightly periods of solitary confinement; but as far back as November 1971, a few days after my arrival at the barracks, Botha, in his role as Minister of Defence, had said that he was 'losing his patience' with Jehovah's Witnesses and was considering asking for legislation to increase the penalties for refusing military service.[53] In the five months between October 1971 and March 1972, the army had sentenced me to ninety days for refusing conscription, to a second term of 180 days for refusing to wear a uniform, and to an additional year for still disobeying the same order. Nel, Botha and the courts had increased the pressure on us in the hope that we would break.

My disclosure to my father outside the court in March and his letters to Parliament and the State President brought unwanted attention and public sympathy, and Nel probably had no choice but to let in the press. He'd had his hands tied. The Parliamentary Select Committee's approval of changes to the Defence Act, reducing punitive measures against conscientious objectors, undermined Botha's plans to have them increased. Nel as Botha's supposed agent could no longer use civilian courts to increase sentences. But I now realised that Nel believed there was still a lot he could do, behind the perimeter walls of the detention barracks, as its commanding officer, where prying eyes could not see. And I was isolated so that no more information could leak out.

First light brought some relief to a confused and exhausted mind and I managed to salvage the remnants of reason and some of my faith, and this brought a kind of peace. I assured myself that Nel held me here in solitary confinement because the army intended to break my spirit. If I permitted that, he would win and I would lose. I knew that I had to keep my focus on this point which held the balance between capitulation and victory.

---

[53] 'Case against serving in the army,' Jean Le May, the *Star*, Johannesburg, 6 November 1971 [#15].

I reflect back on those times as I write about them over forty years on. I marvel at the resources of a nineteen-year-old stumbling alone through such a morass of uncertainty and hardship. I wonder what it was that kept me going.

I once thought that it was tenacity; but I know that while I am sometimes stubborn, I wasn't the most tenacious person back then. Perhaps it was about having a sense of special purpose, a mission? The Jehovah's Witnesses had a very clear dogma, a distinctly marked path through life for their devotees, and all I had to do was follow it. Yet, again, I'm not sure if that was enough to carry me. Did an inculcated 'fear of God' keep me going? Yes, largely so. There was too much at stake if I failed. The Witnesses' guidelines made it abundantly clear that disobedience to their understanding of divinity would have resulted in an expurgation and I would have had to leave the organisation. Yes, this was a major motivation. But it was not the primary one: my sexual orientation already tainted me and I believed that I was doomed to hell because of it – so why would I have continued currying favour with that Godhead as a conscientious objector when I was already damned on another level?

Two entangled notions, of which I knew very little back then, carried me through: *surrender* and *faith*. I absolutely believed that what I was doing was the right thing, not as a promotion of Witness dogma, nor to uphold Godly principles for fear of retribution. It was much, much deeper than that. I had unwavering faith that *my course of action was the only way I could be true to me*. I surrendered to injustice because I was powerless to do anything about it; it was a mere consequence of living my truth. Injustice came from all sides, the military's uncompromising insistence on conscription and their unfair recourse to the might of the law to punish us, and the Witnesses' lack of support and veiled threats of expulsion if we failed. But underlying all of this there was something far more fundamental, radical: the embryonic imperative to be *true to myself*.

I had no control over the outcome of my situation other than capitulation, and that wasn't an option, but *acceptance* was a powerful psychological tool that brought serenity, peace and strength. Casting Mind forward into the morass of expectations, worrying about stuff that might or might not have occurred, was painful. Walking backwards into my future, looking only at my past and reminiscing over memories of freedom, entrapped me. Acceptance of what was, set me on a path of emotional and spiritual freedom. The opening verse to Reinhold Niebuhr's 1942 Serenity Prayer is 'God grant me the serenity to accept the things I cannot change, courage to change the things I can, and the wisdom to know the difference'. Dad's unspoken motto, a simple but profound statement of deeper acceptance, '*It is what it is!*', was a principle by which I have lived ever since.

I'm not going to bluff myself and think that because of a sea-change in my attitude everything became a bed of roses. On the contrary, there were many dark moments and they pressed in and haunted me. They were momentary lapses of acceptance when Mind sucked me into a vortex of depression and despair, and sometimes I sobbed uncontrollably for hours until my being felt squeezed out and I fell asleep, depleted. I was troubled by those times because then I lost power, and capitulation sounded reasonable: surrender to the army, to save myself this anguish? But when I woke up after such long and dismal nights, I understood that the lifelong consequence of living with failure would have been far, far worse than the mental torture of the moment. Realisation of this renewed my resolve.

Other young men believed it was correct to defend their beloved fatherland, or if not quite that, they regarded conscription as inevitable. Many sacrificed life and limb on the Angolan border. I believed in pacifism and love and was willing to sacrifice life and limb in prison. The common strength that carried us all despite different beliefs was our courageous way of upholding personal truth. Who was right and who was wrong? All of us were right and all of us were wrong! – a discovery I made much later.

Nobody monitored my activities in Block 4 and I soon identified people's movements – bucket changes, meal deliveries and tray collections. Apart from those routine visits nobody entered the block, and this gave me time to sit on my blanket at the window for hours, looking out onto the space between the cellblocks. I was too far from either end of the block to see anything other than the brick facade of Block 3, the lawn between the buildings, and a clear view of the sky above. The four parallel blocks ran from southwest to northeast, a placement that let in plenty of afternoon sunlight, and I enjoyed basking in this from my perch at the window.

Hours, days and weeks became a continuum of undifferentiated time, a period of deep personal introspection, interrupted with moments of self-doubt. But it was more than that: time had no outer boundary, no limitation; and I had no idea how long I would spend there. David Hurton, music-oriented psychologist, writes as follows on the idea of structuring of expectations:

> Forming expectations is what humans and other animals do to survive; only by predicting the future can we be ready for it. And because the brain ensures that

accurate prediction is rewarded, we feel good when we're proved right. The link between prediction and reward causes us to constantly seek out structure and predict how events will unfold.[54]

Undifferentiated time strips away any sense of structured future. It seemed that the army systematically chipped away at my own sense of futurity, my self-identity, my survival tools, hoping to make me inept and vulnerable as a person.

Isolation is a heinous strategy, used for torture as well as separation. There was little eye contact with anyone, and without this I had no means of gauging from others how I stood as a person – on track, or losing it. Conformity of one kind or another, and the group connection, are natural instincts, reinforced when we identify ourselves with a group and belong to it. I'd now lost connection with the other conscientious objectors as a group, and I lost the reinforcement offered by that collective belonging. I felt like a dog that had lost contact with its pack and turned into a skittish, neurotic lone hunter.

Sannyāsa is a Hindu state of being – renunciation, the highest and final stage of the ashram system where the *Sannyasi* gives up all material and worldly endeavours and devotes himself or herself entirely to their spiritual pursuits. I wish I could say that I was consciously living a monastic life in detention barracks but, at nineteen, I wasn't ready for that. There is a huge difference between *being alone* and *feeling lonely*. Loneliness is a reaction; being alone is a matter of deliberate solitude. I had to learn to find comfort and meaning in seclusion. Isolation wasn't easy and, at times, Mind played awful games on me. We are complex emotional, intellectual, tactile beings and solitary confinement is a psychological torture, a cruel and unnatural punishment that eats away at the self like cancer. It played havoc with my emotions, it deprived me of mental stimulus, and it stripped me of touch and companionship. I tried hard to *be alone* instead of enduring the awful loneliness.

The endless silence began to separate my once-muddled blend of feelings in the way that silt settles in a quiet pond. Issues were brought into new and difficult focus. I began to question my authenticity and felt more and more hypocritical. Many viewed me as strong and pure, and yet only I knew of the facade and what lay behind. I held on to the Jehovah's Witnesses because I couldn't find a negotiated way out. Had I revealed my sexual orientation, even by way of

---

[54] Sweet Anticipation: Music and the Psychology of Expectation, David Hurton

seeking help, I would have faced instant dismissal; yet I clung on to my association with the organisation because it brought the continuing support of my parents. Besides which, I couldn't fight two great battles at the same time. Dad was my champion. The Witnesses were merely an operating platform, a means, to facilitate his help.

Touch is a vital component of our human experience. The American psychologist Harry Frederick Harlow conducted some very controversial experiments with young macaque monkeys, rearing them in isolation for up to two years. Those experiments severely disturbed the infant monkeys and I look back to the times in solitary confinement and the effects of lack of human contact on me. I sat for hours, gently running my fingers through my hair, caressing my lips and the soft skin around my eyelids. This provided a huge sense of emotional comfort. The continuous caress resurrected a primitive subconscious connection between mother and child. In a way, self-caressing was deeply meditative and rooted me fully in the Now; and the more I learned to live in the Now, the easier it was to survive in solitary confinement.

I realise that we don't touch each other enough. Touching has become a social taboo because we've confused it with sex. Society often views it as harassment, and I guess there is a lot of that about, but the confusion is wrong. Often seen holding hands, black African men do so as a sign of respect and friendship. White South Africans of British roots take their social cue from English society where public shows of intimacy are deprecated. Thankfully, European friends have liberated me from that. I'm now very comfortable with a hug, a consoling hand on a shoulder and the holding of hands, to give support or reassurance during times of spiritual or emotional need. *Maundy*, as taught by Jesus, was an intimate act of touch that served to remind his followers to remain humble and equal, for it was he, the Master Teacher, who washed their feet.

---oooOooo---

The winter months in solitary were the worst. The bars above the cell door opened into the cellblock and the opening that ran the length of the roof admitted a strong through-draft of air. Nocturnal temperatures often dipped to near zero Celsius and I developed awful chilblains on my bare fingers and toes. This condition occurs when the extremities are subjected to prolonged cold and humidity and damages the capillaries beneath the skin, resulting in inflamed, red and often dark blue, itchy and very sore blisters. Trying to keep warm was impossible and the only way I could sleep was to cocoon myself in my blanket and squat in the corner of the cell on my mattress. This way, encased in my blanket, with my forehead on my knees, I could shelter from the cold draft. I conserved the warmth from every exhaled breath and this became my standard sleeping posture.

My weight dropped below its recommended minimum yet I remained reasonably fit due to my walking and exercise. I also found a way to keep a personal journal using the remains of an empty aluminium toothpaste tube as my pencil, writing faintly in the margins of my Bible.

One of the two soldiers with whom I shared a cell had given me a pair of old bootlaces because one of the laces had a tight knot that stopped it threading through the eyelets in his boot. I kept these laces in the side seam of my blanket and forgot that they were there until I started playing with the edging, and then remembered them. Having found them, I imagined how to use them. I began to ponder a way to open my cell door. Cells in all the other cellblocks had a steel grille on the outside of the bars above the door. The configuration in Block 4 was different: the grille was absent and I could reach out between the bars, but not all the way down to the latch.

I obsessed over a plan to reach the latch. First I had to study the identical lock on the opposite door. It wasn't as simple as I had imagined and there was a lot to work out. It had taken many long minutes to thread the laces into the seam and the knot in one of them made it even more awkward. If I used these laces to open my door, it wouldn't be easy to hide them in a hurry. So I looked for another hiding place. My cell had been used as storage space in the past. There were deep gouges in the paint on the walls and there was loose cement between some of the bricks. Gently prising away a bit of flaking paint and scratching a groove into the cement, I created a pocket just big enough to hide the folded laces. I pasted the paint back to the wall with a bit of toothpaste.

The next task involved a risky experiment. With the bootlaces I devised a noose to hook onto the latch outside. They never padlocked our cells. To secure the door, a long steel barrel bolt slid into a housing in the doorframe. A flange with a hole in it was welded to the bolt. This flange met up with a fixed bracket so that, if desired, a padlock could be inserted. (Many of the storage cells in Block 4 were indeed padlocked shut.) I had to snag the flange with the bootlaces, lift and slide it a few centimetres forward to disengage it from the fixed bracket, then move it slightly upwards and backwards to withdraw the barrel from its housing. It was a tricky business: if I lifted the flange too much or too little I could lose traction and leave the latch half-cocked for the guards to see.

Perfecting the design took several prototypes and I could only test them late at night for fear of discovery. I waited a few days for an occasion to study the lock when the cell door was open, and a quick test showed that the bolt moved quite freely. Many attempts failed, not because of an error in the design but due to my lack of skill. It required a lot of dexterity and I feared the laces might snag, or fall outside the door. Both possibilities made me very nervous and I didn't dare take chances until I felt quite safe.

At last, my design was ready and late one night I managed to hook the loop over the flange. I was filled with excitement and fear. A shiver ran through me. There was an equal chance of failing and succeeding. What if I opened the door and afterwards couldn't lock it properly? Lieutenant Jacques always took it upon himself to close my door each night and he opened it again the next morning. He would unavoidably have noticed the displaced bolt. What would happen to me if I bungled?

I'd been brought up in an ethos of honesty, righteousness and adherence to rules. I now found myself about to defy everything my parents taught me, and I knew that there was a high probability of screwing things up. The venture was daring and it got my adrenaline pumping. After a short flurry of nervous lassoing, I snagged the grip quite easily and gently lifted it; but I then realised that I had insufficient leverage and couldn't draw the bolt far enough forward. I quickly retrieved the laces, rattled the door to get the flange to fall back into position, and for a while abandoned the experiment. But the idea obsessed me and I had to succeed, regardless of the dangers.

A few nights later I again easily snagged the flange. I now sought to untie the secured end and thread it through the narrow gap between the door and doorframe to get the advantage of angled distance that I needed. I was scared of losing it. It took a bit of jiggling and coercing, but the more the bolt withdrew the easier it became. Then, a sudden clunk and the door opened! I could hear my heart beating and I didn't quite know what to do next. I spent the remainder of the night figuring out how to close it again.

The latch on the main cellblock door was stiff and unyielding and became a friend in the months that followed because nobody could surprise me as it took them at least a minute to unlatch the door and another thirty seconds to reach my cell. The loud squeaking of the outer latch on the main door to the cellblock was my early warning.

Safety rules specified that a backup person must accompany anyone entering a cellblock and that they had to secure the outer door after entering. Nobody, other than the perimeter guards, carried weapons inside the barracks. Sometimes, someone was equipped with a rubber truncheon, but nothing more. Yet operations in Block 4 were different and the rules seemed more relaxed. I soon observed that they always left the main block door ajar when they came in. Possibly they were wary that they might trap themselves inside due to the sticky latch; perhaps they didn't feel the need to worry since I was the only inmate there. Perhaps they were afraid of the ghosts that were reputed to haunt Block 4. So, instead of working in pairs, the competent Lieutenant Jacques always visited my cell alone.

Regular nocturnal freedom inside Block 4 became a Godsend that allowed me to bathe under the tap at the far end and, during the summer months (the rainy season), I could stand naked in the rain as it poured through the gap in the roof. I became very adept at opening and closing the door, and I even ventured out into the sunshine over the weekends, particularly on Sunday mornings. At that time the entire complement attended service in the little chapel at the far corner of the barracks precinct. There were occasions when they nearly caught me outside my cell but, thanks to the squeaky latch, I always managed to lock myself in and hide the laces before they entered.

One night, however, a guard on patrol around the back of the barracks heard running water inside the block and reported it. This initiated a thorough search of my cell but I had already locked myself inside, was bone dry, and my laces were properly stowed in the groove in the wall by the time they came. I remember the commotion. There was much speculation about the water splashed around the tap and running down the gulley, which proved that someone had opened the tap. Outside my cell, the group of investigators conferred. They concluded that the evidence exonerated me and I had nothing to do with it: how could I have got out of a cell with a bolted door? I couldn't believe how complacent they were over this. To me it was now obvious that the bolt could be manipulated from inside. However, nobody realised that I had the capacity to open the cell door. There could be only one explanation: the ghost.

'Did anybody come into the block?' asked a corporal, awkwardly.

'Yes!' I replied, taking full advantage. 'Very strange things go on here at night.'

I've always been a great teaser with a keen sense of humour that comes from Granddad Bill Sinclair. I lowered my tone and spoke solemnly:

'I often hear noises down near the tap. Sometimes, the water runs for a while and then stops. I must say, it's really spooky.'

I played straight into their vague belief that Block 4 was haunted. I could see that they were suddenly apprehensive about being here so very late at night.

'There are many stories of ghosts in this block,' explained the Lieutenant. 'They've been here a long time and most of the guys are afraid to come in at night. Even when the place is completely empty there are noises. Maybe someone committed suicide in here or maybe they built the block over an old farm graveyard. Aren't you afraid?'

'I get very nervous,' I said, acting my part, 'but I feel safe inside my cell. They've never entered it. I think they're afraid of me! Remember, I'm watched over and protected by a much higher power than ghosts.'

After that incident, I had absolute freedom of the block. Soldiers came in only at mealtimes and bucket changes, but never unexpectedly.

However, on the matter of ghosts, there was an unscripted sequel to the story. I was sitting up at the window one day, enjoying the warmth of the afternoon sun, when I heard heavy footsteps approaching. I quickly dropped to the floor, unhitched my blanket and dumped it on the bed before hopping up at the door to see who it was. I wondered how they had entered without me hearing the squeak of the main door-latch and I assumed that I'd dozed off in the sunshine. I couldn't see anyone, but the footsteps drew nearer. When they were close, I dropped to my feet and peered through the glass eyepiece in the door. The steps came right past my cell and I saw nobody.

It freaked me out considerably. I stood motionless in the middle of my cell staring at the gap of light beneath the door. My senses bristled and I was on full alert. The footsteps stopped some four or five cells farther down on my side of the building. Then came the sound of boxes scraping on the concrete floor of a cell – but I didn't hear the cell door open. The scraping went on for some time. These noises occurred on-and-off for about thirty minutes before I heard the footsteps in the corridor again. I dropped to the floor on my stomach, leaned my head to the side and looked out under the door, but the sound came right past me without any corresponding visual clue that a person had passed by. I was deeply frightened by what I had just witnessed and my skin crawled as adrenalin kick-started my fight-or-flight reaction. I lay there for a while, listening intently, until the footsteps reached the outer door – and the sound stopped as though the entity had walked right through the closed door.

Sundays were predictable as there was a church service for the prisoners in the morning, then a quick lunch before they received visitors in the afternoon. Other than the quick delivery of a meal to my cell around noon, I had the cellblock to myself from seven in the morning until six or seven at night; and I became quite brazen in my wanderings.

On the far side of the corrugated iron perimeter wall at the back of Block 4 were a few houses, accommodation for military personnel and their families, which I remembered from my first arrival at the barracks. The people were generally quiet during the week but, occasionally, on weekends and public holidays, I could hear the adults' laughter and the high-pitched shrieks of playing children. There were many open empty cells on the opposing side of Block 4 and I often hung off the window bars of one of those cells, strapped by blanket, listening to the conversations that drifted across the fence. I occasionally made out a sentence or two but the distance and the fence muffled most of their dialogue. It was good for the soul, and it became a valuable source of information as in piecemeal fashion I gathered up crumbs of current affairs.

Even under such harsh terms of confinement, news still found its way to us. Those who delivered my food and water weren't supposed to talk to me but they did. Sometimes they inadvertently slipped me a really useful piece of information. Lieutenant Jacques lingered most nights, propped up in the doorway of the cell, nonchalant, hands in his pockets, chatting about many different things and, at times, giving me forewarning of impending inspections planned during the dead of night. Over the weeks that followed I grew to know and like him very much. I think the feeling was mutual, and there was definitely something more. The way he spoke to me, the looks he gave me, his body language and gestures and some carefully placed innuendoes, convinced me that his friendliness and kindness extended into places that neither of us could explore. Any move in that direction would have been a reckless dash across a heavily planted minefield.

My father used to send a parcel every month or so, but the last one I received was just before Nel had grouped us together with the soldier detainees in Block 1. Supplies were running out. My soap was long finished and I bathed whenever I could without soap in clean water under the tap at the end of the block. This was a bonus because we had always washed in the water from our drinking buckets. The army provided toothpaste after they discovered letters embedded in the tubes sent by some parents. I needed a safety razor and shaving cream because mine was almost finished.

As the can of Gillette aerosol shaving foam emptied, sputtering out the last few drops of foam, I realised that there was something loose inside. I was keen to investigate but, with only a small pair of nail clippers, it took several days before I liberated a note wrapped in a tight twist of plastic. I disposed of the can and the plastic wrapping in the way that we usually threw away garbage: I first reassembled the tin as best I could and splashed some gravy over it to camouflage the intrusion, and then boldly sent it out at night with my empty dinner tray.

I read the note and immediately discarded it amongst the poo in the latrine bucket. Notes that prisoners kept for sentimental reasons always brought trouble and gave the authorities reason to probe deeper for other contraband. The strip of paper read:

> Family well. No recent news about you so we assume you are strong and healthy. Often write to the Captain regarding your wellbeing but scant replies. Send word of your needs and we will send a parcel.

Dad concluded with some scriptural words of encouragement. He never told me how he got the note into the can, as he probably wanted to protect the identity of his accomplices.

The army clipped our hair once a fortnight. We usually went in groups of three or four, but during my time of solitary confinement in Block 4 they fetched me on my own. They took me to the barber for a quick haircut and then to the doctor for a cursory inspection, before returning me to my cell. These were the only times that I saw the outside of the cellblock and interacted with people other than my guards, and I looked forward to the occasions. I always tried to be chatty and upbeat during those few minutes outside. I didn't want them to sense that isolation had any power over me.

At these times I made it a point to rattle them by dropping a few bits of current news: 'Good game of rugby at the weekend – great win for the Springboks over the All Blacks!' I'd also add a little detail, like the score, just to round it off properly. This had an astonishing affect all round: incredulity on their faces as they tried to fathom out how I came to know such things. They believed that they'd intercepted all communications and yet I seemed to know more than they liked. They kept asking awkward questions about my source of information.

'How do you know that?'

'I'm tuned in to a source that you don't know.' It wasn't actually a lie but I intended it to be misleading and mischievous. It served to give me an aura of mystery. However, after a few visits to the barber and my blasé display of current affairs and trivia from the news, a sequence of events led to something far less amusing.

---oooOooo---

In the freezing cold early hours of the morning near the beginning of July, I was woken, startled, by the squeaking latch of the outside door. It groaned open and I heard numerous people approaching at a pace. I panicked and braced myself for the worst. The cell door flung wide open and a group stood in the doorway. Here were military brass I'd never seen before and many of them were military police. One very stroppy officer who held more rank than Nel burst forward and yelled 'Get out! Get out!'

I obeyed, fuddled with sleep, and still wrapped in my blanket I stepped into a group of about ten officers. Someone pulled the blanket from my shoulders and threw it back into the cell. Lieutenant Jacques stood near the back of the group looking pale and worried. I glanced at him and he raised his eyebrows as if to say 'I'm sorry, this's beyond my control.'

The officer who yelled at me seemed to be in charge. He turned to an NCO and ordered: 'Tear the fucking place apart, everything! And, when I say "everything", I fucking mean *everything*!'

There wasn't much to tear apart. A foam mattress, which they ripped from its canvas cover and shredded with a Stanley knife into fist-sized chunks while somebody else tore the cover along the seams, examining every millimetre. While one lot demolished my bed, the officer in charge turned to me and yelled 'Strip!' I wore only my tee shirt and black rugby shorts. I had nothing else. I removed them and offered them to him but he gestured to another officer to take them. He tore open every seam in my shirt, cut open the elasticised waistband and ripped the pocket off my shorts.

I stood naked. The man in charge turned to another officer and said 'Check him thoroughly!' The officer slipped his hand into a surgical glove and pulled me aside.

'Lift your arms and place your feet apart.'

I did what they told me to do.

He shone his torch across my body.

'Turn around and keep your hands above your head.'

He examined my back, legs and buttocks.

'Turn and face me, hands up, feet apart.'

He came up close and I could smell the cigarettes on his breath. He told me to open my mouth and he shone his torch around, poking his gloved finger into my mouth and feeling along the gums for any hidden objects. He then squatted and, with the same hand, felt around my testicles and along the groove, over my anus and up the fold between my buttocks. I had to put out my hands and raise my feet for him to inspect before he ordered me to stand bent, facing the wall so that he could examine inside me.

They tore the seams off the edges of the blanket, they stabbed holes in my army-issue toothpaste tube, squirting toothpaste everywhere, they sliced the remainder of the toilet roll in half and upturned the latrine bucket into the gully but, thankfully, it only contained urine, and they flushed it away with the water from the drinking pail.

I feared that they'd find my notes and the makeshift pen in my Bible. When one of them took the book by its covers and began shaking it upside down to see what would fall out, I cried: 'Have some respect for the Bible!' The suggestion touched a deep religious nerve and he stopped shaking it, turned it over and riffled through the pages before placing it on the ground just outside the door.

Having cleared the cell's contents, they turned their attention to the room itself. One officer helped another up, to inspect the space above the door. He examined each bar thoroughly while others checked the windows. They poked at some of the gouges in the walls and I feared that they'd find the laces. If they did, they'd put two-and-two together and work out my means of escaping into the cellblock when I chose, as some might well have suspected. I've never been more petrified than at that moment: twenty minutes of tormenting fear and personal indignity; and it all hinged on whether they found the laces or not.

The officer with the torch went inside and kicked out a few blobs of foam rubber that had stuck to the toothpaste on the floor and examined the edges, doorframe and along the corners of the walls where they joined the floor and ceiling. He then called for the Stanley knife and systematically cut away loose cement where the paint had flaked away from the underlying red bricks.

My heart pounded and I looked across at Lieutenant Jacques. He was embarrassed but seemed to be relieved that they hadn't found anything. The expression in my eyes told him that there was more to find and he shrugged his shoulders slightly and shook his head as if to say 'No, Tom! Please don't tell me you've got illicit stuff in your cell.' His face showed that he feared the worst for me.

The piece of paint, glued down with toothpaste over the secret cavity containing the laces, held well and defied detection. The investigator emerged from my cell. 'It's clean,' he proclaimed to his superior officer, as I glanced back at Jacques who seemed visibly relieved.

The stroppy officer in charge turned back to me:

'Who's your fucking informant? Who the fuck gives you information? Tell me! Tell me now!' His jugulars protruded like worms in his neck and now I knew why they were conducting this search. I felt sorry for Jacques. Our nocturnal conversations would surely implicate him. But there was no way that I'd rat on his kindness.

'I don't have an informant! Nobody comes here to share information with me. How could they? I'm alone all the time. The only people I see are the men who bring my food and take away the trays and buckets. They work in pairs so there's no way I could get information from them.'

'You know too much and we don't fucking like it.'

This smacked of Nel's doing and I suspected he'd called in the military police to conduct the investigation. He must have seen me as his Achilles heel and needed to block my source of information, for if I was able to receive it there was a risk that I could also send it.

Through my Scottish ancestry I have Viking blood. I'm longsuffering and patient but there comes a time when I flip. I lose all proportion and turn into a modern-day berserker, and lay waste around me, people scattering to escape my wrath. I'd had enough of Nel and his bullying. I'd had enough of spare-rations, solitary confinement and walking around half-naked like a trapped animal in a cage. I turned to the officer in charge, my hackles up and ready to fight. An officer grabbed my arms but I flicked him loose and pointed at the man in charge, restraining myself from pushing or punching him. I'd never before lost my temper inside detention barracks but at this moment I felt fearless and ruthless.

'You are nothing! You're narrow-minded and pathetic! I've got sources that you'll never know about. Your men speak of ghosts in the block! They're too scared to come in at night. Don't you realise that a higher power takes care of me? Forces far greater than Nel are with me all the time. How else do you think I cope? Not one of you would survive this. D'you think I'm alone? You're idiotic! Search my cell all you want and stick your grubby fingers up my arse but you won't find my source of information there.'

With the others in tow, the officer in charge stormed out. They locked me inside the cell, leaving all my things outside.

I sat and fumed, naked on the icy cold concrete floor. This was the first time I'd been angry with them. The first time I'd been provoked into argument. My heart beat loudly as my mind reeled at what had just occurred. Then, as surely as the approaching dawn, a premonition grew that something awful would come of this.

Events unfolded rapidly that day and everything remains a bit blurry. Vermaak and a few of his heavies came and opened my empty cell. All my stuff was scattered outside. My Bible lay where they had left it near the door. It was a grim reminder of the fury of the night before and I stooped to pick up my Bible, but Vermaak rapped 'Don't touch it!'

He kicked my pants and shirt across with the tip of his boot and ordered me to dress. My clothes were a mess. The edges of my tee shirt were torn and frayed and my shorts hung by a few threads from the elastic waistband. There were holes that exposed my buttocks where the pocket had been.

'Follow me,' Vermaak barked, brusquer than I'd ever heard. He was usually a bit of a windbag and we knew that his bark was worse than his bite. But this time they were seriously pissed off with me.

I stepped outside and asked if I could first put my things away and he again rapped out 'Leave it!'

We exited the main cellblock door and turned onto the narrow walkway between Blocks 3 and 4. I had no idea where we were headed and I followed anxiously. I assumed they were taking me to Nel's office. I wasn't aware that Parliament had amended the Defence Act. I recalled the previous occasion when Nel had referred my insubordination to a magistrate and I'd received an additional yearlong sentence. What were his intentions now?

We arrived at the administration block's *stoep* but, instead of turning right towards Nel's office, we stopped at the green door in front of us. Dark Cells! My heart sank. Vermaak inserted the key and swung open the door.

'Follow me,' he said again. Ungainly camel-legs, knock-kneed, his fat buttocks swaying like two boys playing under a blanket. Behind us, other officers and NCOs. The corridor seemed to lead nowhere. We came to a blank wall. Here the passage doubled back on itself towards the outside *stoep*. My eyes were adapted to the bright sunlight and the semi-dark left me partially blinded. Another blank wall and the labyrinth turned left. Three naked low-watt bulbs lit up the cramped space. Three open cell doors led off this dingy passage and they bundled me into the last one in the row.

Nobody said a word and I asked no questions.

Vermaak closed the door on me and the cell fell dark. A faint trace of light filtered through the steel grille above the door. I looked around as the footsteps retreated down the twisting passageway. The cell was the same as all others, except that it had no rear or outward-looking window.

In the corner were a latrine pale without a handle, three sheets of loose toilet paper and a green aluminium flask of water. Nothing else, no mattress, no blanket, no toothbrush or paste. Stories abounded how previous occupants tried to hang themselves with strips torn from the blankets and mattress covers, so Nel removed them as a safety precaution. I stood looking round in the few seconds it took for the entourage to reach the outside door. There, they flicked the switch and plunged the entire labyrinth into utter darkness, and locked the outer door behind them. I could hear their muffled voices and footsteps as they walked past outside on their way back towards the captain's office.

I cannot begin to describe the darkness. It was thick, solid, oppressive. It summoned up hideous fears and for a long time I could not move. I was shocked and numbed. Somehow I refused to believe it. I wanted to assume that they'd made a mistake, or were playing a sick joke on me and would return to fetch me. But as time progressed it sank in. I was in the Dark Cells.

I reached out gingerly to touch the door; but sense of space was distorted. The door was farther off than I thought. I leaned forward and slid my foot across the floor until I could take a step forward, and reached out again. I touched the cold steel and began to explore it with my fingertips, in the way that a blind person might feel someone's face. The door's familiar shape flickered in my mind like a photographic print, and then all was dark again. I reached up, located the bars above the door, and hoisted myself up as I had done thousands of times before, hoping to find a glimmer of light. There was none. Only dense darkness. I slowly lowered myself back to the floor; thereby, as in a living metaphor, down into a deeper pit of despondence. I hadn't expected Dark Cells.

Nobody'd suggested that I could end up there without the formality of a summary trial and I obsessed over the brutality that this implied. I had no idea how long they would detain me here. Was it going to be hours? Days? I carefully slid my foot to the right until it touched the wall and squatted on my haunches where I remained for a very long time.

Tiny light proof ventilation blocks on the outer wall up near the concrete ceiling provided the only flow of air into the cell. The air was oppressive, dank and smelly compared to the breeziness of the other cells and I fought back waves of claustrophobia. Dark Cells lay in a forgotten corner of the detention barracks where it was very quiet. I'd become used to the silence – but now I had to face the darkness too. If it weren't for the residual acrid smell of fear and the coldness of the concrete floor where it touched my bare feet and the chill of my buttocks through the hole in my shorts as I sat on the ground, this might well have been a sensory deprivation chamber.

Decades later on a tour to Queenstown, New Zealand, Johann and I booked massages at a well-known health spa in the city. Before the pampering began, they offered us a forty-five minute session in their isolation tanks. Having showered, I lay naked in the body-temperature water inside the cigar-shaped contraption. I carefully read the safety instructions, plucked up my courage and pressed the start button. As the lid closed on this high-tech coffin, I remembered Dark Cells and Edgar Allan Poe's story where the narrator, suffering from catalepsy, fell into a deathlike trance and described his crippling fear of being buried alive.[55]

The water in the Queenstown isolation tank had high concentrations of Epsom salts that changed its specific gravity to equal that of the human body. It was a weird feeling lying on the surface of the water and unable to sink. As the recorded voice described the workings of the chamber, the lights faded and the sound decreased. Despite the reassurance that the chamber had multiple safety sensors and would automatically open if it detected panicked movement, I still struggled to subdue the fear that was hardwired in my brain, a stimulus programmed for survival. By taking control of my breath, I subdued my survival instincts and soon enough the deprivation of all sensory stimuli forced me into an amazing trance with an interesting out-of-body experience.

Dark Cells were Nel's ultimate punishment and he'd used this on others before me. I'd heard wails drifting from those chambers in the dead of night; grown men pleading like children confined to the toilet for bad behaviour. Inmates whispered stories of men dragged from Dark Cells, lifeless, as if lobotomised. Rumours had it that in some cases the Doctor admitted them directly to the psychiatric ward of 1 Military Hospital and nobody heard or saw them again. I understood why so many cracked after just a few hours. The majority never lasted more than a few days before begging for clemency. Hearsay suggested that nobody received a fixed or formal sentence to Dark Cells but Nel sent them there until they had changed their attitude and behaviour. Dark Cells was a cooling-off period after some brutal physical attack or acts of violent rebellion towards officers.

As befitted army routine the barracks served meals at fixed times in other cell blocks; but not for me. My lunch arrived, served as usual on a dixie, but without knife or fork. I ate with my hands. Suicide attempts must have been common here so dangerous items were proscribed. I drank from the flask and used the residue to wash my body as I perched over the latrine bucket. Three sheets of toilet paper a day did not suffice and I soon felt soiled.

Bucket changes and food delivery occurred randomly to disorientate my sense of time. It took a while to work out a survival strategy and my first concern was to keep my water unpolluted and the cell as sanitary as possible. On hearing the muffled clank of a bucket on the concrete

---

[55] 'The Premature Burial', Edgar Allan Poe, 1844, the *Philadelphia Dollar.*

stoep outside, I quickly defecated and washed my underarms with a dribble of water before attending to my groin and bottom with the remaining drinking water. By the time they reached and unlocked the cell, I was done. The weak light bulbs in the passage now shone as brightly, to my eyes, as the noonday sun and blinded me. Having done what they came for, the orderlies turned off the lights; and in the space of a few short minutes, before I could adapt to the glare, darkness again swallowed me into its belly.

Without sight, some food items tasted weird and I couldn't identify what they were. One day I received a whole orange. It was an extraordinary sensory experience. I squeezed the peel, spraying aromatic citrus oil over my body before eating the orange, skin and all, except for the pips which I saved. The cell became alive and danced with aroma. My skin awakened to the acidic tingle of the oil. For a spell I was out of the dark and transported to a world lit up with stimuli that filled the void. The orange was a gift of life.

The orange pips became toys and I played endless games with them. I flicked them with my thumb one at a time into the darkness and listened to where each one landed before I set about finding them. This helped me to develop an acute sense of hearing and I learned to locate them as though I had mental radar. Those few seeds helped to save me.

Touch also became increasingly important and I couldn't fall sleep, squatting on the bare concrete floor, until I caressed my body and lulled myself into a trance. I touched every millimetre of the walls and mapped their topography in detail. I discovered the ventilation blocks in the dark and stood on top of a clean latrine bucket to feel the cool breeze blowing across my fingertips. I stood in the middle of the room and touched every inch of my body, exploring, feeling, sensing its shape and imagining its reaction as though I could see it with my eyes.

Sometimes I was inside my body, looking out. At other times I was outside, looking back. Living in Dark Cells was a surreal experience. My conscious mind would often vanish, cease to function, as there was nothing to keep it focussed; and I spent nearly all the time in deep states of trance. I was aware of *being* but everything else lost its cognitive reference. I had frequent out-of-body experiences and drifted endlessly as if throughout the cosmos in a state of limbo. Bucket changes and meal deliveries began to startle me, as if I had woken from a deep sleep. I have no recollection of the time I spent there. Time seemed to fall away and space dissolved.

The body (it no longer seemed my own) lived squatting in the corner in a state of suspended animation. I suppose that this might be what one experiences when, due to an injury, one is completely paralysed yet cognitive. In the body's state of disconnection the room and everything in it vanished. I don't recall being afraid yet I don't recall being happy. I don't remember thinking. I seemed to be beyond worry. I just was. In a strange and bizarre way the experience was, in its sensory nothingness, serene. I can understand why men and women speak of pilgrimages to holy caves in the Himalayan Mountains to live lives of austerity in the quest for spiritual enlightenment, for escape from the burden of thought and form.

One day the outside door opened and more than the usual footsteps approached. Vermaak unlocked the cell door and told me to step outside and to accompany him and his henchmen for a visit to the doctor.

The light was too intense, like being in the presence of a welder's arc light without a protective mask. I cupped my face in the crook of one arm as they led me by the other to the sick bay. The detention barracks, which seemed so confined, now felt enormous and I so frail and tiny. My skin seemed translucent and I imagined that I could see my veins and internal organs beneath it as one can with some nocturnal geckos. I was musky, dishevelled, and my hair and beard had grown a lot. I couldn't find words to speak, as my mind was utterly blank, numbed, devoid of verbal thought.

The Doctor poked and prodded *the body*, listened to its heartbeat and breathing, and certified its fitness. They half-dragged me back to my regular, familiar cell in Block 4, where someone had neatly arranged my things on the floor.

It took a few weeks before I showed any signs of engagement with the world around me. I remember merely crouching on the mattress in the corner, lobotomised and numb. I don't recall eating. I felt neither warmth nor cold in those late winter months. I seemed detached from my body which was like an abstract object in a different realm. I didn't feel dejected or mentally disturbed. I merely felt serene, completely disconnected from the physicality of life.

I heard from someone bringing food that I'd been in Dark Cells for sixty-two days but I find no evidence in my research to substantiate that claim. My father'd kept meticulous records and I used them later in order to construct a timeline from the many newspaper cuttings, letters, documents; and the most likely scenario is that I entered Dark Cells around 7 July 1972 and remained there for a period of no less than eighteen to twenty days. My beard and hair growth seem to corroborate that timeframe as does 3 August 1972, a date that marked the end of my 180-day sentence and the start of the next year in confinement.

I somehow doubt that Nel would have kept me in Dark Cells over that period, yet he was also ruthless enough to have done it.

After my spell in Dark Cells, I became a bit of a hero. Even Vermaak seemed to change his attitude towards me and might once or twice have shown a glint of admiration and a pocketful of shame. Those that brought food and water did so with respect and Lieutenant Jacques hung around longer than usual in the evenings; but I was incapable of finding any warm feelings for him and our conversation now seemed hollow and uninteresting, just like the world around me.

'Jacques,' I once asked him (we'd long been on first-name terms), 'I wish I could put my feet on the grass outside. Is that possible?'

'I can't. I just can't do that for you, Tom,' he replied sadly.

When I realised that I'd now begun serving my one-year sentence, on 4 August 1972, I sank into a complete cataleptic state. I didn't think that I was mentally ill at the time (I still believe that I was on an incredible spiritual high) but I'm sure a medical diagnosis would have accounted for me suffering some form of clinical depression. My apathy extended to my nocturnal escapades in the block and I ceased venturing beyond my cell even though I still had the bootlaces stowed away in their secret chamber in the wall.

During my stay in Dark Cells, and unbeknown to me, a daily newspaper published this:

> Soldiers in detention for refusing to do military training will have their sentences reviewed after 12 months inside... [A defence spokesman said] 'Each case will be treated on its merits. It will be decided depending upon circumstances whether to release a man immediately or to hold him for the full term of his sentence. Once released a man will be exempt from further action against him in connection with service.'[56]

---

[56] 'Army detainees allowed reviews', Defence Correspondent, the *Star*, Johannesburg, 19 July 1972 [#54].

My father immediately wrote to the Director-General of Personnel and drew his attention to my case and the published announcement.[57] I qualified for a review as I had already served fifteen months in detention, twelve of which I'd served in continuous confinement; but a review wasn't forthcoming.

Further, while I was in Dark Cells, my father wrote to Nel asking after my state of health and personal needs.[58] Nel replied: 'Your son is in good health. It is his wish that you send him some handkerchiefs. At present there is nothing else he is in need of.'[59]

'Good health.' What did he mean by that? I was in a wretched state of mental health. I'd been in solitary confinement for about eight weeks, nearly three of which were in Dark Cells. How could he say that I was in good health?

'It is his wish that you send him some handkerchiefs'! What twaddle. I needed new clothes because mine were frayed and torn. I needed toiletries, soap and shaving foam, anything but handkerchiefs. Why say that I needed those? Was it innuendo, implying that I needed something with which to dry my tears after he had crushed me?

The idea of another year in detention haunted me, and in the week that followed I knew I needed to escape. Some soldiers had succeeded. One broke loose and jumped the iron wall from the top of a garden shed in the far corner of the precinct. He was out for a while before they discovered him and locked him up in Dark Cells. Nobody knew what happened to him after that. Daredevil escaping wasn't an option and I had to find a more acceptable way out.

Every enamel water bucket had a thick wire handle which hooked into lugs welded to its sides. To facilitate easy carrying, the manufacturers threaded the wire through a thin metal tube just wider than the average hand that acted as a comfortable grip. On the morning of Monday 7 August 1972, a bucket arrived that had a wooden meranti dowel grip instead of the usual metal tube. The wood was a bit worse for wear and a tiny splinter embedded itself into the underside of my finger as I took it from the orderly.

'Ouch!' I squealed.

---

[57] My father's letter to the Director-General of Personnel, 20 July 1972 [#55].
[58] My father's letter to the commandant, military detention barracks, 18 July 1972 [#49].
[59] Nel's reply to my father's enquiry, 1 August 1972 [#57].

'Are you okay?'

'Hey, no, I'm fine,' I said, biting at my hand to pull the splinter free. 'I've just picked up a splinter but I'll soon get it out.'

By the next morning the skin around the splinter had become inflamed and I couldn't dislodge the offending fragment. I needed a pair of tweezers but, obviously, there were none at hand. As I sat squeezing and scratching, a clear vision popped into my head. I saw myself in hospital. Mom and Dad sat at my bedside. The thought flashed into my mind intensely, making the vision as clear as if I were there. I suddenly had a bizarre and cunning idea and began to formulate a plan. I quickly prised a second, sturdier, splinter off the bucket handle with my fingernail and I hid this with the shoelaces in the groove in the wall.

I lacked courage at first but finally put my plan into action. I marinated the splinter in the latrine bucket for a couple of days. I retrieved it at every bucket change and transferred it to the new bucket. I then took the splinter and slowly used it to pierce the skin between the inner fingers of my left hand, pushing it in deep between the bones. It bled profusely but I managed to stem the blood by keeping my hand in clean water. The splinter stayed embedded and I kept a tight fist for a few more days to prevent it from popping out.

I didn't sleep well as it hurt like hell. It was the first real illness I had in all the time I was there and I reported sick on Thursday morning.[60] The doctor prescribed and dispensed a handful of his pink cure-all antibiotics and tried to prise the splinter out but, by some miracle, it wouldn't budge. I told him that it was much smaller than it really was and he didn't seem too concerned. I felt dreadfully ill, had a headache and threw the pills into the latrine bucket. That night my hand swelled extensively and, by Saturday night, a red stripe began to travel up my arm accompanied by a heavy fever. I knew that I'd a serious infection and blood-poisoning.

I called for urgent medical attention when they brought my supper and the doctor returned to the barracks about an hour later, signed a hospital release note and called for an ambulance. It arrived a few minutes later and took me to the casualty unit at 1 Military Hospital, just five minutes drive northwest of the barracks, where a medic immediately admitted me.

---

[60] In hindsight it's remarkable that under such adverse conditions I hadn't been sick. There was some ongoing allergy and the dreadful chilblains in winter but, other than that, I remained exceptionally healthy. That has to say something positive about simplicity, fresh air, moderate exercise and regular fasting.

Around ten that night, a new doctor arrived to examine me.

'How did this happen?' he asked, in a genuinely caring voice.

'I picked up a bucket of water and a splinter from its handle went into my hand.'

'If you say so,' he replied, and I could sense he knew that there was no chance that a splinter could enter at such an angle between the fingers and penetrate so deeply. I realised that he knew it was self-inflicted.

'How long have you been in detention?' he asked.

'It's over a year but I don't know any more because I was locked up in solitary confinement and Dark Cells and I've lost all track of time.'

'Solitary confinement? Dark Cells?' he asked. 'Tell me about them...'

I told him about my experiences and confided my fears about my future. I remember breaking down and crying because he seemed so caring and fatherly. In that moment I felt like a lost little boy in a shopping mall. I had successfully contained my emotions for a very long time and now, unable to suppress them, they flooded out in a torrent, like water from a breached dam.

'Where are your clothes?' he asked. I was dressed in my frayed tee shirt and tatty rugby shorts. The tear had widened considerably across my buttocks and the elastic waistband had stretched and collapsed, the fabric now held by only a few stitches. My shorts provided little containment and I felt very ashamed of my appearance.

'These are my only clothes. I wouldn't wear the army's uniform because I didn't want to become a soldier; so they took it away. I was completely naked for a while until Dad sent me these shorts a long time ago.' My words seemed to echo through the ward and I felt vulnerable and weak. He listened intently and his face bore an expression of disbelief and shame.

He let me talk for a long time and then asked, 'When did you last bath?'

My hair was longer than usual and somewhat spiky, slightly longer than my patchy beard. My bare feet were filthy, the winter chilblains etched deep groves in my fingers and toes, and they were ingrained with dirt.

'Today,' I said, self-consciously. 'I try to keep myself clean by washing every day in my bucket of water.'

'No,' he said, repeating his question. 'When last did you have a proper bath?'

'On the morning I left home. I've never washed myself properly since then.'

He examined me thoroughly and, as he did so, I became aware of my unkempt grimy state. My body had a musky odour now that I could compare it to the smell of freshly laundered linen. I sobbed again, apologising for my dullness and emotional instability. He was a very kind man and worked with sympathy.

He ordered one of the male nurses (there were mainly male nurses in the army back then) to help me clean up. He walked me to the ward showers and lent a hand to scrub me down because I couldn't do it on my own due to my injury.

The showers were typical army-styled rows of taps along a tiled wall. The hot water was strangely sensuous and ever so welcoming. I hadn't washed my body like this for months. The soap's smoothness on my skin and its fragrance were overwhelmingly alluring to my senses. The nurse scrubbed my back, shampooed my hair and helped me to dry down before returning me to the ward in a fresh pair of hospital pyjamas and rubber beach thongs as slippers.

I felt outwardly rejuvenated.

Throughout my experiences, there was such polarisation in people's nature and character towards me. Some had conscience and feelings; many didn't. The policeman at the courts, Lieutenant Jacques and the hospital doctor were compassionate and fundamentally good people. None of them might ever know just how vital their empathy was: their simplest acts of kindness, their kind words or genuinely interested listening. The doctor helped me during an exceptionally difficult period. I realised then how much I missed other people's affirmation. The doctor demonstrated that I was fundamentally a good person, part of the human race and worthy of care.

The sedative took effect and I fell asleep, for the first time in many months, between starched white sheets with my head resting on a fluffy pillow. It would take a few days for the intravenous antibiotic drip to dissipate the infection, clearing the way for surgical removal of the wooden splinter. In my feverish nocturnal delirium I remember being terrified of the height of the bed and I yearned to squat in the corner as I had done for so many months. A transistor wireless in the nurses' station, tuned to Highveld Radio, broadcast Gershon Kingsley's infectious Moog synthesiser song *Popcorn*, playing it repeatedly throughout the night until it burrowed its way into my brain.

I awoke the next morning in a better mood. Painkillers reduced the ache and I felt reasonably good.

I hadn't noticed the size of the ward the previous night as all the lights were off when I arrived. It was a long rectangular room with rows of beds facing inwards along both of its long walls. Each bed had its own steel locker but there were no curtains to screen it from the adjacent bed. Nurses and doctors performed everything in full view of everyone else. I was in one of the beds just outside the nurses' station, in an enclosed veranda that ran along the northern side of the ward. Michael Humphrey, a nineteen-year-old military policeman, sat guard at the foot of my bed. He'd been posted there during the night, most likely at Nel's request, to prevent me from escaping: a redundancy, in my opinion.

At seven that evening my parents came to visit, and I went through another deeply emotional and cathartic outpouring. Mom was horrified to see how thin I had become; dad said nothing but looked at me gravely through troubled eyes.

'How did you know I was here?' I asked.

'Major von Meiering, the hospital superintendent, rang today to tell us that you'd been admitted for surgery,' explained Dad in his usual matter-of-fact tone.

'We've been so worried about you,' added Mom. 'We didn't know what had happened.'

A few days later Nel tried to prevent my parents from visiting by getting a nurse to banish them from the hospital; but Major von Meiering interceded and, outranking him, gave my parents carte blanche to visit as often as they wished. They travelled the 100 kilometres round trip almost every night and, the more I saw of them, the more I believed I would not be able to go back to the barracks.

Surgery happened a few days after my admission, once the swelling had subsided. With the splinter removed, the surgeon encased my hand in a plaster cast to hold a rubber tube in place. This delivered antibiotic fluid directly to the bones inside my hand. A week later, and I had to undergo a second operation to close the wound. I should have been fit to return to the barracks within a fortnight yet, strangely, there was no word of this. Each morning I expected to be ordered back to detention but the doctor, on his rounds, only said 'Just a little while longer and then we'll discharge you.'

I believe that he tried his best to keep me away from Nel and his detention barracks.

One morning, a nurse came to me and said 'Bring all your things and follow me.' I feared that the day had come for me to return to the barracks and I feared Nel's reactions. But, to my surprise, the nurse turned away from the hospital lobby and led me deeper into the building.

'Where am I going? I asked tentatively, not really wanting to hear the answer in case it was unpleasant.

'The Doctor's transferred you to another ward,' he said.

'Where?' I asked again.

'Psychiatrics,' he replied, and it struck me that the Doctor couldn't find reasonable cause to keep me in his surgical ward and had therefore cunningly helped me by referring me for psychiatric observation, a process that could take weeks to complete.

Ward 22 was almost the last ward, near the back of the hospital, where the army rehabilitated many young men repatriated from the bush along the Angolan border. Many were shell-shocked, broken spirited, boys of approximately my age. The horrors of fighting a terrorist war had fractured their minds, and for many their bones too. This, like all wars, was cruel and pointless. It was as awful on the frontlines for them as it was in prison for me; maybe worse. Some of those soldiers were deeply traumatised and screamed at night, fighting ghosts that stalked them in the darkness of their minds. Some would recover; many never did.

Ward 22 wasn't just for 'large groups of conscripts coming to terms with long periods of compulsory service and the experience of combat [that] introduced new psychological problems into the military.'[61] It also contained many drug users – and gay men too.

There was a popular myth at the time which suggested that homosexuals would get a G5 (Medical Discharge) from the South African Defence Force [SADF]. That was certainly not the case. In fact, the army took a very different view. The army believed that the 'practise of homosexuality is considered to be an undermining factor in the SADF [... that] damages the image of the SADF, undermines discipline, and can lead to blackmail and security risks.'[62] And instead of rejecting gays from service, the army sought to intervene and change them.

Gay soldiers were under extraordinary pressure because they often couldn't hide their sexuality and were victimised. They couldn't share news from lovers back home. Quite often they simply could not keep pace with their tougher comrades (a condition shared by many men of weaker stature). Part of the military's management of gay people occurred in Ward 22. Gay soldiers often found their way to the Psychiatric Ward because of trauma associated with victimisation.

The hospital's psychiatric units were 'largely the creation of Dr Aubrey Levine [sic] [... who] joined the army after qualifying for a medical degree and went on to study psychiatry on military bursaries. He worked under the supervision of Lt General Cockcroft, the Surgeon General from 1969 to 1977. Upon his retirement Cockcroft became active in ultra-right organisations.'[63] Levin had a sinister reputation for trying to 'cure' homosexual conscripts. 'Thousands of [...] gays were subjected to electric shock therapy, hormone treatment and chemical castration through the 1970s and 80s, when national service was compulsory for white males and homosexuality was a crime.'[64] Dr Levin was 'convinced he could make heterosexuals out of gay patients, using electroconvulsive aversion therapy.'[65] Every new patient was 'put on Valium [and the] ward orderlies carried pistols' [66] to prevent escapes. 'Dr Levin also subjected his patients to narco-analysis or a 'truth drug', involving the slow injection of a barbiturate before the questioning began. Dr Levin does not deny its use.'[67] Some gay men

---

[61] http://sadf.sentinelprojects.com/1mil/thug1.html.
[62] Aanhangsel A by Beleidsdirektief HSAW/1/13/82.
[63] http://sadf.sentinelprojects.com/1mil/thug1.html.
[64] 'Gays tell of mutilation by apartheid army, Chris McGreal, UK *Guardian*, 29 July 2000'.
[65] ibid.
[66] ibid.
[67] http://www.guardian.co.uk/world/2010/mar/28/aubrey-levin-charged-sexually-abusing-patient.

'were pressured into surgery by military psychologists after other methods failed. The army carried out as many as 50 sex change operations a year.'[68]

They called this the Aversion Project.

Dr Aubrey Levin left the hospital shortly before the dismantling of apartheid and for a brief span became Head of Mental Health for the old regime. He refused to testify before the Truth and Reconciliation Commission. He then moved to Calgary, Canada, where he lectured at the College of Physicians and Surgeons. In Canada he regularly served as a court-appointed forensic psychiatrist assessing the status of convicted criminals before sentencing.[69] It's hugely ironic that the biggest homophobes often use their homophobia to divert public attention from their own sexual exploits: Dr Levin concealed his record of alleged gross transgression of human rights abuses in apartheid-era South Africa, but while in Calgary was charged with 'sexually abusing a male patient and is being investigated over dozens of other allegations.'[70]

During my stay in Ward 22 I came to know many of those boys and the whole thing freaked me out. There was so much bigotry, such awful judgement, and such egregious cruelty. It wasn't only the army that saddened me. The very organisation to which I belonged, that professed righteousness and love, had compromised itself through needless acts of cruelty and disregard of those who dared to fall short of the rigidity of their interpretation of Jesus' gentle teachings.

I feared going back and facing Nel. I feared Ward 22 and the stuff that happened to the soldiers in that ward. I feared for my own future. The army had every right to detain me until the age of sixty-five. If, however, I secured an exemption from military service, I still faced a rocky future. I had to decide whether to reject my sexuality and hang out with the Witnesses or accept who I was and face the consequences.

Major von Meiering eventually called for me to see him. It was inevitable. I'd been there for over a month.

---

[68] McGreal, 2000.

[69] 'The Real and More Sinister Dr Shock', Richard de Nooy,
    http://richarddenooy.bookslive.co.za/blog/2011/06/15/the-real-and-more-sinister-dr-shock/.

[70] http://www.guardian.co.uk/world/2010/mar/28/aubrey-levin-charged-sexually-abusing-patient.

'We've tried hard to keep you here,' he said to me in a kindly voice as a father would to his son. 'But the situation's getting awkward and I can't intervene any more. I'm really sorry but there is nothing else I can do. You have to return to Detention Barracks today.'

I thanked him for all he'd done. He stood up from his desk and shook my hand. 'Go back to the ward, fetch your things, and then return to the barracks when you're ready. Good luck, Thomas. You're a very brave man. I'll let your dad know you've been discharged.'

I had nothing to pick up from the ward. I said my goodbye to my newfound friends and walked the short distance back to the barracks in my hospital pyjamas and rubber beach thongs. I took it very slowly, lingering along the way. Several army vehicles slowed down. The soldiers looked at me as though I was a crazy patient who had escaped. But I waved and gave them a thumbs-up and they moved on. I turned the corner and walked slowly up the gravel road, along the outside of the corrugated iron perimeter wall, and to the barracks gate. I stood there for a while, looked around one more time, took a deep breath and rang the bell.

Booted footsteps approached. The cover of the peephole swung back and an eye briefly glared at me. Then the jangle of keys and a clunk, and the solid door heaved open.

'When did you get here? Who brought you?'

'I came on my own. I walked here from the hospital.'

I was stripped of my pyjamas and slops and issued with a new pair of black shorts. They returned me to my cell in Block 4. It was the same as I had left it several weeks before. The injury and my prolonged absence had caused concern; Nel had launched an intensive inquisition to determine the cause of these events. He wasn't convinced that it happened the way I described but there wasn't enough evidence to prove that it was self-inflicted. I called the orderly to testify that I had picked up a splinter when he passed across the bucket; but he couldn't confirm what size of splinter it was.

Michael Humphrey's mother Eileen wrote a letter to my mother:

> You do not know me but your husband met my son Michael while he was visiting Tom at Voortrekkerhoogte. Michael is doing his national service and was guarding Tom while he was in hospital. As a mother my heart goes out to you in the agony you must

be going through at the moment with Tom doing that dreadful solitary confinement and I want to tell you that I am extremely sorry at the treatment meted out to Tom. I must tell you that all the people I have spoken to, including [many boys doing their national service], feel that the treatment received by Tom is far too harsh. Unfortunately there are many things done in this country which are said to be done in the name of Christianity and this makes me very sad but please remember there are many Christians who are constantly praying for a change of heart; some as you are no doubt aware are suffering for speaking up.[71]

A stretch of well-kept lawn, some ten meters wide, separated the cellblocks. Blocks 1, 2 and 3 had covered walkways connecting them to the main *stoep*; Block 4 didn't. The gaps between the first three blocks were open at both ends and they had a sense of spaciousness but the nearside gap between Blocks 3 and 4, at the front of the property, had a high brick wall spanning both buildings. The wall probably served as a screen to prevent prisoners from escaping while trucks were in the loading bay, or as a shield to block the sightline between the gate and Block 3. The space at the far end between Blocks 3 and 4 had an enormous tree whose canopy reached across both buildings. The stretch of lawn between those last two blocks was a forgotten and unfrequented part of the barracks and the only person who ever ventured down there was a prisoner who cut the grass once a week.

Each week I sat on my blanket hammock at the window and watched this grass-cutter. It wasn't always the same person, but one prisoner in particular would nod a greeting, grin, and show encouragement with a discrete thumbs-up. He could do no more because an orderly, standing beneath the tree, always watched over him. Sitting up at the window in the sunshine and fresh air I enjoyed an illusion of being outside and free.

One day, however, about two weeks after returning from hospital, I dosed off at the window in my makeshift hammock. One of the personnel, on a rare excursion down that part of the barracks, saw me. Within minutes Vermaak and his entourage were at my cell and marched me off for another of Nel's summary trials on a trumped up charge of 'damaging military property,' namely stretching my threadbare blanket. It was out of shape because I'd used it often at the window, but the alleged damage was just another excuse to get even with me.

---

[71] Eileen Humphrey's letter, 3 October 1972 [#69].

There were vicious undertones at that hearing and Nel scored a cheap victory when he added twenty-eight days to my sentence and I lost the privilege of having a blanket from then on.

In the time I'd spent alone I read every word of the Bible from Genesis to Revelation, not just once but repeatedly. One can however only do so much reading. I remained alone with my thoughts for hours at a time, especially in the dark hours of the night. I used my bootlaces to escape throughout my stay in Block 4 and that little bit of freedom saved me. Meditation wasn't something taught by the Witnesses and I didn't even recognise the word, but stillness and emptiness of mind soon led me to what I now recognise as blissful states of being.

I'd still escape into the corridor at night; but I now used the power of meditation to pass through a spiritual doorway that led out of physical confinement into realms of infinite freedom, peace and bliss. Mind lets go of the illusion of form and Awareness drifts and floats in that blissful realm beyond.

One Saturday afternoon in October I remember taking a rest, squatting in the corner of the cell without a blanket. I entered into a trance and escaped upwards through the bars. Awareness (I suppose I could call it an out-of-body experience) floated above the cellblock for a while as if finding its bearings. Then, like the attraction of opposite poles of a magnet, I had an urge to connect to the power lines outside. The closer I got to them, the greater their attraction – and I suddenly snapped onto them. I stayed fixed there for a while before I discovered that I could shift back and forth. So I tried to navigate my way back home to Edenvale! It was slow and laborious at first. It took a great deal of effort and I feared I might not find my way back. Through trial and error I gained confidence and skill, and I travelled faster and faster along the vast regional grid of power lines. Awareness popped off the lines at a family gathering.

I *saw* them all as clearly as if I was there. I was slightly above everyone, about a meter from the ground, where I observed every movement and heard every conversation – but I couldn't interact with them. I remembered the dress that my mother'd bought for the occasion and the small gifts others brought her. Eavesdropping on multiple concurrent conversations was easy and I lingered there for a few hours. Then, in an instant, as if a switch had been thrown, I was back in my body, squatting in the corner of my cell. I snapped out of trance, heart pounding.

I was startled by what had happened, and a little apprehensive about its validity. Exploring consciousness or the mind in any metaphysical sense was one of the Witnesses' many taboos because it supposedly weakened one's defences and allowed in Satan's power. The experience, however, was far too real to dismiss and it has fascinated me for many years.

Decades later, after my father's death, I got an opportunity to ask my mother about that family party. 'Do you remember having a family party in October of the year when I was in detention barracks?'

She raised her left eyebrow in her idiosyncratic way that showed cautious curiosity. 'What about it?'

'You wore a white dress with dark blue polka dots and navy blue shoes. You bought the dress for the occasion.'

'Yes ....' she replied.

I told her about the varied conversations, the gifts she'd received, who'd sat where. I gave her a detailed account of the day. When I'd finished, she said, 'So who told you this?'

'That's not important, Mom. Just tell me if it's accurate or not.'

'It's exactly how it was. Who told you?'

I didn't answer; but a ripple of gooseflesh crossed my skin. I finally knew that I'd experienced something extraordinary that day.

---oooOooo---

Opposition mounted considerably to the army's management of us in detention. Parliament promulgated its amendment to the Defence Bill, guaranteeing all future conscientious objectors a single fixed-term sentence. I was one of a handful that didn't qualify for parole and I served out my sentence. Sentenced to 663 days in all, I served just 512 because somebody allowed the sentences to overlap; and Colonel van Vuuren, Officer Commanding, Northern Transvaal Command, halved Nel's additional twenty-eight days on Dad's appeal. Of the days in detention, I spent approximately 235 of them in total isolation in Block 4.

Nel eventually transferred me back to Block 1, a month or so before my release on 29 March 1973. But I received another set of call-up papers, requiring me to report for duty four months later. Thankfully, I had already received an Exemption from National Service on 24 April 1972 and this closed the chapter forever.

Once back home, there was no trauma counselling or debriefing from the Jehovah's Witnesses. No emotional counselling and certainly no physical examination. Everyone assumed that I was okay and that I should function the way I had before I left home. Until I began writing this book I never spoke of the details of my incarceration to anyone.

I imagine that my father might have done the same when he returned as a soldier from the Second World War, disturbed by the horrors of battle, fatigued, yet hailed as a returning hero and paraded about like a trophy. It certainly happened like that with me. The Witnesses applauded us, gloated over us and earned much publicity through us. However, a deep-seated animosity grew inside me. I pretended to be okay and I functioned as best as I could but my inner conflict would not subside. The organisation encouraged me to 'keep active in God's service' by engaging in full-time missionary work. People pushed me to apply for a voluntary head office post in the Witnesses' compound in Elandsfontein. Everyone loved me; the congregation members aspired to be like me; but I hated them because I couldn't speak. They had taped my mouth shut.

Looking back at that period of my life, I realise in hindsight the enormous positive impact it had on me. Today, I'm easily led into a quiet mind. I love solitude and stillness. I'm unafraid of authority. I'm resolute in what I choose to do and I defend my right to do it. I champion the freedom of all; I refuse to judge; and I love helping others along their path to greatness. As difficult as that experience was, isolation became one of my greatest benefacting masters. Isolation taught me about simplicity, patience, endurance, surrender and faith.

A last word on 'national service', from a research thesis by Judith Connors:

> Conscription of white males to the South African Defence Force between 1969 and 1994 was one of the measures used by the South African government to uphold apartheid and white supremacy. While it appeared that the majority of white males and their families supported the National Party propagated ideologies of the country at the time and felt it was their duty to render military service, there were some for whom this duty provided a conflict of conscience.

Giving expression to this conflict and finding constructive ways of dealing with it was almost impossible within the highly restrictive, repressive political, legal and social climate of that time. Limited options seemed available to the young men who had objections to serving in the military, namely exile, evasion or deferment: personal choices that drove people into physical and emotional isolation, and which did not engage the state in the resolution of this conflict. Some young men, however, chose to confront the state and object openly.

This began a protracted series of negotiations with ruling authorities, debates within state structures, legislative changes and prosecutions that attempted to prevent and quash the presence of objectors. In the face of this oppression, family and friends formed themselves into solidarity groups around individual objectors to support them in handling the consequences of their objection and in making their stance known and heeded by the government.

And so began a movement for change, which over the years learned the skills of non-violent direct action and constructively challenged the state on issues of conscription and the militarisation of society. This initiative, known as the Conscientious Objector Support Group, although small in scale, ranks as one of the anti-apartheid movements that contributed to South Africa's peaceful transition to democracy. As such it has invaluable lessons to share with movements for change throughout the world that are presently grappling with situations of human rights violations [72]

---

[72] 'A history of the Conscientious Objector Support Group's challenge to military service in South Africa', Thesis, by Judith Patricia Connors, October 2007.

Bittersweet Liberty

In the early 1980s, a friend gave me two taped audiocassette speeches that introduced me to Ram Dass. I remember listening to them repeatedly, enthralled by the clarity of his message that resonated so deeply in my soul. Nobody in South Africa seemed to know anything of him back then, which wasn't too surprising, for we were in the grip of apartheid sanctions and foreign goods seldom reached our shores. Besides which, the old government tried its best to keep us on a straight and narrow Calvinistic path with very little tolerance for other schools of thought. Ram Dass's teachings were refreshingly different; they were modern and tolerant, and yet bore the hallmarks of ancient wisdom. They were radically different from anything else I'd been taught, but part of me embraced them readily as if I had a deep historic connection with them.

Dad came from a Catholic family. My maternal grandfather, William Sinclair, was agnostic. Today, I can understand how Mom's spiritually vacuous childhood might have left her devoid of religious expression and I can sense how she must have yearned for more. When I was three years old, two men came knocking at our front door on a Sunday morning and their visit changed our family forever. These two Jehovah's Witnesses, dressed in suits and ties, brought fresh hope and vision to her doorstep and she accepted their teachings and quickly quenched her spiritual thirst, like dry parched soil soaking up the first of the summer rain. Once satiated, she enthusiastically and without malice embarked on a self-appointed role as religious matriarch and persuasively and convincingly set about converting most of her side of our family to her newfound faith. Grandfather Bill stood steadfast in his agnosticism. My father held back for years before following tentatively and cautiously. Slowly and reluctantly, he half-heartedly joined in, mainly to avoid conflict, which was his idiosyncratic way of living. His side of the family, despite their Catholic roots, remained religiously neutral and never spoke of church and God with us again.

Following my discharge from the Army, in 1973 I became a full-time missionary in voluntary service for the Witnesses. They discouraged worldly wisdom and favoured men and women who devoted themselves to evangelism instead of tertiary studies and solid careers. I accepted an assignment to Groblersdal, a little Afrikaans farming town just less than two hours north-east of Johannesburg by road, where I performed missionary service for two years. After that, I relocated to Bethel, the Witnesses' head office in Elandsfontein, where I performed a host of menial tasks before getting a job on their cartographic team, demarcating congregational boundaries and printing lithographic territory maps and campaign instructions.

An invitation to Bethel is a prestigious honour, received only by a select few from the country's congregations. Doted upon and looked up to as spiritual achievers with leadership qualities, Bethelites are motivated to hold onto their monastic posting; and some do so for life. The effects of such a revered position on one's ego are hard to resist and many become pompous, aloof, snobbish, self-righteous individuals who revel in their elevated status. That's not to say that false ego ruled everyone for there were some who performed their duties with humility and out of selfless service to their beloved Jehovah. My acceptance to Bethel thrilled my mother and made her very proud of me. Father was always a bit more reserved about it.

I performed my tasks conscientiously but my heart was never fully committed to what I did because I did it mainly out love for my mother and a sense of duty towards her, and I knew that any opposition would have hurt her deeply. Besides which, I felt deceitful, living at the organisation's core, knowing the secrets I had to keep in my heart. My teens were times of immense inner conflict, wholly because of my sexual choices offset against the background of the Witnesses' stringent dogma. I once wrote, 'I'm like an allsorts sweet: salty black liquorice wrapped in sweet sugar candy'. I had a dark inner core surrounded by an exterior wrapping of pure sweetness. Where I saw liquorice, others noticed only candy. I masterfully concealed the real me, for the risks of exposure were far too great. Parents and church idolised me but their image bore no resemblance to my covert identity as a gay man and I felt fraudulent, unworthy, and heavily weighed down by my conscience.

In Christian doctrine, there are only two paths to walk: God's or Satan's. 'For the gate that leads to life is small and the road is narrow, and those who find it are few.'[73] I saw myself as the Devil's child clothed in an angel's white-feathered wings. I believed I belonged with the crowd on the spacious road to Hell but strolled two-facedly with friends and family on the narrow road to life. Somehow, somewhere, that masquerade had to end.

---

[73] *The New English Bible*, Matthew 7:14.

The human mind, as incredible as it is, cannot hold onto concurrent conflicting ideas, a theory known in social psychology as Cognitive Dissonance[74]. Test this for yourself. Close your eyes and try to imagine the achromatic colour black and its opposite, white. Try to imagine them at the same time, giving your full attention to both. Notice your struggle at getting this right. In your attempt, you might toggle between the two or imagine them as one, like zebra stripes or alternating tiles on a chequered floor. Notice too that it goes a bit deeper than that – your efforts create stress. We have an instinctive emotional drive to reduce dissonance and often try to do so through justification, blame and denial, which are the ego's ways of rationalising the inner conflict. Rationalising, rather than resolving – and there lies the problem.

Sexuality and spirituality were opposing aspects of my personality and my attempts at reconciling them created dissonance. I blamed my parents for who I was because I had once read that gay men come from families having a strong, dominant matriarchal figure and an insipid, weak patriarch. Covertly, I denied my spirituality because I thought I was a sinner and believed that sinners can't be spiritual. Consequently, I denied my legitimacy as a valuable member of my community because sinners have no place in society. Witness doctrine takes a literal, myopic and conservative view of gay practice and outlaws it without compromise, which meant that there were no mitigating factors and it became impossible for me to seek help without condemning myself and running the risk of expulsion.

A biological definition of sex is that it is an inbuilt drive to mix genetic traits to enhance an organism's specialisation so that it can adapt more readily to its environment (the DNA's urge to replicate itself!). A psychological definition is that there are three stages to human sex: desire and interest; excitement and arousal; and orgasm. Psychopathology and sexual disorder occur whenever there is failure during any one of these stages.[75] Sexual *orientation* is not a disorder. The American Psychological Association says, 'research has found no inherent association between any of these sexual orientations [lesbian, gay and bisexual] and psychopathology. Both heterosexual behavior and homosexual behavior are normal aspects of human sexuality'.[76]

The American Psychological Association adds:

---

[74] *Wikipedia*, http://en.wikipedia.org/wiki/cognitive_dissonance.
[75] *The Encyclopedia of Psychology*: 8 Volume Set, Alan E. Kazdin, PhD, Editor-in-Chief, APA Reference Books, 2000.
[76] http://www.apa.org.

All major national mental health organizations have officially expressed concerns about therapies promoted to modify sexual orientation. To date, there has been no scientifically adequate research to show that therapy aimed at changing sexual orientation (sometimes called reparative or conversion therapy) is safe or effective. Furthermore, it seems likely that the promotion of change therapies reinforces stereotypes and contributes to a negative climate for lesbian, gay, and bisexual persons. This appears to be especially likely for lesbian, gay, and bisexual individuals who grow up in more conservative religious settings.

Most people have a dangerously entangled view of sex. *Sex* is about one's biological drive but *love* is a display of one's strong emotional attachment or affection for another. When entwined, people seek sex as their affirmation of love. Often, when a person feels unloved, they seek sexual encounters in a misguided belief that it will bring them love. It is of course possible to have unemotional sex, intercourse for the sake of meeting one's biological needs, without emotional entanglement, just as it is possible to love someone without the urge to have sex with them. The two are separate but often perceived as one.

Ancient Tantric texts suggest that sex has three purposes: procreation, pleasure and liberation. Spiritual liberation comes to sexual participants at the climax of their act, in an ecstatic experience of infinite awareness, when all opposites collapse into Oneness. Essentially, these practices supposedly awaken Kundalini energy that rises upwards, culminating in Samadhi or integration, oneness. Sex, in this context, is a whole-body prayer to the Divine and is very different from its sinfully-perceived Christian counterpart. Spiritually liberating sex occurs in the narrow gap of non-attachment (where we are neither tugging at nor pushing away the experience) and, while driven by our biology and psychology, it leaves the mind utterly disentangled and the Spirit is at One.

Jehovah's Witnesses, like many other religions, get hung-up over human sexual practices. Trapped in the detail and in a literal interpretation of scripture, they can no longer see the wood for the trees. The early 1970s were times of great confusion for Witnesses around the world regarding 'proper sexual practices'[77] and many were disfellowshipped for failing to limit their sexual activities to 'genital copulation',[78] dogma formulated by a secret Governing Body

---

[77] *Crisis of Conscience*, Raymond Franz, Commentary Press, Atlanta. 2004.
[78] *Watchtower*, December 15, 1969.

that meets in New York City to set such global policies, an authority that nobody may challenge.

On the need for such secrecy, Dr. Haha Lung says, 'Most times a cult's [...] inner teachings are kept secret, supposedly because they are too scared for the prying eyes of non-believers, but mainly because the cult's methods and mythologies are unable to stand up to the light of logic and are unacceptable, if not outright illegal, by society's standards.'[79] Some were disfellowshipped for prolonged foreplay, oral sex and improper sexual positions. The organisation treated people callously and unsympathetically all over the world. Seldom were there signs of compassion and empathy. This was simply a matter of policy: members had disobeyed the organisation's dogmatic rules and it felt justified and righteous in trashing the 'bad apples'.

Reverend Mel White, co-founder of *Soulforce*, cautions Christians, saying that 'Even when we believe the scriptures are without error, it's a risk to think our understanding is without error'. The Bible accepts many sexual practices that we wouldn't tolerate in a modern society and condemns many that we choose to ignore because they seem barbaric, old-fashioned, outmoded and beyond the law. Here is a list of some of them: When a couple are married and he discovers that she's not a virgin, the bride is stoned to death.[80] Ouch! Imagine the Human Rights outcry if organisations practiced that today. Also stoned to death, would be anyone having sex with someone else's husband or wife.[81] The cynic in me sees a quick way to reduce much of the earth's overloaded population if lawmakers passed such a bill. The Bible forbids divorce, and divorcees from remarrying.[82] Many of my friends are in this category. Catching and executing both man and woman when they have had sex during her menstruation[83] would require a special branch of police enforcement to carry out inspections and I'd be loathed to hand this responsibility across to the clergy, given some of their dubious and clandestine sexual practises, especially with choir boys. Then there is a law demanding that if a man dies childless, his widow is to have sex with all his brothers until a male heir is born.[84] Mmmm! There could be a rush to legislate this one. One more bizarre decree: if two men get into a brawl and

---

79 *Mind Control, The Ancient Art of Psychological Warfare*, Dr. Haha Lung, Citadel Press, 2006.
80 Deuteronomy 22:13-21.
81 Deuteronomy 22:22..
82 Mark 10:1-12.
83 Leviticus 18:19.
84 Mark 12:18-27.

the wife of one of them intercedes and grabs the other's genitals, they would have to cut off her hand.[85]

The Bible's apparent condemnation of same-sex practices is contained in a handful of scriptures[86] and I tried to see if I could reconcile them against psychotherapy's contemporary view. Each of these scriptures refers to situations that would commonly be abhorrent today, like the condemnation of male rape in the story of Sodom and Gomorrah, sex that invalidates one's sexual orientation, paedophilia, lascivious and licentious behaviour, ritual orgies and bestiality. These scriptures warn of losing one's spirituality and one's connection to God, not through one's sexual orientation, but most likely through one's lust for power, need for control, and uncapped sexual consumption.

Celibacy is a commitment to avoid relationships and to abstain from sexual practices but it has its dangers if it creates feelings of denial, sacrifice and loss. It then becomes a practice of renunciation and detachment. Perversity, depravity and lust are the opposite as they create an environment of attachment. One pushes, the other pulls. The Hindu avatar Krishna advises, on all such matters, to find and live in the narrow gap of non-attachment. He encourages *sexual continence*, which I think is the real meaning of celibacy.

For years I tried to deny my sexuality by obsessively diverting energy deeper and more fervently into religious service. I constantly strove to attain the sort of holiness expected of us by the Witness organisation. But life had its own plan and I found myself clawing my way up a slippery slope in a vain attempt at attaining perfection. I imagined Jehovah looking down with growing disappointment and disapproval but never once did he seem to reach out his hand to help while Satan took gleeful delight in pouring yet another bucket of oil down the slippery slope to see if I would lose my grip and fall. Life was all about judgement. Others set the rules and I had to obey but the bar was set too high, boundaries were too inflexible, mistakes unforgivable and success unattainable. What does one do when one is stuck? I took the blame upon myself and began to self-implode.

I really needed to talk to somebody during that period but everyone was too busy being self-righteous. Even if they had been ready to listen, perhaps I couldn't have made disclosures for fear of reprisal. I felt trapped and stifled and grew increasingly disillusioned. There was a lot of

---

[85] Deuteronomy 25:11-12.
[86] Genesis 19, Leviticus 18:22, Leviticus 20:13, 1 Corinthians 6:9-10, Romans 1:26-27, 1 Timothy 1:9-10 and Jude 1:7.

hypocrisy about – quite a few elders and Bethelites were just like me, unable to attain the impossible standards set by dogma; and so they led double lives. Apartheid racism trapped some, clandestine sexual activities snagged others and egotism, materialism and a lot of questionable activity far from the reach of the organisation's surveillance plagued many more. Emotionally exhausted, tired of denial and angered by the lack of understanding, compassion or support, I could no longer perpetuate the lie and began to fade from active service.

I hate the circus because I hate caged animals: elephants tied to poles instead of roaming free; lions padding back and forth in tiny cages in mindless surrender to their fate as animals of curiosity kept solely for their entertainment value. These creatures have an awful look of capitulation and defeat in their eyes and I'm sure mine reflected the same emptiness during those years of involuntary surrender. There's nothing more bitter than the sweet song of a nightingale in a cage. I was the bird in the cage.

Cognitive dissonance comes at a high price – extensive stress. Anxiety caused by conflict contributed quickly to my deteriorating health and soon became manifest in a bleeding gastric ulcer that wouldn't heal. I lost weight, looked ill, and felt ill. My term at Bethel had to end prematurely because I couldn't combine living amongst them and my irreconcilable lifestyle. The situation was slowly killing me. Living and working at Bethel lasted less than two years before they reluctantly agreed to annul my four-year contract on medical grounds and I moved back home to convalesce.

The world around us constantly strives to disseminate norms, ideologies and customs to provide cultural continuity and a framework for our integration and participation in society. It makes society social and orderly. Psychotherapy agrees that to socialise a child, one must teach them that *all information comes from the outside*; that *all rewards are external*; and *to ignore their inner voice* when it is in conflict with that of an outside authority.[87] Children then become governable adults.

As with many cults, the Witnesses isolate their members and create walls of fear to prevent them from straying. They teach their dogma exclusively (thereby controlling the outside information); they dictate the friends one keeps, preferably one's brothers and sisters in the faith; what literature one reads (theirs of course); and they discourage worldly wisdom as it is often in conflict with their teachings. They become the only pathway to God (all rewards are

---

[87] *Paths to God, Living the Bhagavad Gita*, Ram Dass, Three Rivers Press, 2004.

controlled by them). They discourage individuality and original thought, and they dampen confidence in oneself, thus holding their members in a space of endless neediness and weakness. Followers constantly beseech God for his intervention and good grace through the only divinely approved agent there is, the Jehovah's Witness organisation itself (they are the sole voice of authority). It fosters a perverse co-dependence: they need their members in order for the organisation to exist and they make sure that their members need them in return. It's as if living in a city with all one's needs met but with sentries posted on the watchtowers along the walls to prevent anybody straying into the wide world beyond. Punishment is meted out to anyone caught venturing too far away. If one doesn't show remorse, they banish one from the city.

Dr. Haha Lung, writes:

> One of the biggest selling points cults and gangs have is that they offer you surrogate families, either offering to replace lost loved ones or else providing us the dream family we've always wanted. That's why cult leaders like to be called 'Father' or 'Mother' and our fellow converts 'Brother' and 'Sister'.[88]

I should have denounced the faith when I left Bethel but I couldn't, I wouldn't and I didn't know how to. I longed to cut all connections with the organisation in order to explore a different world but I simply could not carry through with it for the sake of my family. I was ready and strong enough to write a letter to the elders, renouncing all association, but it would have hurt my family terribly and it would have put them in the intolerable position of having to choose between the organisation and me. Raised in a very loving and close household, I sacrificed self to preserve my family's reputation and unity. The Witnesses' grip is strong, ruthless and often cruel and I feared the consequences of disassociation. Any unrepentant dissident is immediately 'disfellowshipped' and shunned by all. Instead of submitting to disassociation with its awful consequences, I took the softer route and slowly faded from service.

By early 1977, Queen Elizabeth's jubilee year, I escaped my parents' and congregational elders' watchful eyes to explore a burning need to find myself. I left home for a year, going far away, and I travelled the United Kingdom, crisscrossing England, Scotland and Wales on a bicycle for nine months, living mainly in youth hostels and a tent. The last three months were luxurious by comparison, spent riding endless trains across Europe and Scandinavia, using them as a

---

[88] *Mind Control, The Ancient Art of Psychological Warfare*, Dr. Haha Lung, Citadel Press, 2006.

mobile hotel on a Eurail pass. The experience proved liberating and transformative and the world became a very different place.

I thought that I had disappeared from the Witnesses' radar during my trip abroad but my parents arranged a base for me with an elderly Witness couple in Coventry and every time I returned there, they insisted that I attend congregation meetings with them. The elders in Coventry were far too curious about my excursions and one night my host let slip that I had carried a letter from Johannesburg that was more than a thank-you note from my parents to him: it contained a communiqué from the elders back home to those in Coventry, alerting them of my waywardness. I quickly and cleverly deflected suspicion and the red herring led them to send a positive report back to Johannesburg. When I returned home at the end of the year, they welcomed me warmly and soon everyone tried to entice me back into active service – but it was now too late for that kind of reform.

In 1978, I started a secular career in computer science and moved far away from home to live and work in Durban. There, I met my first partner, Johann, which marked the start of a fourteen-year relationship and a lifelong friendship. I know I wasn't an easy person to live with as I carried many scars from the past. I had heaps of guilt and doubt about life and the choices I made but I felt emotionally safer, living a lifestyle that was authentically mine. Instead of denying self for religion, the tables were turned and I denied religion to embrace self fully. The two seemed mutually exclusive and I could only live to one set of standards at a time.

My lack of attendance at all congregational gatherings led me to believe that I was beyond the Witnesses' reach and abandoned as a lost cause, but that wasn't to be. One day, a former Bethelite and once close friend asked to visit me at home to seek my opinion on same-sex partnerships as he suspected he was gay, lived his life in denial and was thus in utter conflict. We spoke freely for many hours and on his way out he made a sexual pass at me and I gently snubbed him saying that it was inappropriate because I was already in a relationship. I will never know if he resented my rejection or whether it was all a set-up to implicate me but, the next morning, we awoke to a loud thumping at the front door. Standing there authoritatively, demanding entry into our home, was a relative, connected to me through my sister's marriage. He was an elder at one of the coastal congregations and insisted that he talk to me about 'a grave matter'.

'No, there is no business of yours here,' I said without hesitation. Johann was still in bed that Saturday morning and I wasn't prepared to disrupt our home at someone else's whim.

I refused to talk to him but he, being the bully he was, insisted.

'You are a Jehovah's Witness and I am an elder and a member of your family and you *will* talk to me.'

Knowing that he wouldn't relent, I agreed to continue the conversation in his car parked alongside the curb. There, he told me that he'd received a telephone call late the previous night, informing him of the meeting and how my visitor tried compassionately and lovingly to advise a lifestyle change for me in harmony with scripture, but that I'd had the audacity to abuse him as he left. The situation was ludicrous. Careful distortion of the facts exonerated my visitor, deflected suspicion away from him, and completely vilified me. I tried to sidestep the issue but the in-law asked a direct and pointed question and I refused to lie.

'Are you a homosexual?'

'Yes, I am.'

They now had the evidence they required to bring me before a tribunal composed of three elders in the Morningside congregation that week where, in secret, they alone determined my fate. I felt like a captured criminal on their top-ten wanted list.

The tribunal's entire proceeding was heartless, uncompromising and lacked any form of empathy or understanding. It was a cold application of principle. They couldn't acknowledge my protection and love for my family, how I sacrificed self, and how hard I had tried to live up to their expectations. None of that mattered. When they demanded I return home to collect my belongings and then leave (supposedly into their care), I told them unequivocally to quit meddling in my affairs, and I walked out before they had time to conclude their procedures. This gave me a huge sense of power by undermining their authority. They were dismayed at my behaviour and protested my exit. There were no mitigating arguments or extenuating circumstances. The committee reached their conclusions in my absence and expelled me.

My mind reeled with contradictions. This organisation, which supposedly upheld honesty and truthfulness and expected its members to be law-abiding citizens, smuggled Bibles and Watchtower literature into Mozambique in defiance of laws banning them there after the *Frente de Libertação de Moçambique* [FRELIMO] took power in 1975 (perhaps that's defensible). They professed a common worldwide brotherhood but during the apartheid years, their black members met separately in black congregations and they accommodated them in blacks-only Bethel residences (an inexcusable perversion of Jesus' teaching to 'render to Caesar the things that are Caesar's'[89]) Hatred lurked in my heart.

They shed no tears and displayed no conscience over the collateral damage that would occur to a hitherto loving, close-knit and wholesome family. I wanted to sue for damages that my family and I would suffer, but I heard that others had tried before and failed. They are a mighty force and I decided it was best to turn my back and walk away. I remember walking home, a short distance up the hill to our apartment. It was a sunny midweek day and I stopped on the pavement, looked up through the liquid blue sky towards a blood-stained heavenly throne, and in a primordial embittered cry, yelled, 'Fuck you, Jehovah!'

My feelings were a mixture of rejection, disappointment, anger and sadness. The cry came from deep inside and its intensity made my jugulars bulge. The sound represented years of pent-up anger, hatred and resentment that were suddenly set free. I stumbled as though intoxicated, fell with my back against a whitewashed garden wall, leaned there for a while and slowly slid down as the rough-hewn surface clawed at my back until I slumped onto my haunches.

Warm liberating tears of release flowed freely.

I had profaned the name of God but no bolt of lightning struck me down. Instead of feelings of blasphemy and guilt, I became braver – and a sudden, immense power flowed through me.

I was free; I was finally free!

Still squatting, I continued my one-sided dialogue with Jehovah:

'Where is your love? How can you sit up there and condone such unfair judgement? How can you abandon me in my time of need? Have I not done everything possible to live up to your laws and rules? Yet you have never acknowledged it, nor have you ever given credit for it. I, as a mere human, would never stoop so low as to put children through this kind of turmoil. I would never split families apart. I would never reject and abandon those close to me. You however are God, and this is precisely what you've done. You've been horrendously mean,

---

[89] Matthew 22:21, *The American Standard Bible.*

inconsiderate and selfish, asking us, your children, to choose between you and the Devil. You've behaved like a divorcee asking the kids to choose between their parents. Show your might for once! Annihilate Satan if you will, and save your sons and daughters! Do it for our sake!'

At that moment I would readily have agreed with Richard Dawkins's verdict:

> The God of the Old Testament is arguably the most unpleasant character in all fiction: jealous and proud of it; a petty, unjust, control freak; a vindictive, bloodthirsty ethnic cleanser; a misogynistic, homophobic, racist, infanticidal, genocidal, filicidal, pestilential, megalomaniacal, sadomasochistic, capriciously malevolent bully.[90]

I was indignant at the profound immorality of it all and couldn't reconcile this with the way of the True God. I stood up, wobbled a bit and walked home. It was a pivotal moment, a marker in time when I gave up the ideology of God and Church.

The full impact struck later that afternoon when I received a telephone call from my mother. Her voice was grave.

'I was told the terrible news that the elders disfellowshipped you this afternoon. I hear you were unrepentant and denigrated the committee by walking out of the meeting. Please tell me this isn't true. Why haven't you told us about this matter before? This behaviour of yours brings unspeakable shame on our family.'

Mom was always adamant about preserving our family reputation and taught my sister Anne and me the strict rules of discretion. Never hang out your dirty laundry for others to see. Having the news of my disfellowshipping known publicly was a source of deep embarrassment for her. Throughout my association with the Witnesses, vicious gossip was commonplace. My mother hated it and used to say: 'Don't telephone; don't telegram; tell a Witness and you'll get your news around.' Long before I had chance to formulate a response to my parents, the coastal relative who brought the matter before the committee of elders had already carried the hot gossip to Mom and Dad – almost triumphantly.

---

[90] *The God Delusion*, Richard Dawkins, First Mariner Books, 2008.

Mom continued: 'Why have you done this terrible thing that's brought such shame on us? What's wrong with you that you can hurt us all so badly?'

'Wait a moment!' I yelled down the line 'How can you only think of yourself and the embarrassment this will cause *you*. What about me? Does anyone care about me?'

She started to cry and I slammed the receiver onto its Bakelite cradle, making the bell tinkle from the shock.

'Fuck! Doesn't anyone care?' I walked about the living room clasping my face in my hands, pacing back and forth saying the words again and again. Then, rage roared to life inside and I raced down the passageway to the main bedroom and ripped the linen from the bed strewing it everywhere. The awful energy of the day had to find an outlet. Attacking the bed was highly symbolic even though I wasn't cognitive of it at the time. I trashed our room in rage and stormed out of the apartment, climbed onto my motorbike and sped off without having a planned destination in mind.

Johann was studying at university for his honours degree and wouldn't be home until late. I hadn't told him about the inquisition as I knew he'd discourage my attendance. I took time off work to attend. Intuitively I knew I should have boycotted the tribunal but somehow, the relief of exposure lulled me into believing that someone there might demonstrate a little love and compassion and offer support and counsel. Perhaps I believed I could present my case favourably and explain how difficult leading a double life had been and how I'd sacrificed self for everyone else's sake. How horribly mistaken I was and I soon realised that all my past fears were indeed correct. Dogma subjugated empathy as the committee cast me aside without compunction.

I knew I had to drive up to Johannesburg to visit my parents but I couldn't without first explaining my absence at work, so I turned the bike around and raced to the office in Durban's city centre. I avoided talking to the receptionist, bypassed the boss's private secretary and knocked on his open door. Kevin Stent is one of those remarkable people that inspire me. He headed the Computer Division authoritatively and decisively but his people skills set him apart from every other person with whom I've worked.

'What's the matter, Tom?' He instantly saw my emotional state and showed immense fatherly support.

'I've got to go to Jo'burg tonight.'

'What's happened?'

'It's a family matter and I'm too upset to explain it properly now.'

'How will you get there?'

'By bike.'

He called his secretary through the open door. 'Sally, quickly book Tom a ticket to Johannesburg on the next available flight and get him a car too.'

'What should I do about my work? How long can I stay away?'

'Your work will wait and I know you will return speedily.'

I thanked him profusely but he shrugged his shoulders as if to tell me that it was the least he could do. A flight within a few hours had a spare seat and Kevin asked if that wasn't too soon, but I assured him that I didn't need to go back to the apartment and that I would go directly to the airport.

'Leave your bike here, Sally will arrange a taxi to take you to the airport.'

I arrived at my parents' door around seven o'clock that night and rang the bell. Mom was in the kitchen washing their supper dishes and I heard her call out: 'Erith, my hands are full of soap and there's someone at the door. Would you get it please?'

Dad opened and I heard Mom question 'Who is it?'

He replied, 'It's Thomas.'

There was no holding back and my emotions poured out. I wanted to hug him but held back because I didn't know whether he would welcome or chastise me. He led me through to their open-plan lounge. Mom by now had dried her hands and joined us. She hugged me and we all cried together. These were tears more bitter than those shed when I went to jail.

'Is this true? Were you disfellowshipped today?' she asked. Dad listened as she led the conversation.

'Yes. It's all true. I was setup. Trapped.' I was deeply saddened and apologetic. 'I never wanted you to go through this. I tried very hard to hide it all but I was hunted down like an animal.'

I told them about the course of events that led to my expulsion and she bristled with resentment because she never liked the meanness this relative had shown. He had a reputation for it and Mom and Dad had endured it more than once. She also hated the idea that he'd gleefully carried the news of my disfellowship to them as if to hang my head as a trophy on his wall of self-righteousness.

'Why didn't you tell us? Why didn't you ask for help? We always promised each other that we could talk about any and every thing.'

'But I've done so, so many times, yet you never listened. You pretend not to hear. Have you ever noticed that I show no interest in girls? Weren't you curious why I couldn't fit into the Bethel lifestyle, fell ill and had to terminate my contract there? Weren't you suspicious of my friendship with Johann when you and Dad came to visit us in Durban?'

Dad's body language showed tell-tale signs of knowing. He didn't seem too surprised. Mom was shocked.

'How long have you known about *it*?' she asked, avoiding the last part of the question which would have been too hard for her to articulate '... being homosexual?'

'All my life, Mom. Forever!'

'How?'

'Every sexual thought, every experience, everything about me is gay.'

'So it was true when Barbara told me what you and Dennis had gotten up to in the garden shed.'

'Yes, Mom.'

'And also when Campbell told the elders about you and him?'

'Yes, yes, yes to all of those things!'

She tried hard to recalibrate her idea of me, given that there were some minor misdemeanours that landed me in hot water. But Mom must have convinced herself that I was beyond reproach and exonerated me from suspicion.

'Why make *this choice*?'

'It's not a choice, Mom. It's who I am. I cannot choose differently. Believe me when I say I tried. I really have...'

'Why don't you just avoid *it* then? Set *it* aside and serve Jehovah.' She still couldn't say the word sex and always substituted euphemisms to make her feel more comfortable.

'I've also tried to live a life of celibacy but I'm just not built that way.' I added: 'I love you both with all my heart and I'm deeply sorry I can't change what's happened.'

'So where did we go wrong?'

'You and Dad did nothing wrong! I haven't done anything wrong! It's just the way it is. I'm still as spiritual as ever. None of that changed.'

I spent a few hours there. I expected to sleep over but realised the first signs of shunning. Mom would normally have made something for me to eat but she didn't even ask. As for sleeping over, that was impossible. I was no longer welcome. We stood at the front door. They stood close to each other. I stood alone outside on the doormat. They would console each other. I was about to leave into the night alone, knowing that I would never associate with them again. We looked at each other for a while with nothing more to say. They were devastated, torn between their love of their child and the demands the Witnesses imposed on them. Mom wept openly. Dad was stoic and spoke the final words of the evening.

'Today, it is as though my son has died'.

Emotionally depleted, I drove the short distance back to the airport, checked into the hotel, sat alone at the bar and got horribly drunk before retiring to bed. I returned to Durban the next morning. Johann was terrified with worry. He'd come home to an upturned flat and I was missing, bike and all. Somehow, there hadn't been time to contact him.

I spent the day telling Johann everything. I'd been a bit uncertain about our relationship before but he was now my only point of reference in a twisted, bigoted world. Johann's parents didn't know about him and it would take a few more years for them to know. His parents became my surrogate parents; mine dismissed him with disdain.

Kevin Stent had the courteous discretion never to ask what family business I had in Johannesburg. He graciously covered all expenses without a word. His kindness and compassion were so profound and deeply influenced the way I managed others throughout my career.

When one is disfellowshipped, the Witnesses announce it to the congregation at their next meeting. There is no appeal process; no way of presenting extenuating circumstances. The committee of elders summarily ignored my lifetime of devoted service and sealed my fate. This is how the organisation regards the matter:

> 'disfellowshipping' is what Jehovah's Witnesses appropriately call the expelling and subsequent shunning of such an unrepentant wrongdoer.... a simple 'Hello' to someone can be the first step that develops into a conversation and maybe even a friendship. Would we want to take that first step with a disfellowshipped person?[91]

The practise was adopted as a punitive measure in 1952 after some very literal interpretation of a few scriptures: 'If anyone comes to you and does not bring this teaching, do not receive him into your house, and do not give him a greeting.'[92] and 'You have become arrogant and have not mourned instead, so that the one who had done this deed would be removed from your midst.'[93]

---

[91] *Watchtower*, 15 September 1981 pp.22,25
[92] 2 John 10, *New American Standard Bible*
[93] 1 Corinthians 5, *New American Standard Bible*

Shunning is 'withholding fellowship' and demands that its members cease all social and spiritual contact with a disfellowshipped person, 'not even eating with them'. They must also shun all disfellowshipped family members living outside the home. Failure to adhere to the guidelines of shunning is a serious offence and disobedient members can themselves be disfellowshipped.

Disfellowshipped persons must believe that they are condemned to everlasting destruction whilst they remain disfellowshipped. They are for the rest of their lives denied all free association with Witness family and friends. The organisation metes out the punishment forever regardless of whether the person ceases the practice of wrongdoing or not. One would have to submit to their reinstatement procedures before the organisation would lift the punishment. To qualify for reinstatement, disfellowshipped members must attend meetings and follow strict procedures of repentance and rehabilitation. Yet, in complying with these rules, they continually submit themselves to the humiliating and undignified experience of shunning until the elders feel that the time is right to submit application to the Watchtower Society for formal reinstatement. Only then would they welcome the disfellowshipped person back into the congregation and shunning would cease.

Disfellowshipping is the harsher of the two punishments used by the Witnesses. Marking is the other. Unlike a disfellowshipped person, a marked person is unnamed and placed under probation and the surveillance of the elders.

As relieved as I was, the consequences of expulsion from the Jehovah's Witnesses haunted me for decades. I had denied my truth for years to prevent disrepute and hurt to those I loved, but the doors slammed closed behind me on that fateful evening and I did not receive the same consideration in return. I was instantly separated from my family who chose to preserve their integrity in the congregation and agreed to the terms of my expulsion by shunning me completely. I was now suddenly a pariah and the consequences of expulsion were amongst the most difficult experiences I had to face in life, including my time in the isolation cell. I'm sure it wasn't easy for my family either, because I know they loved me dearly. Motivated by the Witnesses' doctrine, they chose to abandon me.

The family took comfort in their faith and had each other for support; I did it alone. It felt like a wire brush had scoured my heart. Over the next thirty-two years, up until this time of writing, my sister and her family have never set foot in my home and their relationship with me remains at most a thing of distanced manners.

On one of her more significant wedding anniversaries, my sister telephoned and said 'You know that I can't invite you because of who you are'.

'No, my dear sister,' I replied, 'You've got it wrong! You're not inviting me because of who I am but rather because of who *you* are. This is your choice and not mine. Remember, I'm okay with your choices but don't make your issues mine.'

As for the rest of the family, their reaction has mostly been a varied response from half-hearted nods to outright hostility and ugliness. There were times when I hated them all intensely, especially the organisation that orchestrated it all, and I held the Witnesses culpable for a very long time.

Once when my father was in hospital after suffering a minor stroke, I visited and found relatives and friends in the ward with him. They instantly stopped talking to each other, like the unanimous silence of disturbed frogs at a pond. Each looked down at the floor to avert their gaze. They wouldn't greet me. They dared not make eye contact. They couldn't acknowledge my presence in the room. I walked up to his bedside and held his hand but it was cold and stiff and he played into the shunning game in front of this audience. He was gravely ill and there was a reasonable chance of him dying. Surgeons performed a delicate operation on him that day to scrape the plaque from his carotid artery to prevent long-term side effects and another stroke. They'd done this procedure without blood (Witnesses refuse blood transfusions) which added huge complexity to the process. Yet, even in such dire circumstances, I couldn't get through to him. Everyone sat tight, expecting me to leave. Not one of them tried to console me.

I looked into his watery eyes and saw sadness. He longed for my compassion and love but couldn't reach for it in front of those people. I became incensed and rebuked them all. But to them I remained invisible, the living corpse of a 'dead' man. Finally, I had no choice but to leave.

The instant I exited the ward, I heard their whispered castigation as I walked away sadly.

At the age of thirty-one, Johann and I relocated to Johannesburg where, with two other business partners, I started a successful software engineering company that grew in size and reputation[94]. I now turned to the world of science and technology to find inspiration and

---

[94] *Barone, Budge & Dominick (Pty) Ltd*, incorporated in September 1984.

purpose. Through my lectures at the Johannesburg Planetarium[95], my talks on radio[96] and my television appearances[97], I explored the fascination of the night sky and the mysteries of the physical universe. I owned and flew aircraft, built up a plush home and a collection of nice possessions. We enjoyed many friends, hosted lavish dinner parties and travelled extensively to many exotic places. Money and professional success seemed to be my only goal. The Witnesses had stripped away my sense of self-worth and I had to rebuild myself from scratch, constructing a new persona in order to seek recognition as a valuable and worthwhile member of society. The only way at the time that I knew how, was to build with bricks and mortar and to subscribe to the creed of materialism. I developed an egoistic streak too, believing that the more money I amassed, the more power and respect I would get. I constantly sought affirmation and validation from my place in society but, even then, sexual prejudice and bigotry prevailed and I never truly felt part of anything. Others in my position might have found their material wealth comforting and a sign of success, but my earthly accomplishments slowly proved shallow and meaningless and, as they lost their lustre, raw spirit yearned for something more.

---oooOooo---

Many years later Dad once chose to set aside the rules of not eating together and we met for lunch and a few 'shots' at the Bank Bar, near his offices in Commissioner Street, Johannesburg. Dad was partial to his *dop-en-dam* [Afrikaans: *dop*, a tot of alcohol and *dam*, lake – thus, a single shot of brandy in a tumbler of water] which soon allowed him to drop his defences and lubricated his tongue. In fact, his regular use of alcohol was his Achilles heel that prevented him from attaining rank inside the congregation's hierarchy. It wasn't serious enough to have him appear before the elders but they did scrutinise him closely and kept him in check. I believe his propensity for booze allowed him to bend the rules a little that day because he must have felt that we were both in much the same boat. He was a deep thinker with a quiet voice. He never said much but when he did, he spoke with authority and a sense of great wisdom. Mom encouraged me to think badly of Dad because of his drinking but I later learned of a different side to him and slowly grew to love him dearly.

---

[95] *Johannesburg Planetarium*, University of the Witwatersrand, 1991-2002.
[96] *The Saturday Morning Astronomy Programme*, a one-hour actuality slot on Radio Rippel, 1999-2002.
[97] Scriptwriter and Presenter of *Out of this World*, a six-part, half-hour television documentary on South African astronomy broadcast by The South African Broadcasting Corporation, SABC3.

Poignantly, the pub where we sat eating was the very one I sat in on many previous Saturday afternoons as a young teenager while Dad enjoyed copious *dop-en-dams* with his cronies. Too young to sit inside the bar, I was ushered into the adjacent storeroom to the side of the main counter, next to the machine that spat out ice cubes. There, I could help myself to as much Coca Cola as I chose and indulged in a mountain of French fries while I waited for him to finish. Mom didn't like the idea at all and Dad and I kept it 'our secret,' something special between us, which forged a particular bond between us.

We now sat at the little round table in the smoky room that stank of stale beer, eating our simple bar lunch, when Dad asked, out of the blue: 'Don't you ever think of girls, My Boy?' He always called me *My Boy*, which I think he coined from his favourite song, 'Sonny Boy' by Al Jolson. He often looked sad and pensive when he played that gramophone recording of Al Jolson's song, and so his phrase of endearment became sweet, and I liked it when he called me by that name.

'I've never been with a girl, Dad,' I replied, rather coyly as we never spoke of sexual matters at home. In fact, sex always carried an air of shame, weakness and bashfulness when spoken about.

I remember one evening, when Mom and Dad took us to the drive-in [an outdoor parking-lot cinema] to watch *Gone with the Wind*. During the final scenes, where the couple kiss on the beach in front of the red glow of sunset, Mom turned anxiously to Dad and said 'Make sure the kids are asleep'.

Dad fussed over us, ordering us to lie down on the back seat, covering us with a blanket. 'Go to sleep now,' he ordered sternly.

'But Dad... the movie isn't finished,' we moaned, popping up our heads to watch more. After a few brisk slaps, we got the message and lay down. Mom muttered statements of disdain at the public display of affection shown on the screen as she sucked in little gasps of air in horror each time they kissed. I remember thinking that kissing must be something quite disgusting. Only filthy people out of control had sex together – a mindset later reinforced by Witness doctrine.

In response to Dad's question about me having been with a girl, I volunteered more information.

'No Dad,' I added, stepping way out on a limb, opening my heart to him. I really needed him to recognise me as a nice kid, instead of judging me as some promiscuous and depraved being. 'I could never do it with a girl. I have only been with guys and you'll never understand what invisible force drives me in that direction. It's not something I chose; in fact, it is a million times more difficult than being straight. Everyone accepts you if you're straight but you're instantly condemned if you're gay. I wish I could change, but I can't. Believe me when I say I've tried – but that's who I am and I have to accept it just as it is. You will never know the constant emotional pain and anguish I carry in my heart.'

He slowly put down his drink and looked at me, tears welling up in his eyes. 'The war's a strange place, My Boy,' he said. Then he sank into a long pensive silence and appeared to have drifted away into a dark and unspoken pocket of his past.

'What do you mean?' I asked, after a long pause. I wondered what metaphoric significance there was in what he'd said.

'It drives one to do strange things,' he answered, leaning forward, his elbows on the table, his neck stretched as though preparing to share a solemn secret that he wanted nobody else in the pub to hear. 'I once had a "friend" during the war,' he said, emphasising the quotation marks around *a friend* with gestures of his fingertips.

'Tell me about him?' I asked, disbelieving what I'd heard.

'He was killed...'

Dad said nothing further but I knew what he meant by the euphemism: *my friend*. I tried many times thereafter to get him to talk more but he must have realised that the *dop-en-dam* made him say something he might have regretted, and he spoke about it no more.

I have a little brass button that came from Dad's war memorabilia, which he kept with his medals in a little cigarette tin. Might it be the only remaining memory of his *friendship?* And if so, it then symbolises the opening of a very special place in my heart for my father. It's amazing how so few words have such enormous impact. They haunted and consoled me ever since and I suddenly understood much more about Dad and the pain he must have felt disowning me in the way that the Witnesses expected him to do.

The Jehovah's Witnesses razed my spiritual crop but Ram Dass tilled the soil and lovingly planted fresh seeds in the fertile ground of my receptive heart where they lay dormant, waiting for a new season, a climate that encouraged germination and which nurtured growth. In hindsight, I thought I had abandoned my spirituality but I had actually only abandoned my religiosity. Spirituality found new expression in honesty, gentleness and truthfulness, and it manifested in nature, trees and animals, in stars and galaxies and occasionally, in a few intriguing and inspiring people whose influence was immense.

The teachings on Ram Dass's two cassette tapes were to give me a glimpse of a very different world, one without judgement where he aptly demonstrated that unconditional love was both realistic and achievable. Little did I know back then that he had opened the door to a spiritual space within, where Spirit dwelt in the permanent presence of the Divine. For the moment, though, religion and dogma now lay in burnt-out cinders and a harsh and awful past, a long bitterly cold emotional winter, had finally ended.

For some, coming to full spiritual awareness can be an instantaneous moment of enlightenment. Saul of Tarsus was on his way to Damascus to continue his mission of stamping out converts to the new Jewish sect of Christians when he experienced a vision of Jesus that instantly altered his perceptions of life forever.[98] For others, the road is a bit more arduous because we cling to the character we think we are. What is spiritual awareness? It's letting go, dissolving our deluded illusions of self and remembering who we really are. The *Course in Miracles* states it nicely: 'Your mind can be possessed by illusions, but spirit is eternally free. If a mind perceives without love, it perceives an empty shell and is unaware of the spirit within. But the Atonement restores spirit to its proper place. The mind that serves spirit is invulnerable.'[99]

Siddhārtha Gautama lived four to five hundred years before Jesus and was the son of the ruling king and queen of a small kingdom now situated in Nepal. Raised by his aunt, he was destined to become a prince. He married his cousin at the age of sixteen and spent many years as a prince but felt that life didn't centre on material wealth. And so he quit his palace life, sneaked away and lived as an ascetic, but that didn't satisfy him either so he took his austerities to further extremes by practising self-mortification and eating barely enough to survive. When

---

[98] Acts 9:1–9.
[99] *A Course in Miracles*, T-1.IV.8-11, Combined Volume (Third Edition) Copyright© 2007 by the Foundation for A Course in Miracles.

he fell and nearly drowned in a pond, he realised that this kind of self-deprivation brought him no closer to finding his true purpose. Exhausted, the thirty-five-year-old man sat under a *pipal* tree and sank into a forty-nine day meditation. His companions, believing he had forsaken his path, abandoned him under the tree and left. There, in the shade of the *pipal* tree, now known as the *Bhodi* tree, Siddhārtha reached enlightenment and became the first Buddha and the founder of Buddhism. He discovered a special place between attachment and renunciation. It isn't about one's attachment to material things nor about one's renunciation of them but it's rather about living in the narrow space between them – that special place of non-attachment.

My transition wasn't that fast.

'More is never enough'

Legislative changes and excommunication disentangled me from a triangular web between the State, the Jehovah's Witnesses and my sexuality. But this freedom brought about a different form of entrapment. My family's shunning hurt me deeply and I turned to work and play as pathological ways of numbing the pain in my heart. I defined myself materialistically through a lavish lifestyle and slowly slipped too close to decadence and lasciviousness. I soon lost respect for myself as I became more egoistic and bombastic. I was never truly happy after my disfellowshipping. In fact, I had never been truly happy. It wasn't until a doorway unexpectedly opened to a new way of thinking, that I was able to enjoy a measure of true freedom.

My relationship with Johann ended fourteen years after it began. We divided our possessions and chose to commute our relationship into a friendship that has remained intact until the present. We were both 'damaged goods'. Social bigotry, parental denial and feelings of displacement meant that we could never truly live the lives of our heterosexual friends. We had no children to anchor us. Admired as prominent members of the gay community, Johann and I lived up to our reputation by entertaining and befriending many of Johannesburg's elite homosexual men and women. Our separation sent shockwaves into our circle of friends because they viewed us as strong pillars of hope in an otherwise fluvial world of 'fickledom'. I moved out of our home and lived with Graham and Myrtle for a few months until I found a place to stay far out of town. Graham and Myrtle are both dear friends of ours. She is a full-time mother and artist, and he, a respected Johannesburg architect.

My new home (where I've now lived for the past two decades) is a configuration of a few simple thatched cottages on the slopes of a rocky dolomite ridge. It's an oasis in a sea of Highveld grass. The buildings nestle amongst hundreds of indigenous trees that attract countless birds. Nature abounds in this forgotten pocket so near to the urban sprawl of Johannesburg and Pretoria. Having left Graham, Myrtle and the city life, I lived alone and never ventured off the property unless I was going to work or on an occasional outing. I detached myself from my friends, became a bit reclusive (solitude is my escape and my friend) and had a few attempts at new relationships, one with a very lovely ex-Jehovah's Witness; but due to our common pathology, it was never destined to succeed. Finally, I met Mark, a much younger man with a far less complicated lifestyle. We lived together for over ten years with a few breaks along the way. He was good for me and helped me shed most the tarnished image I had of myself. Where mine was a life of science and fact, his was a life of art and dance.

We balanced each other and lived quite happily until we slipped into a weekend milieu of dance parties and recreational drugs. Slowly, jealousy and fuzziness entered our relationship during that two-year period and it was then that we realised that the relationship was destined to end.

It was shortly after my breakup with Mark, on a beautiful summer's evening in December, when I celebrated Graham's birthday with him and his friends at their lovely Bryanston home in Johannesburg's affluent leafy northern suburbs. Conceited, aloof and mildly arrogant (traits I'd acquired to protect myself from the brutal world that continually bruised me), I arrived in my silver Jaguar with its ivory leather upholstery and quadrophonic sound system and felt at home amongst their other influential guests. The Jaguar was an import from England and only one of a few in the country at the time. It symbolised the height of my materialistic, lavish and mildly promiscuous lifestyle.

Myrtle decorated a few trestle tables that spanned the entire length of their lounge. The dining table in the adjoining room was sumptuous, laden with good food, and easy music and conversation filled their garden, masking nature's twilight summer sounds.

Rapping on her wine glass with a spoon, Myrtle summoned us to the table. Drink in hand, I finished the conversation with the person I was talking to and walked down the rows of chairs looking for my nametag. I sat between two people I hadn't met and as I shuffled into place, the fellow to my right turned, briefly introduced himself and rejoined his group in conversation.

I'm on perfect form when I'm with friends but it's a long struggle to warm to strangers. Close friends know my history, there's nothing more to hide, and I feel safe with them. But it seems as if strangers have this uncanny way of seeing into me and I immediately feel judged. My rational, logical mind knows this isn't likely but my emotional, subconscious mind creates a fantasy about future disclosure of my sexuality and I fret over their reaction to it. My subconscious already plans the scenario of that moment and wonders whether they will remain or will judge me and reject my friendship. This happens regardless of whether I have a once-off acquaintance with them or not. Positioned between two strangers was doubly difficult.

I greeted the woman on my left.

'Hi, I'm Tom,' I said, extending my hand. She said her name but it slid through my brain like a fried egg on Teflon and I didn't have the nerve to ask for it again. We engaged in pleasantries for a while before I asked, 'What line of work are you in?'

It's such an awful social game, exchanging facts about careers, the location of our homes, our kids' schools and the kind of cars we drive. We constantly try to outdo one another, to win a place a rung or two higher up the social ladder. And, regretfully, I was the one who started it.

'I sell health supplements,' she replied, and responding to the rules, she popped the question back at me: 'So, what do you do?'

Safely hiding behind my own importance, which became a red herring to draw her away from discovering the real me, I replied to this gentle, kind and earthy woman: 'I'm a software engineer. I have my own business consisting of more than a hundred programmers at our offices here and in Cape Town. We build systems for the big South African banks and we're now designing and building a billing system for a major mobile phone operator.'

We had played round one of the game and I, having the highest score for the better job, trumped her and rose up the ladder; but there was no joy in winning as it dampened the mood and our conversation became awkward, and soon dried up completely. Material wealth and job status were components of a perfect shell I constructed to protect a vulnerable, doubtful, and somewhat meaningless self. It wasn't my true nature to be rude and it left me conflicted and feeling awkward. Yet, safety inside the protective shell was far more important and drove me to behave the way I did. We were relieved when the entrées arrived as it gave us an exit, so we smiled at each other politely and fixed our attention on eating.

I felt sorry for her because I knew she'd been crushed by my one-upmanship and I remembered what it was like as a young South African living through apartheid's heyday. Witnessing the racial hatred of the time hurt me deeply and I too had sampled a taste of what it must have been for black people when, one day in London, patrons ousted me from a bar after they guessed my nationality: 'We don't want racist bastards like you here!'

I was always a different kind of kid and learned from young to accept teasing and abuse over issues and circumstances that I couldn't control. Since then, I've hated bullies and those who prey on the weak and innocent to gain their advantage, and it now felt as though I had become one of them myself by capping this woman sitting next to me at the table in order to protect myself. I ate silently, sipping my whisky, and she took the cue and did much the same with her wine.

Myrtle wasted no time in opening her buffet and it astonished me to notice the speed of her guests as they scurried to fill their plates with delicacies, as if it was the last meal they'd ever eat. Left on our own for a moment, my table companion plucked up her courage and broke the frosty silence with a question that was so sudden, so out of context and so profound that it took me utterly by surprise. 'What are your opinions about reincarnation?' she asked.

Flabbergasted by her question, I needed to confirm what I heard. I repeated it. 'Reincarnation? You're asking me for my beliefs on reincarnation?'

'Yes,' she said softly. 'What do you think happens to us after we die?'

I didn't know the answer. I hadn't really thought of it before. I knew that Christians didn't accept the belief in reincarnation but I had moved away from that identity and didn't really have an opinion of my own. She appeared to have trumped me and I didn't want to seem foolish, unprepared and ignorant because that would have drilled holes in my defences. Hiding once more behind my pompousness I sniggered before replying. 'You're asking a scientist,' I said. 'When the power's cut, the lights go out and we die. That's it!' Recklessly, I plunged on: 'I assume that you believe in reincarnation, but I regret to say that I need irrefutable, empirical evidence for life after death before I can embrace such an outlandish idea. Until then, I think it's a load of bull. Reincarnation is a vain belief with which we attempt to deal with our own mortality.' And now I was flippantly speechifying, trying desperately to flick her off: 'Ever since, through our evolutionary process, we gained our powers of rational thinking, we've been terrified of dying, of disappearing into obscurity. So we create these fanciful beliefs in God and an afterlife to allay our fears and to give a glimmer of hope.'

Her eyes widened in horror as she tried to retreat. I swirled the ice cubes around the bottom of the glass and swigged back the diluted remnants of alcohol. She'd touched a nerve that connected me to my past in so many ways and she became the focus of my frustration. Belief, faith and surrender were the bearers of confinement and excommunication and I wanted nothing more to do with them. Science was structured and based on experimentation, observation and fact.

'Our purpose is nothing more than a vehicle used by DNA to replicate itself. We are DNA's stepping stone to stronger and more robust DNA. We're a pawn in a biological game and when we're dead, we're dead. First bring your proof of an afterlife and then we might be able to continue this discussion.'

This put the kybosh on the conversation and there was no way of recovering it. I felt even more miserable and the room suddenly seemed oppressive and claustrophobic. The table was too wide, and the room too noisy, to strike up a conversation with someone I knew sitting opposite me, so I sank into a state of mild morbidity and waited for an appropriate moment when I could tender my apologies. I left before Myrtle served dessert.

I flopped into bed at home and mulled over the evening, somewhat huffed by it all. 'People have absurd ideas without having one scrap of evidence. How crazy is that!' The word 'crazy' echoed endlessly in my fuzzy, overtired mind. 'How crazy, and without a scrap of proof!' It was easier to blame the failed evening on somebody else rather than taking full responsibility for my lack in confidence and belief in myself.

Slowly, sleep closed in and in my hypnagogic state, 'proof' and 'crazy' became entangled and undifferentiated. Then, with alarming suddenness, I sat bolt upright and wide-awake in the darkness. A voice had spoken so loudly in my head that it startled me and brought me back to instant sobriety and wakefulness. 'Proof!' it taunted, 'Is that what this's all about? You insist on having proof and she has none so you dismiss her views. But be fair though - you are short of proof too. Your case is as weak as hers.'

There was an irony in this explosive taunt, for it had double meaning. Not only did it refer literally to the propositions about an afterlife but it also was a subtle reference to my internal state of self-rejection and my constant suspicions of others' prejudgement of me. I wasn't ready to acknowledge the latter inference and I stuck with the literal conundrum that messed with my head. I definitely didn't have proof that when we die the power stops and we disappear into obscurity. I didn't have a scrap of evidence to substantiate that we are nothing but DNA's elaborate stepping stone to its own evolutionary survival. There was no way I could disprove her ideas of souls ducking and diving through endless reincarnated forms. Therefore, according to the rules of science, her ideas of reincarnation were as worthy of consideration as my more fatalistic ones. Both constituted working hypotheses until we could find evidence enough to prove or refute them. There were two valid propositions: '(A) – *Repeated Lifetimes*' and '(B) – *One Lifetime*.' Both demanded our scrutiny and our efforts to gather more evidence. Until then, we must suppose that both are equally valid. Scientists come up with ideas and build on knowledge through experimentation and collaboration. Science is after all the pursuit of knowledge, and not knowledge itself.

I leaped out of bed, turned on the lights, flung a dressing gown over my shoulders and walked through the house to my desk. There, I took a sheet of clean, white notepaper and with my fountain pen split it vertically with a thick black line. At the top of the left column, I wrote '*Repeated Lifetimes*' and on the right, '*One Lifetime*'. Then, allowing my mind free rein, I jotted down, under the appropriate heading, thoughts about these ideas as they randomly came to mind. I often use this technique, as it's a useful tool resulting in a much broader view of the subject at hand. It encourages a free flow of uncensored thoughts and I note them as they come up in no particular order.

I don't know what prompted me to hop out of bed in those late nocturnal hours. Perhaps conscience felt I ought to give her a chance to present her case, even in absentia. I realised that proof was elusive and that all efforts to find any that late at night would be futile. I wasn't out to prove or disprove what she'd seeded in my mind but, somehow, I felt compelled to explore the ideas for a while. My investigation wasn't a spiritual one either. It was more of a metaphorical experiment wherein I played around with the ideas of two diametrically opposed paradigms and their consequences for my life in an affluent, consumer-oriented, capitalistic society. My logical mind played with the ideas of afterlife while my subconscious mind toyed with parallel symbolisms that helped solve some of my problems related to my self-rejection and fear of being judged amiss.

My first thought was, 'More is never enough' and I scribbled it down under the 'One Lifetime' heading. It must have emerged first because it perfectly described my lifestyle at the time – the silver Jaguar, a solid career, business owner, wealth, influential friends and how these overshadowed my insecurity, self-doubt and difference. I realised, no matter how much I own, no matter how big my house or car, no matter how much money I have – *more is never enough*. It described my insatiable appetite to consume. I always seemed to need more than I had. The concept of 'more is never enough' was intrinsically linked in my mind to a belief in only one lifetime – a generalisation that wouldn't stand up to the rigours of scientific evidence. My classification was more of a metaphorical way of compartmentalising the consequences of *greed* versus *moderation*. Greed seemed linked to the metaphor of One Lifetime and moderation to the metaphor of Reincarnation. Why so? Because the two metaphors resonated with an internal split between my materialism and its endeavour to mask my fear of not being good enough and my spirituality that lay like dormant seeds waiting for the right moment to germinate. Raised under Christian doctrine, I believed that death marked the end and the soul (such as it may be) moved forward into a state of divine praise (Heaven) or eternal shame (Hell). My life didn't seem worthy of divine praise and this belief influenced my bias towards material opulence. Deeply spiritual beings, like Ram Dass, seemed inclined towards moderation and hence my associating it with the paradigm of Repeated Lifetimes.

My thoughts returned to Graham's birthday party and the polite enquiries the woman and I exchanged about our careers. Asking another about their career is the polite form. We would never ask the dysphemism, 'Are you rich?' as it is rude, and yet both questions seek the same information. Despite our manner and phraseology, we're really asking for information about their material worth so that we might gauge our position on the social ladder relative to them.

'More is never enough' enticed me to achieve more, as does a carrot on a string dangled in front of a reluctant mule, and, as I stepped ahead of others, I kept constant vigil to prevent them overtaking me. This idea led to me to write down in my notes 'Keeping up with the Joneses,' followed by 'Time is money' or, as Oscar Wilde put it, 'Time is a waste of money,' meaning that too much spare time is unproductive and wasteful. I believed that when we've ultimately run out of time, at our moment of death, we will have achieved our maximum productive capacity.

I bought into the idea that 'Time is money' because I believed it encapsulated the essence of a finite lifetime with finite opportunities. Any moment squandered was time wasted: time I could never recover and which was lost forever. It's a paranoia encouraged by a One Lifetime paradigm. Back then, my concept of time was like a cursor on a calibrated scale, a red needle moving constantly and relentlessly forward across the dial, never stopping and unable to backtrack. Somewhere along that timescale, like an opening bracket, was the time and day of my birth, 08:05 on 26 January 1953 (in Johannesburg, for astrologers who are keen to find out more) and – at some unknown position to the right – the matching closing bracket marking my death.

Regrettably, the uncertainty of the second marker left me guessing just how much more time I had before death came stealthily to fetch me. This uncertainty fuelled anxiety, for if I had no knowledge of how and when I would die, I would have no way to plan my resources properly. It's then far better to have a surplus than to live the last few years of my life in suffering. Even if I had surplus, I'd be foolish to share it with others because I might need it later.

Hoarding becomes prudent when one's future is uncertain, so I wrote down 'Save for a rainy day'. It's what Joseph did in Egypt, storing grain during the seven abundant years to provide food during the following seven lean ones. I didn't have a clue how inflation would erode my wealth, how poor political and economic decisions would undermine my investments or how my personal health would stand up to the ravages of old age, so I best-guessed the amount and utilisation of my resources to adequately provide for my future. Therefore, 'Make hay while the sun shines' seemed wise advice if I was to plan my retirement properly to live comfortably and safely in my old age.

A picture began to emerge of the consequences of a belief in having limited time. It revealed embedded elements of fear and panic that force me to devote my efforts to hard work and prudent resource management to allay those feelings and, even if I quelled my emotions, it pushed me beyond meeting my survival needs, catapulting me into a realm of materialism and creating an insatiable greed for more.

However, the belief in having limited time is not only about survival in a materialistic sense. It creates a lust for dominance and entitlement too: 'What's in it for me?' When one fights for supremacy and power, one runs the risk of dealing with conscience, the intellectual aptitude to discern right from wrong.

The world once applauded South Africa for the way it emancipated its people, and the country looked ready to prosper, but large-scale corruption and fat-cat decadence slowly crept in, tarnishing its reputation. When Kenny Kunene, a flamboyant South African businessman, celebrated his fortieth birthday, he demonstrated the excesses of the new post-apartheid elite when he served sushi from the bodies of half-naked women. It reminded me of Tinto Brass's very controversial 1979 film, *Caligula*, featuring Malcolm McDowell, Peter O'Toole, Helen Mirren and Sir John Gielgud. In advertising the movie, they posed the question, 'What would you have done if you had been given absolute power of life and death over everybody else in the whole world?' Born on 31 August 12 AD, Gaius Caesar Augustus Germanicus 'Caligula' became at 24 the most powerful man in the world, the third Emperor of Rome. The historian Lord Acton postulated that 'power tends to corrupt, and absolute power corrupts absolutely' and this was certainly true of Caligula. Raised in an autocratic world, Caligula became more despotic than any of his predecessors. He used social perversion, debauchery and brutality to mock the Senate and to flaunt his power, eventually demanding that they and the whole of Rome worship him as Jove, the Supreme God of the ancient Roman Pantheon. When writing about moderation, Democritus (4th Century BC) stated that 'The animal needing something knows how much it needs, the man does not'.

Another glaring example of this is the near state of warfare South Africa faces over rhinoceros poaching. Hundreds of these majestic animals lose their lives annually for the harvest of one tiny commodity, *cornu rhinoceri Asiatici*, their horn, which certain Chinese, Vietnamese and other Asian cultures claim as a life-saving remedy and aphrodisiac. Rhinoceroses will soon become extinct if the slaughter remains unchecked but the syndicates behind the illicit trade have had to cauterise conscience to gain their bonanza. This is more than a carrot on the end of a stick: the prospects of wealth lure them into using military-style tactics to achieve their aims. They have no feelings regarding this animal's pending extinction. They're out to make money. You might argue that this is an exceptional example of ego's desperate attempt to gain material advantages over others and that it doesn't fit into the general scope of living, but that's simply not true. Opulence, rampant consumerism and the belief that 'More is never enough,' drive a self-invested, egoistic world towards unsustainable exploitation of the earth's resources. This *is* the same as rhino poaching, just on a slower, less discernible and less emotive scale. Would we exploit earth's resources so greedily if we knew we would return repeatedly, lifetime after lifetime?

Everything in nature is in balance. Through the processes of photosynthesis, primary solar energy is converted to more usable forms of sustenance. Beginning with plants and other micro-organisms there's a complex interplay of give and take to nourish animals higher and higher up the food chain. Biodiversity and specialisation exploit competitive ways to survive but there's always a symbiotic balance. This, however, seems not to be a human trait. We've generally forsaken symbiotic balance for control and dominance. We subjugate and exploit earth selfishly. We are happy to take yet seldom do we give. There came a time in human evolution when we were no longer able to live harmoniously alongside all else. Our unique abilities to reason, analyse and strategise set us apart and ensured our survival in greater numbers. In densely populated parts of the globe, the land was no longer able to support us, and nature's symbiotic balance broke down. We were then forced to adopt a new paradigm hitherto unknown – *productivity*. Necessity is the mother of invention. Agriculture, mechanisation, technology have changed the landscape and squeeze more out of less. But this paradigm of survival has overtaken us and, in the world of consumerism, the wheels of economy are oiled by productivity – 'More is never enough'. Where once productivity centred on food, it slowly changed and much of our productivity now comes from intangible commodities, especially those found in the cyber world.

Productivity (or rather the lack thereof) is often a hotly debated topic in Africa. There seems to be a slack work ethic, a lethargy and a reluctance to put one's shoulder to the wheel as people seem more willing to do elsewhere in the world. Africa is a big continent and to the rest of the civilised world, it may appear to be archaic and barbaric. For millennia, Africans lived off the land. Living in tribal settlements, people hunted and gathered until the resources declined in their area, forcing families to uproot and relocate to better-resourced locations. People in Africa lived in accordance with the rules of symbiotic balance until the northern empires extended their colonial reach into the continent and began to exploit the land to their own ends. Suddenly, the land was no longer that – the land. New landowners had title to the land. Hunting and gathering slowly diminished. Indigenous people were put to work. Unaccustomed to the necessities of productivity, native Africans sought the means to life from the new metaphor for the land, the landowner. Migrant workers sought better opportunities and clustered in cities and around first world industrialised sites and soon, the balance of nature collapsed. Now, displaced, westernised, stripped of their ancient culture, these people still turn to 'the land' for their survival: Government, the modern landowner, is expected to provide houses, sanitation, potable water, electricity, jobs, health care, money and more. No wonder the idea of productivity hasn't fully permeated into the collective mindset.

Today's consumer world is obsessed with *material value*: fancy cars, fashion garments and technology seem to have displaced antiquated, outmoded cultural values. The belief that 'More is never enough' is a primary emotional motivator splitting the world into *those that have* and *those that have not*. Conscience is again cauterised as society tries to justify the juxtaposition of decadent lifestyles against the suffering and impoverishment of others and in this case it's not hard to see the cruelty inherent in the idea that 'More is never enough.'

It was a long night up at my desk. My musings had strayed far away from a need to accept or deny the notions of one or more lives. I no longer focused on whether spirit transcended death or if DNA tenaciously sought its own survival. I was now onto something different that explained why I had become the kind of person I despised. I'd joined a new 'sect' that was hell-bent on power and wealth and I knew it wouldn't provide the nurturing climate for spiritual seed germination. I paused for a moment, yawned, stretched, and squiggled down a few more ideas under the 'One Lifetime' heading: 'Life is not a dress rehearsal,' and 'There's no time to smell the roses'.

These notions reinforce my belief and entrenched my fear that I had only a fixed allocation of time and, if I didn't use it wisely, I'd end up regretting it and suffering the consequences of lost opportunities. This fear discourages time spent frivolously on unproductive endeavours. These driving ideologies once pushed me to grow my business. Every year, it had to outperform the achievements of the previous year. I was similarly unhappy if I hadn't increased my wealth over time. Every new vehicle had to be better and more expensive and every holiday more exotic. I mixed in higher and higher echelons, competing for status and recognition, overtaking those that lagged behind. Thinking of this, I wrote 'All's fair in love and war,' which hints at the fundamental principles entrenched in capitalist ideologies. It's a dog-eat-dog world and the millions of people in my group were quite at liberty, even expected, to elbow competitors aside to secure the biggest slice of the cake. Damned are any ideas of sharing for there is no room for weakness in capitalism. Those who lack tenacity, aggression and assertiveness must be content with the crumbs that fall from the table. I summed it up by writing 'The guy who dies with the biggest toys wins'.

My next entry was 'Money is power' and directly beneath it 'Power is freedom'. Money buys anything. If I had enough money, I would have the freedom to do whatever I chose. With money, I could solve problems, gain respect and elevate my status. Money would bring liberty and I could never have too much of that. I was constantly seeking more equity, more land and larger investment portfolios. Ownership is paramount, despite the fact that we can never take our stuff to the grave. The acronym for 'More is never enough' is MINE and I smiled gently when I wrote it as an abbreviation, thinking how apt it was. Our frequent use of possessive pronouns reveals the extent of our obsession over ownership. *My* house, *my* car, *my* partner, *my* body, *my* money and an infinite list of other possible uses of this part of speech that shows how conditioned I was in needing to own things and how easily I had slipped into the habit of not sharing them: 'No, you can't have any because it's *my* money'. It's our general addictive need in a capitalist world to control everything around us.

I doodled in the margin for a while as Mind fell into a moment of stillness. Then, I recalled a particular meeting of our company's board of directors. The board had set a target, to achieve a high thirty-five percent growth in profit year-on-year around the time when companies in the IT [information technology] sector enjoyed exceptional returns across the globe. At the end of the period, we bemoaned the meagre twenty-five percent we had actually achieved.

Emotions ran high at that meeting. Some felt we hadn't done enough and there was a general air of shame in the room. People began seeking a scapegoat, a member of the executive team who had underperformed. I sat seething, loathing the greediness of it all, and wondering why the board couldn't see how remarkably well the company had actually done. In that year, it contributed towards the financial needs of two hundred families in the form of salaries. That money rippled out into the community providing education, homes, food and clothing. During the fiscal year, the company paid its executives and directors hearty amounts and allocated generous dividends to its shareholders. I was ashamed that we felt cheated and hated our obsessive ideology that 'More was never enough'.

I began to realise that my ranting that night was not about denouncing the world but recognising my folly for having bought into those worldly ideals. I realised that my generalisations were not about the way things were around me but that they were directed at me, particularly as a comment about the way I used these mechanisms as a defence to protect a very vulnerable and frightened self. Many believe that the merits of capitalism far exceed those of communism and socialism and I have no academic authority to judge which one makes better sense. I also knew that each of these systems have individuals that uphold their principles and others who selfishly exploit them. I further indulged my train of thought knowing that the 'world' I criticised was really a criticism of self.

The problem with continued growth is sustainability. To grow a business one has to grow markets and, to do that, we require more people with more disposable income. India, Africa, South America are all targeted as emerging markets, places of huge middle-class population growth, but population growth isn't of itself enough: businesses and government must first shape people into becoming consumers. Advertising creates needs and fuels desires. Sales satisfy those desires, thereby increasing profits. Profit brings power. However, we can only eat limited amounts of food, indulge in finite periods of recreation, travel only as far as time permits, and this doesn't suit businesses who rely on increasing consumption growth. Their purpose is to take as much money as they can from us without turning us into paupers, for if they did, we would fall out of the consumer bracket and become liabilities to the system. Thriftiness isn't encouraged in a consumer-oriented society.

One facet of life that seems infinite and therefore very lucrative is the field of healthcare. Sadly, health does not build medical and pharmaceutical empires; sickness does. Because there is no limit to the amount of infirmity we can bear, especially if that illness is psychological, these companies quickly become monolithic empires since every ailment presents an opportunity to sell a pharmaceutical cure. In 2006, according to IMS Health (2007), 'antidepressants were the most prescribed amongst all classes of drugs, with a total of 227.3 million prescriptions in the United States. They were third in revenue, with a total of $13.5 billion'.[100]

My decadent bloated lifestyle wasn't natural, and unhealthy living soon took its toll on my body. I wasn't in the best of health. Obesity is on the rise as are many other killer diseases associated with opulence. The idea of 'More is never enough' is deeply entrenched in our brains, turning many of our attempts at healthy and simple living into internal wars of willpower and wits, often leaving us with a sense of loss, deprivation and sacrifice. To give our bodies a chance to recover, we must fight against a lifetime of consumer programming, so it is little wonder that healthy living seems impossible in comparison with the easy way we slip into eating junk, smoking and drinking.

Take a moment to notice and you will surely concur that real, wholesome, healthy food hardly ever reaches us in fancy wrappings. Evolution taught us to recognise what's good for us when we see it. Designed to fool our senses into believing it is good enough to eat, junk food is hidden by manufacturers inside colourful, shiny wrappers. Additives, like monosodium glutamate, bluff our taste buds into believing that the substance it masks is healthy, even if it is just synthesised rubbish. I avoid eating anything too artificially tempting and my rule of thumb is, the glitzier the packaging, the more sinister the substances hidden inside.

The statement, 'More is never enough,' also alludes to our copious need for sensory indulgence. It permeates into all aspects of modern life, including our sexual needs, recreational pursuits, health, wealth, and sadly even our spirituality. It seems as if we have a habitual, morbid disposition towards dissatisfaction underlying all the things we do.

I've been a vegetarian for over thirty years. It's a personal choice and I make no fuss over it but there have been occasions when I've dined out in lovely restaurants in the company of friends and had to be content with a salad and French-fries while they enjoyed the chef's finest culinary cuisine. When the establishment caters predominantly for the carnivorous, I'm okay eating whatever I can from the menu and I know it creates a little awkwardness for others but I can still enjoy the occasion no matter the simplicity of the meal I'm eating.

---

[100] *Talking back to Prozac*, Peter R. Breggin, M.D. and Ginger Ross Breggin, E-Rights/E-Reads Publishers.

Living the paradigm of 'More is never enough' seldom made me happy with my body. Affluent societies increasingly want slimmer waistlines, whiter skin tones, darker skin tones, curlier hair, straighter hair, longer, shorter, thicker – whew, the list is endless. One day, three women in their mid-thirties walked past in the mall and from their voice tone I could hear that they were jubilant about something and shared it excitedly amongst themselves; but I noticed a strange incongruity: their faces showed no signs of joy. Botoxed into paralysis, they couldn't smile, at least not externally, because their plumped up glossy lips and paralysed cheeks struggled to crease into even the tiniest grin, and I began to giggle because they looked like three ventriloquists. Later, I thought about the adverse side effects of their vanity, not just on their bodies but also on their social interactions too. More than ninety percent of our communication is non-verbal. Granted, we convey about a third of our content through our voice tone but that still leaves a whopping sixty percent that people read from other things like body language, styling and accessories.

There are many social-science studies that suggest an increase in children's inability to recognise personal threat because they're slowly losing the art of reading the non-verbal cues given off by those who wish to exploit them. A lot of our communication now occurs electronically in typewritten form that is stripped of the nuances of voice tonality and body language. The more we obscure our natural ability to transmit and receive vital information, the more we become new-age non-verbal communication cripples.

Longhand cursive writing is also rapidly becoming a dying art. Our writing style, conveyed by character slant, roundness, sharpness, size, rhythm, arrhythmia and pressure, often reveals more about us than the words we've written. Sometimes, as I page through my personal journals without having to read the content, I'm able to sense the mood I was in at the time simply by observing the writing style. With the advent of typewritten text, we've lost the communication content that was carried in our handwriting. Typing, and I'm not criticising its usefulness, feeds into the notion of 'more is never enough' by offering speed, volume and immediacy to our communications.

'More is never enough' infiltrates into our so-called acts of generosity too. Take the acts of giving, be it gifts on birthdays, Christmas or even corporate acts of kindness to the less fortunate. Giving in this sense always impoverishes the giver and enriches the receiver. There are seldom pure acts of generosity in this kind of giving because it alters the balance of power. It is designed to increase the influence one person has over another. The old adage states that there's no such thing as a free lunch. Corporate acts of giving almost always have an attached price tag – brand awareness, publicity and influence. Would companies give generously if their giving was altruistic and anonymous? Politicians seeking power often uplift the destitute in their constituencies in order to buy votes. Acts of giving can create competition, a need to outdo each other, which can quickly spiral into realms of ludicrous expenditure. I once listened to a woman's snide comments about her husband's simple yet tasteful birthday gift. 'Is this it?' she exclaimed, obviously expecting much more and trying in vain to hide her bitter disappointment. 'It's the *thought* that counts,' he replied sweetly, only to be cut to size by her lightning fast reply: 'Yes, I can see that. This small gift shows how little you *think* of me – what little regard you have for me'.

The phrase 'More is never enough' applies to the material world, in the same way that 'Now is never enough' applies to time. It is a concept I never considered until my friend Bridget pointed it out to me. Few seem content with the present moment. The majority of us in the modern consumer-oriented world constantly strive to fill our time with better experiences, more pleasure and bigger adrenalin rushes.

A recent example of this happened when a few friends decided to take their first bungee jump from a gangplank hanging between the twin cooling towers, 100m off the ground, at the now defunct Orlando Power Station in Soweto. It was exhilarating and their adrenalin pumped. 'Wow! What an awesome experience! I *now have to* do the Golden Eye Bungee Jump at Verzasca Dam, Switzerland... Imagine that, a 220m fall at 120km/hour... 7 ½ seconds to complete the distance! Isn't that just awesome?' Of course it is but first savour the experience you've just had. Live the present moment fully, right now, without casting your mind out into the future where only fantasy and possibility exist. Their overwhelming desire for more seemed to trivialise their jump, and their yearning for the next disappointed them a little because it wasn't the big one. Having consumed that jump, they set their sights firmly, longingly and quickly on the next, affirming that 'Now is never enough'.

I suppose we're socialised to think that way. Taught from infancy, I looked out towards my future believing that's where my real value lay. Systematically, society programmes me to believe that I had no value until I'd graduated from school. Having done that, society pushes me to look forward once more towards tertiary education. Even then, armed with various qualifications, I never actually stopped looking to my future for value. My career was a future-value proposition as were annual holidays, expertise at work and finally, even the prospect of retirement. It's all part of that future-value mindset which I spent a lifetime chasing. I was so busy looking forward that there wasn't much time to experience life as it was in the moment.

By the time I'd approached my golden years, I'd come to an abrupt and awful realisation that life had almost passed me by. I made a quick about-face and started looking remorsefully and regretfully backwards into my past. There, I'd hoped to catch glimpses of those rare moments when I actually did experience life for what it was. Expectation and reminiscence are both products of a belief that 'Now is never enough'.

Swept up in this reflection on life in the now early hours of the following day, I realised how far I had strayed from my core values in those intervening years and how I lacked the bravery and tenacity to explore the real me. I began to understand the paradox within and how I had wrongly pinned my hopes on a set of ideals that I believed would protect me, if not define me. Self-hatred slowly melted as I realised that I had lived by a set of ethics and values to which I did not really subscribe. The person I had become was not the real me; he hid behind that defensive mask. Surely, there was another way of living, a different code that would bring out the best in me. I seemed to have painted myself into a corner out of a fear of living a single unfulfilled life and then disappearing into obscurity. Slowly, a picture emerged about the consequences of my staunch view of how I thought things worked. I was rude and dismissive to the woman sitting next to me at dinner that night and it saddened me to think that the constraints of my belief had reduced us to pawns in a game, encouraging egotism, consumerism, competitiveness, all underpinned by fear. How else was I to find meaning in my world? It was a very morbid thought and I stopped writing for a while, stretched my tired body and felt grim. If my fear of not being good enough, not having enough and not living enough was perpetuated by my belief in living merely one rather unsatisfactory lifetime, how differently would I be living if I changed my belief to one of multiple, repeated lifetimes?

My fountain pen seemed to hover indefinitely in the empty space under the 'Repeated Lifetimes' heading and I didn't know what to write. Trapped within conservative Christian doctrine, I'd been taught that reincarnation was an abhorrent and foreign idea. The church taught that I had but *one lifetime* in which to elevate myself from ancestral sin, to a place of holiness. It's not a task for the fainthearted because, just as it is in the competitive world of commerce, so too is it in Christianity where Satan prides himself in using a miscellany of irresistible, enticing temptations, designed to cause our downfall. The whole of my life, it seemed, was like a gigantic game of Snakes and Ladders.

There was no place in my world for weakness and conscience. When I believed that I supposedly lived only once, I neatly abdicated responsibility and expunged my need to worry about the consequences of my actions. I bequeathed to subsequent generations a plundered planet, and they had little choice but to find a solution or face their untimely annihilation. My choice of belief rejected any notion of soul and relegated spirituality to the realms of the mildly insane – those deluded beings who believe there is a God that offers them hope.

Opening up to the possibility of reincarnation was very difficult for me to do. I didn't know the intricacies of the belief and I recoiled at the mere thought of it. The column on the right of the sheet was full of notes but this one on the left remained blank as did my mind. It took concerted effort, bravery and finding a place of non-judgement inside before any ideas began to flow. I nearly abandoned the exercise because I was both tired and disillusioned by what I had explored thus far. But it was that grim sense of hopelessness that spurred me on.

The idea of reincarnation must establish a premise that there is part of me that was never born, and which cannot die. That part repeatedly takes on form, having multiple experiences in many different contexts. A belief in multiple lifetimes might mean that I could live future lives in a stark and decimated home that I had once plundered. Gentleness towards the earth and sustainable living could be worthwhile virtues to cultivate if I knew I would live here again sometime in the future.

There were so many questions and not enough knowledge to answer them so I noted some of my concerns in the empty column: What part of me lived on? Would I have my same sense of identity, my present personality? Why couldn't I remember previous incarnations? What is the purpose of my returning? Infinite cycles of birth and death might themselves become an entrapment. Wouldn't this too become infinitely boring and ultimately pointless? Would it indeed foster a different mindset, engendering gentleness and symbiotic balance for me? Infinity, that's a very long time... It is said of infinity: once every thousand years a little bird perches on a gigantic granite mountain to wipe its beak. When the bird's repetitive wiping completely erodes the mountain, that's the beginning of infinity.

I had to start somewhere on my exploration of reincarnation and so I settled on the idea of time in relation to it. If it were true that part of me *never* experienced birth or death, time would be on my side at last. In an episode of the BBC's *Doctor Who, Mawdryn Dead,* (1983), the Doctor says 'Well, there's a probability of anything. Statistically speaking, if you gave typewriters to a treeful of monkeys, they'd eventually produce the works of William Shakespeare'. I quickly wrote, 'In all eternity, time is in oversupply and worthless, like grains of sand on the beach'. Whilst that idea immediately threw up opposition in the form of boredom and repetition, I suddenly understood that it provided me a means to slow down my frenetic and obsessive life of trying to hide. If reincarnation were true, it would give me time to create all I wished for and equally as much time to relax. I noted the first positive idea that emanated from having repeated lifetimes: 'Take your time, for there's no rush'. I became a little more enthusiastic and jotted down the next point: 'In all eternity, there *is* time to smell the roses without experiencing feelings of guilt and remorse.' A belief in reincarnation could give me time to experience every possible opportunity, to live as uncountable different characters, in countless homes, experiencing every culture. This gave me immense relief because I realised that who I was, was only one of many more – who dare judge any of them? For now, they were all perfect. I would also then have no need to hoard because, in limitless lifetimes, the earth would be my endless material repository. My fear of death would vanish and with it my grim feelings of obscurity, pointlessness and vulnerability. Birth and death would be my doorways leading from one experience to the next in an endlessly playful game.

More upbeat by the ideas that now flowed more freely, none of which I'd thought of before, the faster the ideas came to me, the more repugnant my idea of my one-lifetime became. A single lifetime brought panic and fear, and drove me forward relentlessly, anxious to achieve the maximum I could in what little time I had, all primarily designed to obfuscate the vulnerable self beneath. Reincarnation had the opposite effect and soothed me by assuring me that in a universe of infinite abundance everything has its proper place and time; including the being I manifested as at the time.

In my original world where the end marked my ultimate finality, I tended to blame others for diminishing my chances of success and I might even have been motivated to take revenge, to regain what was once believed lost or for which I felt entitled – particularly the years with my family that Jehovah's Witness dogma had stolen. In contrast to the old belief, this newfound one made vengeance now seem pointless and meaningless. With ultimate resources infinitely at my disposal, it would probably encourage me to adopt an attitude of sharing instead of hoarding. I might quickly learn to live in a world detached from ownership and away from the fear of loss, deprivation and judgement.

Neither able to prove nor disprove these postulations, as there is no empirical evidence, I realised that I stood on the cusp of something new with far-reaching consequences for the way I lived my life, if only I could make a brave new choice. I never thought it possible, but suddenly I found myself favouring some of the gentler side effects I believed might arise out of a paradigm of reincarnation. But what about proof? I was back to *faith and surrender* and they weren't my best of friends.

I thought about finding proof for a long time in those early hours until I resigned myself to the fact that it was a futile pursuit. If I blundered and chose badly, I would probably never know as I would just die into obscurity; but I intuitively sense that reincarnation opened up a pathway to a peaceful garden, and I like the lifestyle that this garden offered. I wasn't too concerned about my future after death but, rather, searched for a deeper meaning about my purpose in life. Being content with who I was, was paramount. I needed to learn to like me. The two metaphors and the ensuing reflections of the night changed forever the way I thought about myself. I hadn't adopted a new religion but I had come to realise that there were more ways of looking at life. Where once was hatred and self-doubt, now stood compassion and a possible way forward. There was still much to learn, more to explore, plenty to change but the climate for germination had arrived at last.

I longed to get back to Graham's party and share my insights with that woman but it was nearly sunrise, the party was long over, and I never did. She probably still thinks badly of me and she may never know what an amazing impact she had on me that night.

I found peace in my past, and reconciled it with my newfound idea of me as a fundamental entity, whole, complete and content, an immortal being of infinite possibility, playfully experiencing itself through all manner and means of incarnation in benign and endless loops of differing form. Finally, I had come to accept myself.

---ᴜᴜᴜOᴏᴏ

There were positive and negative consequences to our meddling with drugs: It ended a superb relationship by injecting jealousy and suspicion. Substances clouded our vision and we couldn't quite discern what was real from what was imagined. But it also peeled away my conservative view on life and I experienced Mind in ways I believed impossible before. Hallucinogenic drugs brought a strange clarity to an otherwise befuddled brain. I saw new possibilities and different ways of thinking. It was as if the drugs had shaken something loose inside and awoke me to a different world beyond. Others in our group were not quite so fortunate: two died from overdose; about two-thirds disappeared into darkness, losing everything they possessed, including their dignity; the remaining third were the lucky ones who managed to shed the shackles of addiction and rebound anew, albeit after nearly coming to the dark and sinister edges of sanity.

After my devastating breakup with Mark, I eased into an involuntary life of celibacy for about six years that afforded me a period of intense introspection and self-discovery.

---oooOooo---

Just as a side note to this chapter, I often wondered whether my new, more open-minded view of life without ego was truly achievable. Perhaps it was just a pipedream, a naive and infantile wish for simplicity; the sort of paradise that Jesus had in mind for us during his thousand-year reign after his second coming. There seemed no evidence for such a change anywhere in the world, until I witnessed something outstanding shortly after Zimbabwe's general elections in March 2008, when I accepted an invitation to host a hypnosis workshop for a group of medical and allied health practitioners at the Island Hospice in Harare.

The years after Graham's birthday party saw many changes in me. I took early retirement, explored different philosophies, mixed with people in many different walks of life and established a different circle of friends. Part of that transformation urged me to give something back to society instead of just taking, the way I had done before. Many years later, this led me to use hypnosis in a non-medical, therapeutic way. At first, it intrigued me and I wanted to know more. It was similar to the intrigue that started me on a path of understanding the inner workings and the programming of computers. I had been so gullible in my past, and was so easily and naively led down a cul-de-sac of belief with its dire consequences. Now, I fervently wanted to understand the powers of persuasion and influence so that that I might never be misguided again. I read widely and studied those topics in depth, delving into advertising methods, cults, the black art of ninja warfare, body language, political manipulation and of course mentalism and hypnosis. In time, I became a well-known expert on those subjects. To me, hypnosis was a different sort of programming language. Instead of using software tools to program computers, I learned to use hypnosis to help others reprogram the most sophisticated computer of them all, the human mind.

I must confess I was, at first, a bit anxious going to Harare because of the political unrest and trouble that existed between the main political rivals after their elections. Tensions were running high at the time and a few friends fanned my nervousness into flickering flames of fear by suggesting that I was being reckless, travelling when the mood could easily erupt into civil violence; and yet I knew the urgency of teaching when Zimbabwe lay in ruins and I decided to cast caution to the wind and go. In the wake of the elections injury and trauma abounded; medics and pharmaceutical supplies were scarce. Concerned health practitioners asked me to run the course to equip them with a new set of tools that could bring relief to those in abject need, without requiring much more than a skilled practitioner.

I generally avoid reading newspapers, seldom listen to the radio, and I rarely watch TV but I had a fair idea of how derelict the Zimbabwean infrastructure had become; and it came as no real surprise to drive along their potholed roads, witnessing at first hand the decayed municipal services, pavements, and government property that I saw. People, out of pure desperation, sold street signs for scrap metal, used manhole covers as cooking skillets and stole bulbs from traffic lights to light their homes.

I stayed with my cousin Heather and her husband Dave in the guest cottage at their home in one of the plush Harare suburbs. They hadn't had municipal water for eighteen months because the pipes were broken and, due to insufficient pressure, only houses in low-lying areas received water. This common problem forced many to buy fresh water from entrepreneurs with roving tankers, plying their trade up and down the streets of the higher-located townships. Dave and Heather had a borehole that augmented their domestic requirements but though it was steady it pumped out a mere dribble from the nearly depleted underground reservoir, delivering only about one litre a minute. Toilets were flushed with buckets of water drawn from the partially empty swimming pool and everyone took turns to squat in the bath in one of their three bathrooms, to wash from the trickle of hot water that spluttered from the tap.

During the day, government regularly diverted electricity away from residential areas to industry and most homes had no choice but to generate their own. This created an eerie drone throughout the neighbourhood like some invading swarm of gigantic and invisible insects.

Prohibited from retrenching workers, storeowners kept their inactive businesses open in darkened shops. Row upon row of empty shelves, fridges and freezers stood silently in those cavernous premises. Shopping malls in Harare became like ghost towns. The people everywhere suffered; poverty was rampant. A year before those elections I travelled to Kariba, a hydroelectric scheme built in a deep gorge along the mighty Zambezi River, to spend time with the family at their holiday home on the banks of that enormous sea-like dam. The local fish factory is a short distance from their home and we went there one afternoon to find fresh fish for lunch. Lorraine had to fend off hoards of emaciated people who had gathered in the parking lot, each with their container, waiting patiently and often hopelessly for the trash of discarded fish remnants after we had taken the prime fillets. These people boiled up a broth made from bones, innards, heads and fins to eat with their staple diet of *sadza*, a thick dry porridge made from milled corn. Under such hardship there isn't room for consumer materialism and 'It's not enough' quickly replaces the phrase 'More is never enough'.

Zimbabwe's plight struck terror into the hearts of relatively prosperous middle-class South Africans but, strangely, this wasn't quite the case amongst the same category of people living inside its borders. Middle-class Zimbabweans became financial prisoners and had little choice but to stay and navigate their way through the disaster. The tough life forced people to band together in order to survive. Decades under such living conditions knitted communities into tight groups. Social networks, not the cyber kind but real camaraderie and a spirit of togetherness, sourced, shared and distributed most of the basic food supplies that arrived in the country. Those networks offered benevolent help and support in many different forms across a wide swath in the community. Rural Zimbabweans were regrettably so poverty-stricken, malnourished and dying, and in such a state of pure desperation, millions were forced to flee across the South African border to seek asylum and a new life.

Word got out during my stay that a private hauler managed to bring a truck across the border laden with sugar, salt, flour, fruit, vegetables, milk, eggs, soap and every other conceivable thing including diesel fuel. The truck parked at a farm just inside Zimbabwe, and as it was too risky to drive the laden vehicle to Harare, a convoy of other smaller vehicles couriered the loot home. There it was distributed through a system of barter trade and, where cash changed hands, the transaction was usually in US dollars because the local currency had become worthless due to hyperinflation, escalating at rates of several hundreds and sometimes over a thousand percent per day.

Most people abandoned the banking system and turned their lifesavings into commodities. Heather bought a consignment of refined sugar worth a fortune and stored it in her garage at home. When word got out that the local baker had sourced enough ingredients to bake bread, Heather took piles of sugar in used plastic ice cream containers to the baker's shop. Everyone met at the stipulated date and time, and goods swapped hands quickly before the shop closed. Government scouts constantly combed local business premises to detect such illegal trade and a corrupt and draconian judiciary often meted out disproportionately harsh penalties and jail sentences to those caught doing it, yet everyone had to, to survive.

This subculture worked really well. There was an informal import and export system; free-market forces determined prices and profits; it encouraged entrepreneurs; it was self-governed and founded on a spirit of generosity. It operated below the government's radar, for the people and by the people. Everyone knew that their system of trade added nothing to the fiscus and they seemed quite ready to give what they could to those less privileged in their community to keep society functioning. As a result, schools continued to function, as did other essential services that operated independently of their decrepit government-administered counterparts.

There was a sense of thriftiness and of making do with what one had. Conservation was vital. The Island Hospice, where I conducted my courses, operated mainly on stuff we in Johannesburg would have readily discarded as junk. Here, elaborate, shiny packaging and branding weren't important. Every container was recycled. They often bought in bulk and divided it into smaller portions, sharing and swapping wherever possible. Nothing went to waste.

Many of the delightful people I met in Harare gave of their time generously and I experienced a community spirit like none I'd witnessed elsewhere before. I got the sense that nobody could find it in their hearts to hoard when others were going without. They were concerned about the wellbeing of others, which seemed embedded in the very fabric of their society. I'm sure there were some greedy ones who tried to profit from the system by exploiting others but I suspect that the community soon knew whom they were and quickly and fatally sidelined them. This self-governing, self-regulating system encouraged common conformity.

Zimbabwe was an embryonic New Order of self-rule but its elected officials were as yet impotent in effecting real improvements. Even so, despite the challenges in that country, it gave me hope because it showed that something other than 'More is never enough' is still possible. Thomas Jefferson once said, 'I believe that banking institutions are more dangerous to our liberties than standing armies. If the American people ever allow private banks to control the issue of their currency, first by inflation, then by deflation, the banks and corporations that will grow up around the banks will deprive the people of all property until their children wake up homeless on the continent their fathers conquered'. I think the same principles hold true for our elected leaders too.

Changing Perceptions

My spiritual awakening started in 1996/7 when, one Saturday, I decided to take a different route home from our Houghton offices. Completely stressed at the time, I tried to cope by immersing myself in work. I had an idea to create a radically new and innovative Integrated Electronic Settlement system, which I proposed to my business partners to secure development funding. It processed credit card payments at the cash register instead of using a separate bank-owned device and would be enormously beneficial to retailers and banks. Markus, a colleague and friend, slowly helped me piece the software together over several years. He was in a very bad headspace at the time as his marriage was crumbling and he was afraid of losing his sons. I was in a similar headspace as my relationship with Mark had already ended. I was lonely, embittered and lost. Work gave both of us meaning and purpose and we worked well together, feeding off our common pathology. To put my madness into context, I awoke each day at three o'clock in the morning, and left home by four to be at my desk by five. Markus and I would have coffee together and continued working throughout the day until eight or nine o'clock at night. This routine continued for years and I often worked on Saturdays when the team were away, returning home via the highway by about mid-afternoon.

The incident at Graham's birthday party already opened up new possibilities in thinking but I was trapped in repetitive cycles of work at the time and too busy to explore much else owing to those pressing deadlines. I'm a thinker, subconsciously chewing on new ideas until I am comfortable with them. New scope of thinking usually undergoes many iterations of review before I can fully embrace it. Sometimes I reject it and never implement new ideas, preferring to stick to the old, tried and tested ways instead. When change does occur, it's usually a slow steady transformation, like a slow cross-fade in a movie.

For some inexplicable reason, I turned off the highway one Saturday afternoon and drove home along suburban byroads. I cannot explain my motive for taking the longer route but it took me past Maritz Brothers College in Sandton where they were hosting an esoteric fair and I pulled in to look around, even though it was way out of my nature to visit an event of this kind. I walked around, had someone read my palm and surreptitiously jeered at some of the other whacky ideas on display. I wanted to buy a cold drink and went through the rear door, signposted to the school's tuck-shop, but it led to an open-air amphitheatre where a man spoke to a crowd sitting on the raked concrete steps. Not wanting to disrupt his presentation, I waited politely for a gap, bought my drink, and joined the audience on the steps where I listened to the remainder of his talk.

After a short intermission, he began again with the words 'All your problems are an illusion. If you want to change your life, you need to change your thoughts. Hell then instantly transforms into Heaven and we then experience Heaven on Earth'.

During my youth I was taught much about Heaven and Hell, but I had never heard the suggestion that '…your problems are an illusion'. I remember thinking, derisively, 'Yeah! Right! You haven't seen my problems! Mine aren't an illusion – they're as real as they get!'

Nevertheless, as this man expanded his arguments, I couldn't fault the flawless reasoning behind them. I wanted to talk to him afterwards but too many people gathered around and I decided to tear a strip off the fringe of his poster, which listed his telephone number. I slipped the tiny piece of paper into my wallet where it stayed for another six months or more. It surfaced again one day when I was throwing away some old receipts and it rekindled my desire to make contact with him.

My call to him happened nearly a year after the fair: 'I took your number at the esoteric fair about a year ago and intended calling you sooner, but somehow I never got around to it until today. I'd really like to have a discussion with you because elements of your talk stuck in my mind and I want to get a deeper understanding of what you said.'

Terry Winchester said he was holding a talk at his home the following Saturday and invited me to join in. His workshop led to many subsequent discussions at his home and I later came to realise that his teachings are ideas taken from *A Course in Miracles* combined with some group hypnosis based on José Silva's popular alpha reframing techniques[101]. This set me on a twofold course: to embark on a series of spiritual studies of my own and to understand and learn more about hypnosis and hypnotherapy in order to help others.

---

[101] *You the Healer*, The World-Famous Silva Method on How to Heal Yourself and Others, José Silva, 1989, New World Library

I've noticed over the years how certain people, caught in their cycles of emotional despair, often turn their attention to healing others. In my case, helping somebody else became an oblique way of helping myself – because I didn't know how to turn my help inwards directly towards the Self and I thus found reflected wisdom in helping others.

I didn't realise the consequences of exploring my spirituality at the time but, the more I embraced it, the more it led me away from old friendships and, as a result, I became more detached and reclusive and spent a lot of time retreating into solitude. A further consequence was loss of appetite for material things, and I slowly came to resent the effort I'd put into furthering the aims of the IT business.

Undergoing spiritual transformation was like a caterpillar morphing into a butterfly. As I went through the chrysalis phase, I gradually lost my former identity. It took a long time to rearrange my being before I emerged with a new identity. There were times when I felt detached, lonely and adrift, and I remember trying to go backwards, hanging out with former friends, but I no longer felt as though I belonged there. They remained the same while I had changed. I didn't know where the transformation was leading me and I couldn't make new friends during that transitional period because I had no clue of who I would become. My former purpose progressively faded in importance – and yet I clung to it, seeking the security it had once offered. I felt deeply unsettled, perhaps even afraid, yet an unseen force carried me through as naturally as my biology had taken me through puberty.

I remember having a very lucid dream in which I found myself clinging to a branch of a dead tree in the middle of a thunderous and torrential river. Close to death, I gripped the brittle limb, petrified that my sapping energy would fade and it would carry me downstream to my death. As I clung to the safety of the branch I heard it crack and, to my horror, it splintered and slowly tore away from the tree. With all the energy I could muster, I scrabbled down to the trunk where I lay exhausted, water flooding over me. I felt safer on the sturdy trunk but my ordeal wasn't over. Just then, the river dislodged the tree from the muddied banks and the entire thing tumbled into the churning water. No longer my refuge, it became a perilous object intent on killing me. I had no choice but to kick myself free and surrender to the river's angry might. It tumbled and bashed me, nearly drowning me, before it disgorged my aching body into a quiet and peaceful pond.

I realised that the river symbolised the river of life and the tree was a metaphor for our IT company and all my material attachments that I believed kept me safe. The tree however, was dead; and clinging to it proved futile. Had I bravely let go sooner and faced my issues, I would probably have come to rest in the quiet spiritual pond with less anxiety and drama. The journey through the rapids represented my spiritual transformation, which was tough at times, and I often believed I had made a mistake – but there was no going back and, in the end, I was grateful that it forced me to surrender to the forces of the river of life. The universe instinctively knew where it was taking me.

During those corporate days I created meticulous short, medium and long-term plans, even as far forward as five years; but now, I really don't *know* what I'll be doing tomorrow. If at the age of thirty I had tried to formulate a roadmap of where I expected to be thirty years later, I would have failed dismally because I would have dreamed of palatial homes, fast cars and frequent travel to exotic locations and I most certainly would not have imagined the simplicity, happiness and joy that I experience now.

The warmth and joyfulness of spring irrupted into my life during my mid-forties, and those years became a time full of possibility where Ram Dass's seeds broke ground and flourished. Somewhere on an overseas trip in the late 1980s, I found my first book by Ram Dass, which rekindled something deep inside me. I later bought a lot more of his material, sourced mainly from his tape library in America, and every piece had a profound effect on me and I fell in awe of the author and greatly admired him for his unwavering devotion to his guru Maharaj-ji, Neem Karoli Baba, and his simple and easy adherence to Baba's clear spiritual beliefs.

Ram Dass dared to do things differently, and soon he came to mean to me an icon of what I could be one day. His life and work inspired me and I mimicked him a lot, walking in his footsteps, like a boy following his father along wet sea sand stepping into the capacious indentations of his feet. I told his stories to others nearly as well as he told them himself, because I wanted people to know him, to find liberation through him in the same way that I had.

I suppose everyone goes through similar growth in one way or another. We emulate our superheroes in the hope of becoming them, or like them. Although I never met him in person, Ram Dass coached me invisibly into a world of new understanding where I now find safety in being spiritually fully present. There is a connection between us, a kindred spirit that pulls and tugs and binds. Our lives have parallels: he left his Jewish roots, I my Christian heritage; he sidestepped mainstream society and, in his footsteps, so had I although my journey took longer; we were outcasts; we both had pilot licences; some of our spiritual epiphanies came through hallucinogenic drugs; and we defended our beliefs fearlessly.

Emulating Ram Dass was helpful but I soon realised I didn't want to become a bad impersonation of him: I needed to be authentically me. I've been to many artiste revival shows and watched talented actors impersonate some of the big names in show business, like Freddie Mercury, Shirley Bassey, Michael Jackson, and others. Those performances, as wonderful as they were, were never a patch on the originals. Stepping up alongside Ram Dass took considerable adjustment of thought over a long period. I could no longer walk behind him, for if I held him in awe, I judged myself as less. I chose therefore to explore and articulate my uniqueness and stepped forward to walk beside him.

The first thing I had to change was my anger, embitterment and resentment towards my family and the Witnesses. The first useful readjustment of thought was that if it weren't for the Witnesses, I might have followed Granddad Bill's agnosticism and might have then permanently fallen into a world of material philosophy, finding value only through the multitude of material trappings offered by a tempting consumer-focused society. The Witnesses were one of many stepping-stones across the river to softer, greener pastures. The Witnesses left a legacy of some very useful character traits that I still like in me. They taught me about faith, and a lot about service to others. They gave me the guts to resist a world of materialism (despite being drawn into it for a season of my life) and they showed me how to stand up and defend myself with courage, even under pressure. They taught me to be fearless and, although I don't have anything more to do with them, I can now acknowledge their positive influence with gratitude.

My expulsion marked my graduation. It no longer symbolises an ending but a beginning, a metamorphosis from which I emerged a changed person. But insects undergo multiple transitions between egg and adult and I still had much further to go towards full spiritual maturity.

Ram Dass helped me to realise that, contrary to many of the world's secular beliefs, reliable information comes from within, that true value is internal and that the highest authority one has is one's inner voice, God's voice inside.

Ram Dass and the Witnesses are now part of a Divine Dichotomy, two methods through which I experience God, both mutually exclusive yet jointly exhaustive. The Witnesses gave me a subset of worship, a uniquely condensed, literal view, one modelled around *fear* – the fear of being born into sin and eternally indebted to a higher power where salvation comes through an earthly agent, one having sole mandate to set the rules of acceptable behaviour that leads the obedient to deliverance and the defiant to conflagration. The Witnesses claim a naive literalism, expecting behavioural compliance instead of encouraging inner wisdom. To me, Ram Dass symbolises the non-overlapping remainder, a teaching of *surrender* – surrendering to one's highest authority, one's Inner Source that is a constituent of God, never born, which cannot die, sinless, magnificent and imbued with infinite creative potential. These teachings are not uniquely Ram Dass's but ones that span time from early Vedic texts to more contemporary beliefs that lie beyond the reductionist views of the Jehovah's Witnesses.

One view *looks up at God* from the place of human form; the other *is God*, tangibly experiencing Its potential through human appearance. These are opposite sides of the same coin. One may view the coin from one side or the other but the metaphor of the coin illustrates the illusory construct of God in the human mind. To understand God more fully, we can't think of God as *this* or *that*; we have to let go our idea of the coin completely and see God as the Nothingness that allows the coin to exist.

The Witnesses and Ram Dass are two sides of my relationship with God and both are my teachers. The Witnesses hold their beloved Jehovah in awe thereby preserving the greatness of the Godhead as an external, almighty being. This view presupposes that everything outside the Godhead is corruptible – look what happened to God's Angel, Satan, in whom was found iniquity and who used his free will to defy his maker and corrupt Earth. These views, this side of the coin, prevent us from an easy diminishing of the idea of God. But there's a dangerous consequence: we will always remain less than the Godhead, struggling to attain the impossible goal, the state of sinlessness (oneness with God). The view on the other side of the coin presupposes that sin is an illusion. We are eternally at one with God, incorruptible. The only way we separate from God is through our erroneous belief that we are our bodies. Bodies come and go, they are corruptible, in the sense that they get ill, die and decompose. Mind is also corruptible in that it may project fantasies through the body and onto the material world beyond. But our essence remains untarnished and at one with the universal Godhead at all times.

Deepak Chopra's book *How to Know God*[102] gave me a vital clue in understanding this. He postulates that if you ask someone who God is, you ought to know whom you are asking because that person's state of mind will influence his or her idea of God. Ask a person that lives mainly in a flight-or-fight response mode who God is and they will probably describe God as a parenting protector that looks out for their safety and survival; ask an enlightened being who God is and he will probably say 'You're looking at God'. I finally understood that there is only one Divine Being but multiple perspectives, each view determined by one's vantage position relative to God.

Even though I saw Ram Dass as a being of equal magnitude, it took about a decade before I could fully embrace him as my spiritual mentor and guru and it filled me with gratitude that he and other great men and women were willing to share their experiences with us. They have held a lantern to light our path so that we can find our way home more easily; but in this long process I also learned to be vigilant, cautious, and I promised myself that I would never let others delude me again.

He that hath ben ones begyled by somme other ought to kepe hym wel fro the same.'[103] This original form of the proverb 'once bitten, twice shy' keeps me alert and wary and prevents me getting sucked into cults again. I had hitherto never met Ram Dass in person and knew nothing of him except for what he published. In my heart I knew that, one day, I should meet him face-to-face to validate him. Being with him in person would give me time to gauge him intuitively – after all, he comes from the great land of bluff and hype, and selling of ideas, America. I knew my intended visit had nothing to do with him and everything to do with my previous experiences and me. I also realised that my wariness should be about the message and not the messenger. Still, I felt that I needed to meet him although I knew the risks were great, for it would either cement our relationship forever or throw a hand grenade into it and blow my idealised image of him sky high. If the outcome was negative, it could leave me more disillusioned and further hurt than I had been at the age of twenty-six; and I sensed that compounded experiences of loss might plunge me into a lasting cynicism.

It is easy to sweet-talk others, to rise in popularity and fame, but it is quite a different matter living up to one's own beliefs, to *walk the talk* and to practise what one preaches. I had seen this Jekyll and Hyde behaviour before in congregations and it was easier for me to overlook it

[102] *How to Know God, The Soul's Journey into the Mystery of Mysteries,* Deepak Chopra, Harmony Books, 2000.
[103] William Caxton's earliest translation of *Aesop's Fables,* 1484.

amongst ordinary Jehovah's Witnesses but less so amongst their elders and head office personnel. I remember many examples of men and women, including myself, who said one thing from the congregation's podium yet, in their personal lives, shed their richly embroidered cloaks of righteousness and became ordinary worldly folk at best and at worst, misanthropic and crooked members of society. Not that I put Ram Dass in this category; but I reminded myself that I had once put my trust in iconic religious men and an organisation that ultimately let me down, leaving me disillusioned and hurt. It was now a time for prudence.

Validating my Guru

The opportunity to meet Ram Dass arose in March 2007 when I found time enough to go to Hawaii to attend one of his retreats on the Island of Maui, his home county. Time and place come together at moments in a life, long-postponed appointments happen: sometimes by chance, or fate, or – in this case – after much planning.

My journey to my teacher took me on a lateral traverse, flying more than 24 thousand kilometres to the furthest inhabitable place from home. If one pushes a spike into a polystyrene model of the earth, starting at Johannesburg and piercing the globe's centre, the closest land to where the spike would emerge is Hawaii. In the way of things my pilgrimage was leisurely, blended with tourism and other activities. I crossed the equator three times, travelling from Johannesburg to Singapore and then south to Auckland to visit Johann, and back north to Honolulu. Sight-seeing, surprises, challenges, reunions, and a rendezvous with the one who influenced me so greatly. Yet a sober solemnity characterised the journey and I kept my mind focussed sharply on matters spiritual.

Singapore was like a sauna, saturated humidity and temperatures in the high twenties. I walked a lot and my first trip by foot was on a random route from the Miramar Hotel in Havelock Street and across Marina Channel's east estuary. I soon discovered, a short distance from the hotel, the ornate Chettiars' Temple in Tank Road, named in honour of Sri Thendayuthapani (also known as Lord Muruga). The temple, built in 1859, is the oldest Hindu temple on the island and is breathtakingly beautiful. Its *gopuram*, the monumental tower at the entrance to any South Indian temple, is elaborate, colourful and depicts Hindu mythology in a myriad of detailed sculptures.

This wasn't the kind of journey that lent itself to enjoying a few crisp gin and tonics in the shade of a hotel veranda so I stopped at the temple to meditate. The hour or so spent in the stillness of the temple's open courtyard, away from the heat of Singapore's busy streets, rejuvenated mind and body. Then, off by foot, around the north-western boundary of Fort Canning Park to

Dhoby Ghaut's Metrorail station in Orchard Road, for a short underground train ride to Little India.

Why Little India? Mainly in search of a tasty vegetarian curry lunch. But there was a secondary purpose: Ram Dass's teachings leaned towards Hinduism and this encouraged me to defy the Witness' ban on studying 'heathen' spiritual philosophies. I strongly desired to widen my philosophical and spiritual understanding beyond the myopic Witness view of Christianity. After I met Terry Winchester at the esoteric faire in Sandton, I developed an insatiable appetite for oriental teachings, reading texts on Hinduism, Buddhism and Taoism: I loved the simplicity of Sri Ramana Maharshi's *Advaita Vedanta* philosophy where liberation is found by recognising the identity of Self and its relationship to the Whole. I became curious about some of the mystic practices Paramahansa Yogananda described in his book *Autobiography of a Yogi* and in Baird Thomas Spalding's six-volume account of the *Life and Teaching of the Masters of the Far East*. The Tibetan Dzogchen lama of the Nyingma tradition, Sogyal Rinpoche, eloquently encapsulated his brand of Buddhist teachings for me in his book *The Tibetan Book of Living and Dying*. And Lao Tzu, the ancient Chinese philosopher's *Tào Té Chīng* inspired me greatly. All of these books encouraged a wider acceptance and understanding, and my respect for other beliefs quickly extended outwards like ripples in a pond. Had it not been for two additional manuscripts, I might have turned my back on Christianity forever: Neale Donald Walsch's trilogy, *Conversations with God*, and Helen Schucman's *A Course in Miracles* offered me a renewed view of Christianity that wasn't too contradictory to the new eastern teachings I was learning.

Deep inside my brain still lay a lair of Witness doctrine. Reading literature other than that off the Watchtower Bible and Tract Society's printing presses was already a giant leap forward but visiting different sites of worship took immense rebellious courage and defiance. So brainwashed was I that on one of my early trips to London, I wouldn't go inside Saint Paul's Cathedral because it represented a part of apostate Christendom, believed by the Witnesses to be 'Babylon the Great, the Mother of Prostitutes and Abominations of the Earth.' Johann was furious with me.

My quest in Singapore was to find interesting eastern places of worship and it wasn't long before I stumbled upon another temple, Shree Lakshminarayan Temple in Chandler Road. Its location is an unlikely site down a narrow side street in Singapore's Indian neighbourhood. The compact four-storey building, opened in 1969, is nowhere nearly as ornate as the Chettiars' Temple but it was abuzz in comparison. The entrance is directly off the cramped cement pavement and the building stands proudly over its humble neighbours, the Kerbau Hotel and the 'Oversea Cosmetics Shop'. The temple's facade is dirty white, relieved with rust-red painted triangles.

So, once more off with my footwear, which was a great relief – I promised myself never again to travel with new shoes. As I walked barefoot over the cool tiles I mused on Emmanuel's clever simile, 'Death is like taking off a tight shoe',[104] If that cool floor was anything to go by, how delightful death might be for the unafraid.

Devotees moved about in throngs in the temple courtyard. Others stood patiently to take their turn with the priests at the *garbhagriha*, the temple's inner sanctum that houses the *murti* or image of the main *devata* (the deity). They handed the priests offerings of food, flower garlands arranged on enamel or pewter plates, and prayers written on small slips of paper. Since I was on my way to visit my guru, I thought it would be appropriate to have a scarlet cotton sacred thread, a blessing thread, tied around my wrist. My ego had sadly opened its lustful eye because it wasn't really the blessing I sought. Ego needed to be seen at Ram Dass's retreat wearing a holy thread as a marker for others to notice.

I approached an official at a trestle table near the doorway and asked how I could obtain a blessing. He pointed me to the long queue outside the sanctum and I put a tip into his tin box and took my place in the slow-moving line. The woman in front of me carried her year-old grandson on her hip and told me that she was bringing him for a special blessing We chatted as we shuffled forward, while down on us, from their alcoves on the sanctum's outside wall, gazed brightly painted porcelain deities. At last we turned a corner and I saw the priest, officiating where he sat midway along the back wall.

One by one, worshippers took their turn before him, conveyed their requests, knelt down, and let the priest intercede on their behalf. I smiled at the business of religion, how reliant we have become on agents who arbitrate between God and us. We often fail to realise that we have direct access to God, and we readily relinquish our spiritual wellness to our priests in much the same way that we place our physical health in the hands of our doctors. Perhaps we do it because that's what they taught us to do; or maybe it's because we believe that we're not worthy enough to approach God directly. A cynical part of me considers that religion made us

---

[104] *Emmanuel's Book: a manual for living comfortably in the cosmos*, compiled by Pat Rhodegast and Judith Stanton, Bantam, 1987.

needy of its priesthood, in order to give those castes of arbitrators a meaning and a purpose. Whatever the reason, by doing it we absolve ourselves of personal responsibility.

I had nearly reached the head of the line when I got an urge to satisfy my curiosity, and I twisted to peer up at the deity that was lodged in the alcove. I imagined that I'd see the familiar Lakshmi, Hanuman or perhaps Lord Ganesha but I reeled, shocked by the grotesque image. There in that cramped space stood a female *murti*, slightly taller than life-size, with long black hair cascading to her buttocks. She thrust a long and pointy tongue down to her chin, and it dripped with blood. Decapitated heads and severed arms girdled her loins. She wore a necklace of human skulls and held the head of a man sliced from his body by her bloodied sword. At her feet lay Shiva, murdered.

A wave of weakness washed over me and I glanced around. I felt as though I'd sinned. I half expected to see my mother, or Jehovah, staring at me in damning accusation. I wanted to run but it was too late for that – I didn't want to draw attention or offend anyone behind me in the queue. I felt sick to the pit of my stomach and a thousand fearful thoughts flooded my head. I panicked, imagining that I'd unleashed some demonic force, like Pandora, when she opened the jar that bound within it all the evils of the world.

But here was the priest! I took my place in front of him, certain that my face betrayed the classic roadmap, signs and pointers, of the path to eternal hell. Indeed he seemed bewildered as he looked at me, and asked how he could help. Perspiring profusely, I stammered: 'I was hoping for a blessing to take with me, on my way to see my guru.'

I didn't want to kneel in front of this deity but I complied, even though I kept a wary eye on that cunning and devilish woman. The priest chanted something in Sanskrit, bowed in reverence, turned to face me again, daubed holy ash on my third eye and tied a heavy black thread around my wrist. He made three knots with a deft movement of his hands, uttered a blessing, and – with the kindest and most compassionate touch – held my hands warmly in his as he looked me straight in the eye and said softly 'Good lucks! This is a thousand good lucks'.

I ran from the temple, scattering shoes as I scuttled to find mine amongst hundreds of other pairs at the entrance. I sprinted, barefoot, across the blistering tar into the shade on the far side of the street. I leaned against an iron picket fence near a cluster of bicycles, and I slipped on my shoes. Heart still racing, I turned my attention to the black thread bracelet on my right wrist. I recollected my egotistical intention: how cool to rock up at Ram Dass's retreat wearing a scarlet sacred thread. How chastened I felt now! My mind was a tangle of guilt and present wisdom. Nothing seemed, for now, to make much sense. Had I just been rebuked by God? I struggled to rip off the band but, as if by some magical force, it wouldn't budge. After a futile struggle I decided to leave it until I could cut it loose in the hotel room.

I don't remember much of the rest of the day but, once I'd returned to the hotel in the early evening, my panic had subsided. My mind had settled down and I decided to wear the bracelet until I fully understood the teaching that it presented. Somehow, I suspected, I wasn't getting the message. I spent the evening writing and reflecting. I was horrified at the Witnesses' power to shape my brain with fear, for here, some thirty years later, I was filled with guilt just because I'd received a blessing from beneath a painted plaster deity. Sinister in appearance, no doubt of that, but one of many faces of the life within us; and the priest was gentle, and benevolent.

I avoided further temple visits and frittered away my time on eating, drinking and catching up with some Singaporean acquaintances I'd met on a previous journey to New Zealand. I then winged my way down south to spend time with Johann at his luxurious guesthouse – Umoya Lodge – some hundred kilometres south of Auckland. This was near the Miranda Bird Sanctuary, on the Firth of Thames.

One of Johann's guest suites had an unusual outside bath on a secluded wooden deck. From the deck, on a gentle hill, the view looked out across soft green rolling valleys. The night was clear and cool, and I immersed myself in a tub of steaming hot water and gazed up at the starry sky. From these southern latitudes the Southern Cross is almost directly overhead, and I understood why it became such a prominent motif on the national flags of Australia and New Zealand.

The stars are familiar friends to me. From a decade of public lectures at the Johannesburg Planetarium, I've come to know them well by name. I recognise them by the company they keep in familiar stellar patterns across the sky. A plethora of data ran through my brain, as I lay relaxing in the warm water: facts about star distances, how colour and size indicate stellar age and how binary pairs orbit each other, locked into an interminable dance around a common centre of gravity. Our two neighbouring irregular galaxies, known as the Magellanic Clouds, were particularly beautiful in the dark skies away from Auckland's city lights. They reminded me of the Persian astronomer Al Sufi's description of them as *al-Bakr* 'the sheep'– a detail that I like – because one can only see them south of the strait of Bab el Mandeb at the southern tip of Arabia, Al Sufi meant, in particular, the southern Arabs' sheep.

I lay there for a long time gazing at the sky until the skin on my fingers and toes crinkled. I listened to the distant calls of the small brown native Morepork owls and wondered if there wasn't another way for me to *see* the stars. I had only seen them before through scientific eyes, so I pulled the plug to release some tepid water, topped it up with hot and slid in a little deeper to help induce a trance, thinking that hypnosis might provoke a new way to view the wonders of the night sky. I kept my eyes closed for some time, to stabilise the trance, before slowly opening them. I tried to avoid looking at anything specific, for otherwise I would have engaged left-brain analysis and missed any possible trance experience. I soaked up the water's warmth, and I allowed the visual splendour to wash over me: the celestial canopy received by an altered state of mind, glimmering jewels bright against black velvet, the two fluffy white blobs of our neighbouring galaxies, the dark tract of empty sky near the foot of the Southern Cross.

A meteor streaked by and I thought 'How small everything is!' That statement surprised me for I had always used adjectives like majestic, vast, colossal, and immense to describe stellar objects. Now, in trance, I viewed their apparent and not their actual size. Compared with the earth most of these structures are mind-boggling in their size, but in comparison with the Universe, they're miniscule. To my subconscious mind, every pinpoint of light became a microscopic, subatomic particle of God. I looked at the sky, enthralled, as each star transformed into a tiny fairy-like friend and soul mate.

Aided by hypnotic hallucination, the stars weren't just seemingly small but actually small. My eye muscles became fatigued, I relaxed them for a while, and the star field turned into a three-dimensional very close space, so close in fact that I lifted my arm and touched each star with the tip of my finger. The only way to describe what I saw is to compare it to an autostereogram where, hidden in a spatter of apparently random dots, until the viewer focuses the eyes correctly, is a three-dimensional object. Once that's revealed, the brain locks onto the three-dimensional image and the eyes are free to move about and look at its parts without disrupting the illusion. This is how I saw the night sky, as a 3-D image right there at arm's reach instead of way out beyond the solar system. The furthest entity in this three-dimensional celestial cluster seemed a little more than a meter away, and I touched the stars and cupped them in my hands. They were shy beings that retreated gently whenever I reached out too quickly but soon became braver the more I engaged with them.

Each pinpoint of light established a unique rapport with me. One by one, they came closer to look at me, each a tiny soul ready to reveal its personality. Some were sweet and innocent, others dodgy and cunning. I saw the universe differently: each star a unique soul clustered within galaxies of souls, each cluster a microscopic, subatomic building block in the overall celestial fabric that comprises God.

I spent a couple of weeks with Johann and toured New Zealand's South Island before flying off, backwards in time, to Honolulu, capital city of the 50th state of the USA. New Zealanders are genuinely nice and sincere people but Americans present you with a veneer of superficial pleasantry. 'You're welcome, have a nice day!' becomes a tired and threadbare salutation, and you just know that they're probably cursing you under their breath. I got my first glimpse of American consumerism as I walked through Honolulu's terminal building. Posters along the route from the aircraft to the cordoned Immigration area tout Hawaii as a dream summer vacation. I remembered the old cliché: 'been there ... done that ... worn the tee-shirt'. These billboards are checklists for good-time experiences one should have on the islands: food eaten, places visited and souvenirs collected.

Border control officials wore blue disposable latex gloves to protect them from the nasties lurking in travellers' luggage. A detection machine stared into my eyes; other devices scanned me in strange spectrums of light, making me look like a NASA topographical map of an alien planet. There were sniffing machines trained to ignore the smell of last week's socks, their olfactory prowess bent on finding more threatening odours. The New Zealand authorities conducted security inspections with finesse even when invading your personal space, but their American counterparts are just the opposite – authoritative, brash and bullying. The whole American Homeland Security System projects fear. A booming voice repeated an announcement in American twang while I stood in line to have my passport stamped, until it echoed in my brain: 'Homeland Security Alert System is Code Orange'. So what? Why do visitors need to know this?

Officialdom cleared me by ten o'clock that evening and I boarded a bus to Waikiki. A young New Zealander also tried to catch the bus but the driver quickly turned him away because the size of his surfboard offended the carrier's luggage rules. He was banished unceremoniously even though there were only three of us on board.

I slept for a few hours before flying out to Maui the next morning.

I boarded a twin-engine Cessna Caravan in Honolulu at ten a.m., as the pilot's only passenger. Security rules enforced after 9-11 forbid passengers from entering the cockpit and the pilot took great trouble demarcating it as 'the area bound by an imaginary straight line across the backs of the pilot and co-pilot seats'. No part of my body could intrude into that space at any time during the flight. I chose to sit in the first row against the window on the right, where I could look into the cockpit and still enjoy the scenic views out to the side. Once airborne, I saw Pearl Harbour to starboard, just beyond the fighting might of military aircraft stationed at Hickam Air Force Base, which shares its runways with civil aviation in and out of Honolulu. We banked gently to port, flying parallel to Waikiki's popular beaches, and then climbed up and out across the ocean. The pilot was busy for a few moments before his cockpit duties eased and he and I soon began to chat our way across the sea while he shared his jumbo packet of crisps through the invisible cockpit wall.

It is a wonderfully scenic flight and one I will never forget. Having acquired a private pilot's licence, I spent hundreds of hours in the air. Many of them spent in a microlight giving me a sense of freedom like none other, suspended high above the ground in what's equivalent to flying, seated in a plastic patio chair dangling beneath a garden umbrella. This flight was routine yet very symbolic. I was on a spiritual high, flying on an ethereal journey into my future; below, the material world in which I now showed little interest – Waikiki the symbol of capitalism; the other islands in the archipelago making life seem so small compared to the vast Pacific Ocean that gave definition to the 360° horizon.

We flew over Moloka`i, one of the islands along our flight path, and soon the pilot pointed out Maui in the distance, separated by a narrow sixteen-kilometre stretch of sea and, on our starboard side, the comma-shaped island of Lāna`i. These are three of the four islands comprising Maui County, the fourth being Kaho`olawe where, on 6 February 1965, the US Navy detonated a 500-ton TNT explosive charge on its south-western tip, the first of a series of three test explosions on the site to simulate nuclear blasts. As we approached Maui, I saw clusters of hotels and resorts along its popular western shores as they disappeared southwards along the curved volcanic coastline. The sparsely populated northern pineapple farming slopes of Puu Kukui, Maui's smaller peak, rise just over half the height of its sibling volcano, Haleakalā. Maui could easily have been two islands had it not been for a bridge of land running ten kilometres from north to south between the two volcanic peaks.

As we rounded the northern shores of Puu Kukui, I could see a busy airport off to our right. Commercial jets were parked on the apron but we were still at high altitude and I assumed we'd been put in a holding pattern to favour some larger aircraft. Instead, to my surprise, we flew right past.

'Isn't this where we're supposed to land?' I asked.

'No, sir! We've got another twenty-five nautical miles to go.'

A dull panic came on me as I realised that I'd made a mistake. I had spent some time exploring the island's topography on Google Earth before leaving home but had failed to zoom into either airport, for had I have done so, I would have quickly realised the travel agent's error. I'd booked my trip through a South African travel agent, a woman who hardly knew of the existence of the island of Maui let alone its topography and she'd arranged the flight from Honolulu to Maui's remote secondary airport, Hana. I will never know why she chose the Hana airfield over Kahului's main civilian airport where most tourists disembark, but she did; and I never questioned her authority. My mind churned with alternative plans, including a drive back to the town of Kahului in a hired car or perhaps hitching a lift with someone else.

Fortunately, I had given myself four days on Maui to acclimatise and get orientated prior to Ram Dass's retreat, so I had plenty of time to rectify my error. I had no choice, sat back, and enjoyed the magnificent views of the northern rugged coastline as it drifted by. I knew that the retreat was located along this stretch of land and tried to identify it from the air but, somehow, real-life terrain didn't quite match the satellite images in my head and I could not spot it.

Signs of civilisation progressively diminished the closer we got to Hana, and the tropical forest growth on the fertile volcanic slopes thickened. I caught a glimpse of a microlight flying low towards us and then beneath us, and I plotted its course backwards to get a first glimpse of Hana's airfield, a single tarmac runway lying parallel to the shoreline. It was cut into dense forest with no neighbouring signs of life. My worries intensified but I had little choice other than to take things as they came.

The pilot performed his final approach checks and descended straight in. It was a perfect touchdown and we rolled to a halt at the end of the runway where he turned, backtracked and parked in front of the tiny terminal building. He unloaded my bag, wheeled it to the veranda, said his goodbyes and walked across to meet an elderly man and his teenage son. Father and son hugged each other, exchanged a few words, and with three firm pats on his back, his father despatched him into the pilot's care.

Leaving my bag on the wooden bench outside, I walked into the terminal building to find it unoccupied. The square room contained a single check-in counter, a small stall where one could buy sweets and chocolates, and a car-rental booth. Not one of these was staffed. I quickly sprinted back outside to catch the man's attention before he drove off in his thunderous white Dodge pickup truck, as he was my only link to the outside world and, without him, who knows how long I would wait for someone else to pitch up. Already seated, with engine running, he leaned his bare tattooed arm out of the window.

I spoke first. 'Excuse me sir!' I began, somewhat short of breath, 'I seem to have made a mistake and I'm not sure how to fix it.' I told him my situation and asked how I could get back to Kahului. He explained that attendants work at the terminal building only when large scheduled flights come in and he expected none for the rest of the day. He also said that a journey by road would take hours, I might get lucky and hitch a lift, but it was already mid-morning and the possibility was slim.

'Is there a hotel nearby? Can I walk there? How far is it?' During my barrage of questions, I had a growing feeling that I might have to sleep at the airport until staff arrived the next day, for only then could I make other plans to get to Kahului.

Jerome, as I later discovered, is a native to Maui and worked as a road maintenance supervisor. The back of his truck was loaded with stones, a barrel of bitumen, and a variety of picks and shovels. He was far from his team, as he had left them to drop off his son who was flying to Honolulu. He made a quick call to his wife and generously offered to accommodate me for two nights in the back room of his house. I was astounded at his kindness and hospitality and marvelled at his trust in me, for back in Africa we would hardly invite a stranger into our home – the security risks would be too great. I too placed all my trust in him, for he could have taken advantage of my situation, but I instinctively sensed that this encounter was safe and I smiled at the universe's arrangements and embraced them as an interesting teaching.

Thus the universe brought me to Hana. Here I stayed with Jerome and his wife Josie in their simple house on a street littered with vehicles in various states of decay, where barefooted children played, observed cautiously by an emaciated lactating bitch. Neighbouring houses had junk piled everywhere, cars on trestles, rusted parts, flat and perished tyres. This poor housing settlement (according to American standards) lay on the forested outskirts of Hana Bay, about one kilometre north of Hana Township.

Mahatma Gandhi said that 'the greatness of a nation and its moral progress can be judged by the way its animals are treated'. African rural townships have scrawny dogs roaming about freely, some in season or pregnant, mangy coats, thin and malnourished, feeding on scraps and belonging to no one. In Paris, it is quite the opposite, other than having to dodge their residue on the pavements. Parisiennes treat their dogs like Roman emperors at the height of decadent rule. Some of the dogs of Paris have their own rooms, wear diamond-studded collars and are cherished members of the family. In Hana, most dogs were caged or tethered. The dog in the house on the opposite side of the road was chained to a steel peg in the yard and, by the state of the ground beneath it, it was obvious that this dog had spent most of its life inside that relatively small circle. The cute little white neighbouring dog stood on top of its dilapidated wooden kennel in a cage no bigger than two square metres, to get a better view. It wagged its tail furiously and its eyes called in vain for rescue. It longed for a comforting pat on the head.

The room they offered in their house was rather more than that. It was a completely separate timber-clad cottage, scantily furnished with one double bed and a few built-in benches along some of its interior walls. It was completely devoid of curtains, which was okay because of its secluded location at the forest's edge. Josie made up the bed with a set of dark green fitted sheets and a floral pillowcase.

I walked the strip between their house and the village several times to buy supplies, to eat supper at the Spa Hotel, and just for pleasure. The kids followed me, curious about my accent, but not quite brave enough to ask anything except the gentlest of questions. Hana has a small population of some seven hundred residents and constitutes one of the most isolated villages in the entire county. It's no more than a stopover for tourists travelling to the lava flow sites on the southern side of the big volcano.

The Catholic Church remained shut during my visit. I smiled at the contrast between this place of worship and the busy Hindu temple I visited in Singapore, and I tried to reason why it kept its doors closed to the public. On an extended walk along one of the backstreets behind the school, I found a caravan (a mobile home) where I bought the most scrumptious vegetarian sandwich I've ever eaten. It bulged with Italian cheeses, artichokes and other delicacies, and dripped with fresh, fragrant olive oil. I ate it on the beach, just a short stroll away. The beach is devoid of sand and is a tumble of black volcanic rocks worn smooth by the ebb and flow of the ocean. Green ferns, moss and small trees cling to every perch between the black boulders on the landward side. Seawards, tiny colourful fish inhabit the spaces between the submerged rocks and boulders. The contrast between the black and green, and the ever-moving blue water, creates a kaleidoscope of postcard scenes.

I sat there for a while, engrossed in nature's charm. A young man in his early twenties strolled up to me and I invited him to sit on the bench. He was looking for a cave on Red Sand Beach, near the southern boundary of Hana, a place he wanted to sleep in for a few nights. He'd been bumming around for four years. His clothes were filthy and in tatters, his skin stained with ingrained dirt, and his teeth encrusted with a heavy build-up of yellow tartar, plaque and nicotine. But his face showed signs of freedom and life. He sat and talked with me while he coloured in the letters on his cardboard sign that read 'Need any kind of work for cash – please help!'

I asked how much he made.

'About a hundred bucks a day,' he cheerfully replied.

We talked for a while longer before I had to leave to get home before dark, and part of me envied his simple lifestyle. I reflected on how much he lived in *the now*, a little like I had done when I travelled throughout the United Kingdom and Europe back in 1977. Even so, there popped into my head another of Dad's sayings: 'no matter how poor you are, my boy, there's always enough money for soap'. I grappled with my rationalising ego as I pondered whether I would neglect my personal hygiene to the same extent this young man had done. Beneath the grime was a very good-looking person. And yet my long-indoctrinated mind whispered that looks, too, can be deceptive: the old adage of a facade that hides a crumbling interior, a Jekyll and Hyde identity. When speaking of the hypocrisy of the scribes and Pharisees in Jerusalem, Jesus referred to this as 'unmarked graves,'[105] normal and ordinary on the outside but full of dead men's bones within.

As I walked back in the last mauve hues of twilight, I saw something glinting in the dark green grass: a fallen pewter angel some five centimetres tall studded with several diamante stones. She held a star in one hand, her feet pressed together and pointed like a ballerina. I slipped her into my pocket and wondered how long she'd been lying there waiting for me to pass, and who might have had the privilege of her company before. I felt reassured by her symbolism, and safe in the hands of the angels. Much later, this guardian angel was to become a fitting symbol as the centrepiece on the front cover of a book of affirmations that I gave to Mark after his near suicide attempt.

---

[105] *The New English Bible*, Luke 11:44

The next morning, I phoned the airport to enquire about possible ways of leaving Hana. They told me that I could hire a car for 200 dollars a day or catch a return flight to Kahului for 97 dollars. It was an easy choice and I booked my ticket, packed my bags in the early morning on the third day, thanked the folks for their kind hospitality and drove back to Hana airport with Jerome in his white Dodge pickup.

A quick shuttle flight in a tiny four-seater Cessna took me at low level back along the rugged coastline. I felt wry about this flight: Hale Akua Shangri-la Resort lay midway between Kahului and Hana, a little more than thirty kilometres from either end, and it seemed such an awful waste going there by air.

Only later did I learn that few people travel the 80 kilometre trip along the Hana Highway as it takes around three hours to complete. The road winds through tropical rainforests and crosses no less than 59 bridges, nearly all of which have single lanes. Traffic is slow. This short but twisting, turning route snakes its way around more than 600 curves between the two urban centres.

At last I arrived, intact, at the resort. I settled in, and reflected that despite my panic over the ill-planned excursion, I was safely here and with a good story to tell. I was one of a group of about thirty who had gathered at Hale Akua Shangri-la. It lies midway along the Hana Highway on the rocky cliffs of Maui's northeastern shoreline, but it no longer functions as a resort. New owners have, since then, converted it into an organic farm where they teach natural and permaculture farming methods, based on models found in natural ecologies.

'Fear is that little darkroom where negatives are developed', said Michael Pritchard. I certainly believe that we attract the things we fear the most. Many years ago, after a long walk through some of the backstreets of Paris, I returned to Pascal and Katie's home, and having heard of my day's adventures, both were horrified at where I'd been. 'People die there!' said Pascal, with a grave look of concern on his urbane features. I hadn't sensed danger and I guess my innocence shone through which rendered me invisible and thereby invincible. My unexpected trip to Hana could have been frightening, but I believed all would be okay – and so it was. It symbolised the leap of faith I took by visiting Ram Dass and I understood that this too would end well; I instinctively knew that I'd soon weed out my seeds of doubt about him.

On the first day of the retreat, I came back into the empty hall after lunch to take my place where I sat all morning. To my surprise, Ram Dass was already sitting there in his wheelchair just a few metres away from me. I hadn't expected him and, for a moment, I didn't know what to do: should I leave or should I enter? He smiled and I acknowledged him. I walked across the room and sat down on the floor where I had left a few of my things. This was my first encounter with him in person.

Ram Dass seemed to drift in and out of a deep meditative trance, which induced the same feelings in me, and I closed my eyes and quickly slipped into my own inner space. The room tingled with vibrant energy and I snuggled into it as though it were a cosy blanket. I sat there silently for a while but my body then began to quiver and shake uncontrollably as a profound deep emotion rose within. I feared that I would cry and tried desperately to suppress it to prevent embarrassment; but the more I tried to contain it, the quicker and more powerfully it welled up inside. My futile struggles lasted a few short moments and I hung my head low, tears streamed from my eyes and dripped into my lap and my breathing deepened, interjected by occasional soft sobs.

I looked up at Ram Dass after a while and he was smiling at me with a look of absolute understanding, love and compassion. He beckoned me to come to him and I did. The room was small and I reached him quickly, squatted on my haunches next to his chair and let him embrace me tightly with his good arm. I gazed straight into his liquid eyes and said 'I've loved you for a very, very long time'. He smiled some more. I had nothing else to say and neither did he. We looked at each other for a few moments until others drifted in.

I have never before felt so at home! My heart embraced him unconditionally as teacher and guru and in an instant my mind abandoned all its concerns over his legitimacy. I saw no trace of ego, pretence or showmanship. What I saw instead is a being of incredible love, dedicated to his guru, Maharaj-ji who instructed him to 'Love, Serve, Remember', which he faithfully does.

Ram Dass, unable to facilitate the entire day, due to his age and confinement to his wheelchair after a stroke, had Deepak Chopra present the five morning sessions. The two men's styles differed considerably: Deepak, suavely dressed, equipped the room with modern computer, plasma monitor and a well rehearsed PowerPoint presentation that ran like an oiled machine. It seemed so out of context for such ancient wisdom. Deepak never stayed for lunch, nor did he fraternise with the crowd, but had his entourage quickly whisk him and his wife away directly after his daily talks. Ram Dass did the opposite. He hugged anyone who wanted to, he sat in his wheelchair and, without much to say due to his expressive aphasia, poured love into the hall. When he spoke, he did it personally; and he frequently spiced up the event with a few well-known, well-loved one-liners that elicited oohs and aahs from his devoted audience.

I learned from Deepak that 'All Enlightened Beings have a past; Sinners have a future' and I affirmed my beliefs that all information is carried by light, photons of neurological energy, to our brains; that there is no individuality at the quantum level; and that nothing exists without an Observer.

Many seemed to attend the retreat to see Deepak. Amongst the attendees were some hardened conference junkies, those out shopping for new experiences and more knowledge. They compared notes with each other during the breaks and played one-upmanship by speaking of conferences they'd attended that others hadn't. When Ram Dass announced that he would be handing everyone a *japa mala*, a string of hand-turned wooden beads containing a single thread from Maharaj-ji's blanket, there were gasps of awe across the room. As he carefully lifted the first string from his wicker basket, a woman startled me by leaping fast to be first in line to receive her holy souvenir. I'm sure she had in mind the elevated spiritual status that this would bring her when she recounted her story to friends back home, leaving them envious for weeks.

A day later, I wrote in my Journal[106], 'Oh dear, it seems that all I write about is my obsession with the negative... but being with Ram Dass is pure joy and he's a living presence of love, compassion and selfless service to all'. I continued: '...the stuff I write about is stuff that I need to express. I use the word *express* in its medical sense, a healing way of expressing pus from a boil so that it might bleed a little and then rapidly heal. It lets me understand others and thereby myself. I observe failings in others so that I can judge myself, change my course of actions and grow'. I believed I never judged others in order to denigrate them or to elevate myself, and I tried to differentiate between judgement and observation and used the latter to give me a point of reference in order to better myself. Wayne Dyer puts it this way: 'When you judge another, you do not define them, you define yourself'.

One morning, during the retreat, I awoke to a fresh insight: Spirit can't perform comparative measurements – it cannot judge! Judgements are only possible in a world of separated forms by comparing two or more objects and assessing their individual worthiness against a set of

---

[106] Journal #15 in a sequence of Journals that I began writing on 26h May 2002.

predetermined values so that we might establish their ranking. Even in trying to judge intangible things like words, thoughts and actions, we can only do so by examining them against a set of beliefs, laws and principles to ascertain their fairness, lawfulness and appropriateness. However, anything compared against itself is always equal to itself thus making judgement redundant and pointless in this instance. Since we are all One, it seems futile trying to find differences between us because none exists. God is the superset and we are a subset of it. Nothing exists outside the superset, for if it did, God wouldn't be omnipresent and omnipotent. In fact, separation from God is only a concept possible in the illusory space of our minds and never in reality.

Others once judged me amiss and I loathed myself because of it. Their judgement separated our family, and in my mind back then it separated me from God. It focused so narrowly on one thing, thereby completely overlooking other redeeming qualities, dismissing them entirely. Draw a black dot in the centre of a sheet of white paper, hold it up and ask someone what he or she sees and, invariably, they will notice the black dot. Few see the perfect sheet of white paper. We look for and obsess over blemishes, often missing the purity of what surrounds these. Judgement seems to be in our nature, a deeply ingrained need to calibrate and question where we stand relative to others. The parable of Adam and Eve, symbolically eating from the tree of the *knowledge of good and evil*[107], is a metaphor describing the origins of judgement. The moment we created and calibrated scales, against which we measure and compare our experiences, we entered into an illusion of separation from God. Feelings of guilt lost us our paradise home, Eden or nirvana. Judgement, as we've seen before, is only possible when items to be compared are separate from each other.

Goethe said, 'The greatest evil that can befall man is that he should come to think ill of himself.' I slowly befriended the persona I once hated, and began to see myself differently, as a component of the divine. I had done so much judging and others had judged me badly, but now I found God anew in a place of non-judgement and realised that neither sexual choices, ethnicity, class distinction, cultural differences, religious persuasion nor material status could ever set us apart from each other, and certainly never from God. Spirit binds us. We *are* the *image and likeness* of God spoken of in Genesis[108]. Nothing can ever offend God because God is love and divine love is unconditional. Our Spirit, being a facet of God, must therefore also love all forms unconditionally and bring them home together as one. When we give up

---

[107] *The New English Bible*, Genesis 2:9.
[108] *The New English Bible*, Genesis 1:26.

judgement, our world takes on a very different form. Heaven comes to Earth, the Paradise that once was lost is regained, peace pervades our minds and we return to a state of nirvana. *A Course in Miracles* states that 'The ego cannot survive without judgment'.[109] And we cannot regain Eden while we feed the ego.

I spent a lot of time during Ram Dass's retreat contemplating the question of judgement, and I later amalgamated it with my understanding of non-attachment. Nowadays, with more wisdom, I try to weed out all forms of judgement – but it is a very difficult thing to do because it is so insidious. Believing that all actions are fundamentally equal, I no longer reference myself against others but stand alone in the midst of my own experiences, trusting that each one brings me into a closer relationship with my true nature.

A Course in Miracles further speaks of judgement as follows:

> Judgment, like other devices by which the world of illusions is maintained, is totally misunderstood by the world. It is actually confused with wisdom, and substitutes for truth. As the world uses the term, an individual is capable of 'good' and 'bad' judgment, and his education aims at strengthening the former and minimizing the latter. There is, however, considerable confusion about what these categories mean. What is 'good' judgment to one is 'bad' judgment to another. Further, even the same person classifies the same action as showing 'good' judgment at one time and 'bad' judgment at another time. Nor can any consistent criteria for determining what these categories are be really taught.

It concludes:

> It is necessary for the teacher of God to realize, not that he should not judge, but that he cannot. In giving up judgment, he is merely giving up what he did not have. He gives up an illusion; or better, he has an illusion of giving up.[110]

Marcus Aurelius said, 'If you are pained by external things, it is not they that disturb you, but your own judgment of them. And it is in your power to wipe out that judgment now'.

---

[109] *A Course in Miracles*, T-4.II.10.3, Combined Volume (Third Edition), the Foundation for A Course in Miracles, 2007.
[110] *A Course in Miracles*, MFT-5.III.10, Combined Volume (Third Edition), the Foundation for A Course in Miracles, 2007.

If I were to judge my experiences, I would limit myself. Where I find myself today is a karmic consequence of every thought I've had throughout eternity; where I will be tomorrow, depends upon what I think today. This tempts me to think only wholesome thoughts so that I might elevate myself to a more righteous place but isn't this just another form of judgement? If I'm to suspend all judgement, I have to accept that every thought is proper and every action godly – including murder – but how can this be so?

Imagine another sheet of clean white paper with a straight horizontal line drawn across its middle. The line represents society's norms and values. The space above the line represents 'good' and below the line, 'bad'. The further above the line, the better it gets and the greater the distance below the line, the worse it becomes. We could plot all our experiences on the page. 'Feeding the poor' would probably go close to the top edge as a very noble and good thing to do; 'rape and murder' would be very near the bottom. Every human experience can be plotted somewhere on the sheet and I'm certain that most of them would probably lie in a narrow band close to the baseline, for most of our experiences are average, not too bad but not too good either. Notice how difficult it is to find neutral experiences, ones that we could plot on the line itself. Observe too, that few of us have had experiences far away from the line, as it takes exceptional people to have exceptional experiences. Mother Theresa's work in Calcutta would be near the page's top edge and Robert Mugabe's activities in Zimbabwe near the bottom. Notice how ready we are to accept the baseline's position on the paper without question. Who decided where to position it on the page? Why shouldn't it be higher up or lower down? We buy into society's norms as part of our socialisation. Our parents influence us and thereby determine the line's position but so do our teachers, priests, politicians and all Holy Scriptures. Philosophical paradigms position the line through sets of rules, laws, codes of conduct, ethical and cultural values, and dogma. When we are young, we have very little say over the line's position and we may be so brainwashed as adults that we never consider challenging it and moving it elsewhere.

If you are a conservative thinker, you will probably lobby to move the baseline high up the page. As a liberal thinker, you will certainly motivate a baseline nearer the bottom. A conservative stance leaves very little area above the line but an enormous space below it and the converse is true of a liberal view. Conservatism narrows the definition of good and liberalism widens it. Let's take a contentious example like sex before marriage to illustrate the ridiculous nature of judgement. To the liberalist, sex before marriage is acceptable human practice amongst consenting adults; but conservatives forbid it. Depending on one's vantage point, sex before marriage is either a punishable offence or a jolly good time. Who is right, who is wrong, the conservatives or the liberals? Or should we be taking a more neutral stance?

A Course in Miracles refers to this judgement conundrum and gives us a clue to solve it: 'It is necessary... to realize, not that he should not judge, but that he cannot'. Judgement is possible only in a world of duality. It is impossible in a world of unity or oneness. God cannot judge; it's an impossible task for him to do. Not only is it impossible for God to judge but it is nonsensical too. How can he create a calibrated scale of comparisons when all he can do is compare himself against himself? God is Love and love cannot judge love amiss. Judgement, as the *Course* says, is an illusion. We can conclude by extension, therefore, that good and bad are illusions too.

If we cannot judge, we may not draw a line anywhere on our clean, white sheet of paper, for by so doing we instantly divide the page and give birth to separation and judgement. Jesus said, 'Pass no judgement, and you will not be judged; do not condemn, and you will not be condemned...'[111] The moment we extend a line across the page, we judge ourselves because we must take a position relative to it.

Imagine that the Divine Mother is sitting with a sheet of white paper on her lap and at her feet is one of her children. She asks the child, 'What experience are you going to have as you go out to play in the divine cosmic sandpit today, my darling?'

'I thought I would play the game of "feeding the poor", my Divine Mother.'

'Well, off you run to play then ....' she replies lovingly. As her child leaves with the other cosmic kids, she takes her felt-tip pen and places a tiny black dot over the location of 'feeding the poor' on her sheet of paper.

The next morning, she asks her child, 'Did you learn much from feeding the poor, my angel?'

'Yes, Divine Mother, I learned about compassion and suffering.'

'And what kind of experience do you intend having today, my darling?'

'Please may I play the "murder" game today?'

---

[111] *The New English Bible*, Luke 6:37

'Of course sweetheart.'

After an eternity the entirely blackened sheet of paper will reflect every experience her child had while playing in the cosmic sandpit.

Spiritual Evolution

A battle ensued between two rival branches of an Indian royal family three thousand years or so before Jesus' appearance on Earth. The king had two sons. His first was born blind and thus had his kingdom ruled by his younger son. These brothers had sons of their own who became jealous over the disparity between what was and what should have been, had the normal laws of succession been followed. After much skulduggery to usurp dominion from the younger brother's heirs, and their failure to pull it off, the two branches of the family draw battle lines to fight for ownership. The place is Kurukshetra, North India. Both factions appealed to Krishna, an avatar (God in human form), for help. Leading the aggressors (one of the blind son's descendants) is Duryodhana. Arjuna (one of the younger son's descendants), a pure, noble and chivalrous man, leads the defendants. Krishna agrees to help: one of you can have all my weapons and all my armies; the other can have me without my weapons and armies. Duryodhana, true to character, chooses Krishna's might; Arjuna chooses Krishna as his advisor, who rides beside him on his chariot.

This battle, documented in the Bhagavad Gita, is more than an historical account of the battle at Kurukshetra; it is a profound text about our spirituality and the battles we face internally. Arjuna doesn't want to kill people he knows: it will certainly break down family ties and cause irreversible rifts. And yet he knows that he must set aside family love and loyalty and act out of a different set of motives to fulfil his *dharma*.

I had to make choices with serious consequences that pushed me upwards. Forced, like Arjuna, to confront issues, I had to transform profoundly in order to question the public norm of going to the army and opposing that which others never dreamt of challenging. In order for Spirit, by choosing this incarnation, to allow the Witnesses to excommunicate me and for me to go into battle with my family and 'kill' them, I had to endure these experiences. 'Anyone who loves his father or mother more than me is not worthy of me; anyone who loves his son or daughter more than me is not worthy of me.'[112] But the Gita isn't just about moral law versus social law; it's about Higher Consciousness.

Many years ago, I bought a copy of the Bhagavad Gita and it went into my library, where it stayed for years though I never read it. I bought it after listening to Ram Dass's taped speeches about the Gita and I knew that it was essential study material, but it never really caught my attention. One day, when searching on my shelves for a different book, I rediscovered it and thumbed through it, diverting my attention away from my original quest, as one can so easily do when riffling through books. After dipping into it for several minutes, I placed it on the little table in my meditation space where I keep a collection of spiritual literature that I currently use, hoping that I would muster enough enthusiasm to work through it. I think it was all the Indian character names that put me off, as it reminded me a little of reading the first few books of the Bible containing the endless list of genealogical data of who begat whom.

It's a little book and I popped it into my luggage to read en route to Hawaii, but never did. In December 2010, Yvonne and I took her boys to Sodwana Bay on the far northern Natal coast for some deep sea diving and, once again, the Gita came with me. Not being much of a sun lover, I settled into an easy chair in the dappled shade under the thatched eaves of our chalet while they went out to sea, and I read it at last.

The first few pages confused me and bored me a little but I had nothing else to read and pressed on. It hooked me when I started reading the third *śloka* (song) and I started making notes in the margins. I was soon in awe of the profound teachings of this ancient Indian text and I knew the Gita would become a fundamental foundation to my spirituality. It is the spiritual essence of India's great epic, the *Mahabharata* and its name literally translates as *The Song of God*. Traditionally sung or chanted as mantra, its verses were passed on orally for centuries before appearing in written form.

It is a conversation between Lord Krishna and his warrior friend the pious prince Arjuna. Krishna fills Arjuna with courage by concisely, sensitively and exquisitely placing his life and duty within the cosmic order of the universe. Krishna essentially advises Arjuna, *to do everything with non-attachment* – and this taught me just how destructive judgement is. Attachment is a vice whereby one clutches, clasps, clings to tangible and intangible objects,

---

[112] Matthew 10:37, New International Version, 1984.

desirable or undesirable in their nature. In fact, attachment applies to all worldly things like our possessions, our bodies, beliefs, rituals, ideas, and even our emotions. Non-attachment is often confused with detachment but, instead of it being a synonym, I see detachment as the opposite vice to attachment where one gives up, rejects, snubs, discards and throws out desirable and undesirable objects both tangible and intangible in nature. Renunciation, austerity, celibacy, vegetarianism can all become a vice. Non-attachment is significantly different.

I once heard the story of a devotee who visited his guru to seek enlightenment and the wise man told him to cease eating meat. The devotee obeyed faithfully for thirty years, fastidiously and fanatically avoiding any food contaminated by flesh. After thirty years, he returned to his guru, bitterly disappointed at not having attained enlightenment despite his assiduous commitment to a vegetarian diet, and he asked for further advice. His guru's words were, 'Eat meat!' One could argue that the devotee attached himself to the outcome of enlightenment, which caused his suffering, or one could say that he tried too hard to push meat aside and fell into the trap of detachment and renunciation. Perhaps his vegetarian guru's secret was careful navigation in the sacred zone of non-attachment. My practical definition of non-attachment (although maybe naive) is this: attachment is the inability to say 'no' to something; detachment the inability to say 'yes' to it; and non-attachment is having no bias or preference for saying 'yes' or 'no'. While my definition and the phrase '*it is what it is*' may be an over-simplified view of non-attachment, I apply this to most things in life to help me stay in that zone of holy-indifference; and it then becomes a useful start to a more refined understanding of what Krishna advised Arjuna.

To achieve higher states of personal consciousness, I had to undergo my hardships.

As I winged my way across the American continent after visiting Ram Dass in 2007, I reflected on the gentleness of my experience in Maui. There were no ceremonies, initiations or baptisms to mark the occasion of meeting Ram Dass but it felt as if it was the opening of a new chapter in my life.

In the Hindu scheme of *āśrama*, a boy lives with his parents until he is five years old and then falls under his guru's tutorship until he turns 24, a phase of life called *brahmacharya* or the Student Life. *Grihasta* is the second phase, the Household Life, during which he selflessly carries out his domestic duties until, at the age of 50, he begins to withdraw from the world, entering *vanaprastha* or the Retired Life. From 75 he completely dedicates himself to spiritual duties, entering the final phase of his life, *samyassa*, the Renounced Life. I liked the way my timeline roughly followed these phases and wondered how I would utilise my Retired and Renounced period.

On the long flight home, I reflected on a very awesome moment of pure synchronicity – one that I took as a convincing act of divine approval: I had held a large amount of stock in our computer company and planned to retire at the age of fifty. Believe me, one doesn't want to grow old in the fast-paced world of information technology and software engineering! Of our three founding members, I was the first to reach that age; but my birthday came and went and buyers were few and markets tight. There were young black entrepreneurs who sought arbitrage opportunities from white business owners forced by legislation to sell large chunks of their enterprises in order to adjust ownership ratios in keeping with the racial demographics of the new South Africa. I tried for four years to secure a fair deal but none came to fruition and I felt trapped.

I had a heavy heart when I left Johannesburg to come to Maui because there was unfinished business that dimmed my spiritual light. On the flight out, en route to Singapore, I'd thought a lot about the stagnant equity sale and how this cramped my freedom to explore new horizons. Intercontinental flights are tedious and I'd had enough to eat and drink. I decided to meditate. I suddenly became inspired to take a huge leap of faith and emerged from my trance state to write my insights in my journal. I clearly knew now how to solve my problem and set myself free: I decided to give my shares to the two remaining senior partners for a nominal amount upon my return. I know that sounds crazy but it was a spiritual and emotional choice and not a financial one.

My freedom was much more valuable than any amount of money, and I needed to liberate myself and to follow my heart instead of my head. I liken the universe to a strong-flowing perennial river full of abundant opportunity and us as residents along its banks. For anyone living along the river, building a dam is a futile effort if one can readily tap into its abundant resource at any time, drawing what one needs from it, when one needs it. Having taken richly from the river, I hold no fear about doing so in future. My dreams are a creative force that takes me further, not the money. I was quite ready to immediately let go my trappings, give away my equity, and move on unencumbered; and I somehow deeply trusted my partners' integrity and knew that they would never leave me destitute even if I had squandered money – and far less so if I handed them my equity and subsequently fell on hard times. Happiness and purpose come from Spirit and not from money in the bank. I paid attention to Krishna's advice to

Arjuna, to be 'established in eternal truth, self-controlled, without any sense of duality or the desire to acquire and hoard'.[113] The extent of one's success is inversely proportional to the degree of one's self-doubt and I had no hesitation about my future.

I felt good about my decision but, on the second day of Ram Dass's retreat, I was called from the hall to receive a telephone call from South Africa. I worried that it might be from someone with bad news. On the contrary, it was our company's financial director, who advised that I should return home at once as a cash buyer offered to purchase my equity at a fair value and I needed to be there to conclude the deal.

'I simply can't come,' I said, and signed and returned a hasty Power of Attorney by fax, giving him authority to conclude the transaction in my absence. I'd put years of effort into selling, but a solution came only now once I'd surrendered and let it go. The moment I chose to solve my problem by giving away the equity, the universe stepped in and brought the matter to a proper conclusion. I let go my attachments and the universe organised the sale. It reminded me of Neale Donald Walsch's writings in his *Conversations with God* trilogy, 'What you resist persists. What you look at disappears ... The act of resisting a thing is the act of granting it life'.[114]

Synchronicity surprises me time and again and I notice that if I truly want something, it never materialises until I abandon my neediness for it and only then does it manifest, often with such speed that it leaves me ill prepared to receive it. Synchronicity is a wonderful side effect of being in a non-attached space.

As the aircraft touched down on the runway at Johannesburg airport, I knew that nothing would quite be the same after my face-to-face encounter with Ram Dass. It empowered and readied me to embrace my calling that floated on the air like the notes of a long-remembered, favourite song. My journey had come full circle and so had my spirituality from its painful beginnings. I had permanently gained a day by travelling around the world but, more than that, I gained a lifetime of wisdom and understanding.

> Where sin once was perceived will rise a world that will become an altar to the truth, and you will join the lights of Heaven there, and sing their song of gratitude and praise. And as they come to you to be complete, so will you go with them. For no one

---

[113] *The Bhagavad Gita*, 2:45, translated by Eknath Easwaran, Nilgiri Press, 1961.
[114] *Conversations with God, an Uncommon Dialogue*, Book 1, Neale Donald Walsch, Hodder.

hears the song of Heaven and remains without a voice that adds its power to the song, and makes it sweeter still. And each one joins the singing at the altar that was raised within the tiny spot that sin proclaimed to be its own. And what was tiny then has soared into a magnitude of song in which the universe has joined with but a single voice.[115]

The next three and a half years were awesome. I worked with people from different parts of Africa and across all cultural and commercial divides. I honoured sitting with some as they died and with others as they healed from their awful mental and physical traumas. By suspending judgement, I received them with love and compassion. I try to meet new acquaintances as divine, magnificent beings regardless of their physical form: 'Hello, divine being! What's your experience like in there?'

I made an observation in my journal: 'I don't write much anymore, not because I lack motivation but that I don't have much to say'. I continued:

> I'm absolutely content! Nothing worries me and nothing angers me; everything inspires me. I see such beautiful potential in everyone and they feel safe enough to explore it in my presence .... Thank you, Buddha and all ascendant Masters, that I have grown so much. I like who I am. It's the first time in this lifetime that I've been so comfortable being me. I love my compassion. I love my grace. I love my generosity and integrity. I love being. I love life. Thank you, Ram Dass, for teaching me everything that is important in my spiritual life. You've taught me to love everyone unconditionally, to serve selflessly with grace, and to remember God and my oneness with the Divine.

This awareness brought instant satisfaction. The *Course* says 'Nothing at all has happened but that you put yourself to sleep, and dreamed a dream in which you were an alien to yourself, and but a part of dream. The miracle does not awaken you, but merely shows you who the dreamer is. It teaches you there is a choice of dreams while you are still asleep, depending on the purpose of your dreaming. Do you wish for dreams of healing, or for dreams of death?'[116]

---

[115] *A Course in Miracles*, T-26.IV.5, Combined Volume (Third Edition), the Foundation for A Course in Miracles, 2007.
[116] *A Course in Miracles*, T-28.2.4, Combined Volume (Third Edition) Copyright© 2007 by the Foundation for A Course in Miracles.

In 2004, while still active in the computer business, I made contact with Malcolm Hendry-Holland to learn hypnotherapy under his tutorship. This liaison slowly developed into a very interesting and close friendship. He and his Austrian life partner, Christa, lived in Cape Town. I often commuted there on business and frequently included weekends in my trip to attend their classes. Malcolm had charm, charisma, and a suave, confident style, enhanced greatly by his deep resonant Scots brogue. Christa was the motivator behind the formation of their school as she had studied extensively under Gil Boyne and Anne Spencer, big names in the American field of hypnotherapy. People often asked why I chose to study such an apparently obtuse subject like hypnosis after a lifetime in Computer Science but it seemed like a natural migration for me. I spent ages programming lifeless machines and really wanted to help others find the peace and the tranquillity I discovered, so, inspired by Terry Winchester's work[117], hypnosis became a powerful programming tool that I could master, to help reprogram the most sophisticated software of all, the human mind.

Malcolm was a very interesting man to converse with because he had widespread experience in many fields of life. He was never ostentatious or pretentious. He was also a Freemason (although few knew that) upon whom they bestowed the highest rank, the Third Degree of Master Mason. Grandfather Bill Sinclair was also a Freemason and a Scot but I knew very little about his practice. All I remember from my early teens was that some family members were surprised after his death to find a little suitcase amongst his possessions containing his Masonic regalia. Ancient secret societies like the Freemasons and the Rosicrucian Order fascinate me and I would love to peek at their teachings but I cannot get myself to enrol, as I'm so averse to closed organisations – possibly because of my Jehovah's Witness background and the secrecy surrounding their governing body.

In September 2005 Malcolm asked me to conduct a few of his elementary hypnotherapy courses in Johannesburg because he and Christa were finding it difficult to travel too often and an increasing number of people were becoming interested in the subject. I gladly accepted his offer and honoured his trust in my skills, my competence, and my self. Just over a year later, he developed lung cancer from earlier exposure to asbestos, and he died. Christa asked me to conduct all their courses in Johannesburg and I enjoyed teaching for the next five years. Soon after Malcolm's death, Christa sold her school to new owners and they retained my services as a freelance instructor in Johannesburg.

---

[117] http://www.mindframe.co.za/

Too many people seek knowledge and certification across a diverse spectrum of New Age modalities in a misguided attempt at transforming the lives of others when actually they are symbolically and in essence trying to nurse themselves back to health, a fact borne out by the handful that actually went into serious practice out of the hundreds of hypnotherapy students whom I taught.

Sue is a former friend and a collector of New Age qualifications. She has a wall covered with framed certificates: Shaman, Sangoma[118], Reflexologist, Reiki Master, Aroma Therapist, and many, many more. Her vast array of diplomas reminds me of Idi Amin's[119] impressive but worthless self-bestowed title of '*His Excellency, President for Life, Field Marshal Al Hadji Doctor Idi Amin Dada, VC, DSO, MC, Lord of All the Beasts of the Earth and Fishes of the Seas and Conqueror of the British Empire in Africa in General and Uganda in Particular*'. How many seekers of truth fervently read and study in hopes of finding meaning in their meaningless world. Regrettably, knowledge never provides one with real meaning and purpose. One can't *cognitively know* Truth, one has to *be* Truth.

I was interested no longer in adding more information to an already soggy, saturated logical brain. I sought instead to explore ways of giving people a glimpse of their true self through experience and not through knowledge. I know that what I've just stated is a spiritual oxymoron, for one's true nature lies even beyond experience; but it is a pathway less explored in the western world and has better chances of dissolving one's material illusion of self. Other hard-to-learn, mind-stilling techniques and the use of soma[120] may produce better and deeper awareness, but hypnotically induced trance seemed to give me my best and most reliable set of tools to open the mind to new realms of possibility and spiritual epiphanies. I certainly don't have a myopic view of hypnotic trance and I take no moral high ground regarding the use of soma, as some of my most profound moments of deepest enlightenment came through its sacred use.

During those fun teaching years, I formed a new kinship with other like-minded folk also interested in pursuing their spiritual path, and it occurred to me to host a regular open day

---

[118] *Sangoma* is a traditional herbalist, counsellor and diviner found in the Nguni tribes of Southern Africa.
[119] *Idi Amin Dada, President of Uganda* from 1971-1979, with a legacy of economic mismanagement and gross human rights abuses.
[120] The sacred spiritual use of hallucinogenic drugs like Ayahuasca, Hikuri, San Pedro, Peyote, Mescaline, Lysergic Acid Diethylamide (LSD), Marijuana and a plethora of Psilocybin Mushrooms.

where we could hang out with one another. After much deliberation, I despatched an email to everyone who might have been interested:

> *A Circle of Friends*: This is your personal invitation to an ongoing series of events, starting Sunday 28 January 2007, and regularly thereafter in the auditorium at my home. Some of my family, many of my friends, former students, colleagues and clients have repeatedly asked me to convene a group where we can meet together in a spirit of truth. They share my view that we have seen through the frayed fabric of this materialistic, ego-invested world and have, in one way or another, begun personal journeys in search of something new – a different paradigm that resonates at the level of our Inner Being. I kept agreeing to the idea but just as quickly avoided doing anything about it. It's a tenacious one however and nags me incessantly but I shy away from it because I doubt my suitability. Under whose authority and mandate do I stand as facilitator for the Highest Truth? The very last thing I would want is further investment in my ego but then I remembered: I'm not the inventor or the patent-holder of Truth. It belongs to us collectively and has been thus for all eternity and I now feel honoured and humbled by this prospect. Please come if you are moved to join us and I respect your choice if you decide not to attend.

My former life slowly faded into the obscurity of the past as old friendships transmuted into mere acquaintances. Months went by and I began to settle into my new, simple lifestyle. Word of my work permeated into the world around me and growing numbers asked for help across a wide range of issues. I initially took a consulting room at Weleda's Homeopathic Pharmacy and after a few years relocated to a bigger space at the Wellness Centre in Bryanston. The latter was an enormous leap of faith, introducing Spiritual Hypnotherapy to a group of high-powered medical staff who worked at the centre. The gamble paid off and I soon became a respected member of that community and still receive regular patient referrals from them. I wanted to bring spiritual awareness to mainstream society, and it worked. There might have been a time when I thought pursuing spirituality was a weakness, but I soon changed my mind about that when I realised how many top-achievers sought something more than what money could buy.

This all-too-common situation [says Charles Tart[121]] easily makes for an ineffective and stuttering kind of spiritual search, two or three steps forward (that spiritual idea or experience rings true in my heart!) and two or three steps back (scientifically ridiculous — I must be stupid or crazy!). One day our heart and head open towards the spiritual, and then the next day our (apparently) scientific mind rules it out as an illusion and delusion.

He goes on to say:

So here you are, a human being with a yearning for something higher than simple material gratification, something 'spiritual.' Yet modern science, the most powerful knowledge-refinement system in history, which has led to enormous power over the physical world, seems to tell you in no uncertain terms that you yearn for nothing but fantasy – superstitious, outmoded nonsense that will make you feel less fit to live in the 'real' world …. [Yet] something in us yearns for the higher thing we vaguely call 'spirit,' but we don't want to feel stupid or crazy …. I've talked to innumerable people who consciously thought of themselves as spiritual seekers, who were often quite knowledgeable about spiritual matters but, nevertheless, had something in them holding them back, doubting, sabotaging and invalidating their own spiritual knowledge.

The Circle of Friends (satsang[122]) started well but later hiccupped, the numbers dwindled, and I concluded that it wasn't what people were looking for and decided to let it fizzle out on its own if that's what it had to do. Late one Sunday afternoon, I received an unexpected, anonymous text on my mobile phone quoting Gandhi: 'It's unwise to be too sure of one's own wisdom. It is healthy to be reminded that the strongest might weaken and the wisest might err'. I immediately took the message to heart and applied it to the Circle and to me. Was someone politely trying to point out something by inference, which I had missed? Had I inadvertently stepped into the realms of ego and become someone I wasn't? The text bothered me a lot. I took it seriously, my mood slowly changed and my sense of grace was being undermined. As time passed, I felt powerless, ordinary, phoney and uninspired. Life was like driving my car with the handbrake on – a strong vehicle with a full tank of fuel but smoke

---

[121] *The End of Materialism,* Charles T. Tart, New Harbinger Publications and Noetic Books, 2009.
[122] *Satsang* (Sanskrit sat = true, sanga = company) is a concept in Indian philosophy that involves (1) the company of the 'highest truth,' (2) the company of a guru, or (3) company with an assembly of persons who listen to, talk about, and assimilate the truth – *Wiktionary.*

pouring from its wheels and an engine about to seize. In hindsight, I'm astounded at the rate and depth of my decline over such an apparently insignificant message. I now realise that I applied it directly to me and it touched a very sensitive nerve: it challenged my validity to practice. When I reread my invitation to the Circle, I noticed that even back then, I had major doubts about my suitability to host the event, which kindled those feelings of stupidity and craziness of which Charles Tart speaks.

Discovering the Real Me

Taking to my spiritual journey was like a drunk trying to find his way home on a dark and misty night. Smudged by ego's intoxicating, hedonistic blur, I almost lost my way. I feared falling to the ground. For then, lacking co-ordination, strength and willpower it would have been difficult rising up and continuing. I might have lain there in a crumpled heap on some cold concrete sidewalk anxiously hoping I wouldn't be abused, and yet too ashamed to ask for help. A strong intuition urged me to stay on my feet to avoid danger. Instinctively I knew I needed to go home to the spiritual safety of that haven. I also had a general sense of the route I should take to get there. But the oppressive fog of worldly trappings played its part to obfuscate the way. There were times of inactivity as I struggled to find and focus on the next landmark in the misty haze. Once I had that fuzzy goal in sight, I mustered just enough courage to let go my safe anchorage and teeter to the next secure waypoint.

I'd fought off the thugs that tried to hold me back on this perilous trip home. I'd staggered into the oncoming lights of materialism and at the last possible instant, returned to the safety of the pavement. I was grateful to the good Samaritans who compassionately showed me the safest and quickest path to where I needed to go. Sometimes, when the mist lifted, I walked briskly and with purpose as though not drunk at all. But there were times when I lost all sense of direction and believed I'd never make it home.

The moment I doubted my aptness to host the Circle of Friends meetings, I'd lost my bearings and a growing sense of hopelessness clawed at my heart. The night seemed more oppressive and the mist thickened. But I hid my fears well, fooling those around me into believing that I would be okay. Nobody, unless they knew me well, ever guessed there was a growing, stagnant, subterranean pool of doubt. The self-doubt of my youth once had a deep taproot but I thought I had weeded it out, and my faltering thus seemed strange and out of context. The spiritual high that emerged after attending Ram Dass's retreat slowly dampened and earlier feelings of spiritual phoniness emerged once more. I didn't doubt my capabilities or wisdom; I challenged my authenticity and validity. I kept asking myself, 'Why me?'

I readily recognised and admired others who courageously accepted their spiritual purpose, but somehow I felt afraid to walk down the same path. I once wrote of my spiritual inertia as a 'fear of spiritual narcissism'. Narcissus was a young Greek man who, in ancient mythology, pathologically fell in love with his own reflection in a pool of water. I became afraid that I might succumb to my ego in a similar way. The following quotation seemed to sum it up for me:

> The Inner Critic makes each of us a child. As we become the child [...] we lose our sense of self. We are no longer self-contained, self-respecting adults. We look to others for validation. Our self-worth is based upon their opinion of us. Thus, everyone around us becomes a mother or a father whose support and approval is desperately needed to protect us from the constant criticism of the Inner Critic.[123]

University degrees, diplomas and all other certificates conferred by professors and teachers recognise academic effort and attest to the student's competence to practise. Those who embark on a spiritual path have to attest to their own readiness, which becomes an act of self-certification and self-validation. This can be a risky business when dealing with one's ego. I suspect that I was looking for an external endorsement from a respected person of authority who could vouch for my fitness to do my work; but no one besides God could ever give me that. I had grandiose visions, held captive behind bars of doubt, that left me at a standstill and I needed some help.

I so wanted to speak to Ram Dass personally about my dilemma, even just to chat over a cup of tea or via Skype, but I vacillated repeatedly, questioning whether I should or shouldn't ask him. I kept making the same excuses why I shouldn't go: he's probably inundated with requests; he won't have time to see me; there are more important people needing his time; and many more.

When Johann invited me to his graduation ceremony at Auckland University, I immediately reckoned I could take a few days round trip from New Zealand to Hawaii to visit Ram Dass, so I set aside my fears and wrote requesting an audience with him. Weeks passed without an answer and I was embarrassed at having had the temerity to ask. Time ticked by and I needed to book my flights and so I abandoned the idea of seeing him and paid for my return tickets to New Zealand instead. A week after that, I received a reply from Raghu Markus in Malibu,

---

[123] *Hal and Sidra Stone*

writing on behalf of Ram Dass, asking if I could plan my visit around mid-September, a quiet period at the Ram Dass house. This suited me perfectly as it was in the middle of my New Zealand trip and easily allowed me to fly north to Maui. Instead of a chat over a cup of tea, Ram Dass proposed a five-day stay in his house and I was overwhelmed by his generosity and accepted it graciously. Yet trepidation and self-questioning gnawed on the old bones of self-doubt. I now felt even phonier at having secured an invitation to live with my teacher in his house.

On the previous occasion that I travelled to New Zealand, I took far too much luggage and now decided to try a different strategy. I filled a small backpack with some simple essentials for my trip to Ram Dass and placed it in a larger suitcase along with the other items I needed for Johann's graduation and the much colder, wetter and unpredictable weather of *Aotearoa* (the Māori name for New Zealand meaning 'The Land of the Long White Cloud'.)

I arrived in Auckland completely jetlagged, a feeling I look forward to and quite enjoy as it produces disorientation, mild delirium, feelings of intoxication and it often separates me from my body in a manner similar to the way I felt after my time in dark cells. Consciousness and Body seem to coexist independently of each other. It induces sustained trance states and I'm fascinated by the thought-loops in my brain as it obsesses over trivial problems and ideas that seem unsolvable. With my mind in this strange state and my body feeling like a mechanically marching wind-up toy, I seem to operate in a completely different realm outside the normal space-time continuum.

The days in New Zealand prior to visiting Ram Dass brought constant challenges that ironically helped me to solve a lot of the doubt I carried within myself.

Years of self-validation were an attempt to disentangle a multiplicity of doubt. It took enormous past resourcefulness to reframe the notion of having been 'raised in sin'. Functioning in a straight world is a homosexual nightmare demanding endless suggestive counterattacks to find one's place in society. And, one should not step blindly into a world of alternative beliefs about one's relationship to the Godhead without a generous dollop of humility, lest one gets entangled by ego. It's good to tread cautiously because there's a fine line between self-deprivation and self-importance, and it's along that narrow path in between the two that one should aim.

As often as I devalued myself, so did Johann. We tried to help each other through the hardships of gay life during our many years together, validating ourselves individually and collectively. But our closeness produced a jealous competitiveness. My successes exaggerated his weaknesses and for a time the same applied to me too. However, the more I embraced my new non-judgemental attitude of pure acceptance of what is, the less jealous I became of his achievements. He chose a more formal academic path through life. I never formally qualified beyond matric. Where his enterprising entrepreneurial endeavours systematically failed, mine seemed to have the Midas touch. This occasionally opened the way for anxiety to prick its ears, raise its hackles and growl a little. Whenever we meet, our third day together is predictably the moment of conflict.

Johann graduated, extending his qualifications in the world of psychology and counselling. I was running a busy and acclaimed hypnosis practice but without much academic ado. So he often pointed out my lack of formal education and questioned my unqualified ability to carry out my work properly and safely, given the stringent framework imposed on practitioners in his field. His barbed statements often penetrated deeply and touched nerves of self-doubt but they also forced me to create counter arguments and to build a clearer picture in my head of what I was trying to accomplish. He diagnosed patient's mental ailments and prescribed sessions of curative counselling; I offered clients an alternative way of looking at life and they diagnosed and healed themselves. This insight gave me a renewed sense of purpose, my objectives came into clearer focus and I became determined to continue.

I arrived in Honolulu on 6 September 2010, one day before my departure from Auckland (because I crossed the dateline), and stayed in a hotel in Waikiki for a few days to mentally prepare for my onward journey to Maui.

Yvonne, my soul mate and present life partner, sent a message of hope and encouragement to me: 'I hope Ram Dass will help you find within you the strength to believe in your extraordinary capabilities and acknowledge the magnificent being that you are'.

I wrote this in my journal:

> I ask myself again and again, "Why am I here?" Is it to seek personal endorsement and recognition for the spiritual work I do? Is it perhaps my need for validation, to cancel out an ancient notion of feelings of unworthiness? I'm like a toy duck, stuck in the vortex of the bathwater as it swirls down the plug – I'm afloat, I look happy and

buoyant but I'm actually quite trapped. It's as though there's an invisible force holding me back. Many friends try to reassure me but no matter what they say, nothing seems able to break this force and I suspect the only way to do so is from within.

Frankly, part of my reason for visiting Ram Dass was a hope of receiving his unambiguous approval, validating my path and confirming that I was justified in trusting my instincts and sharing my spiritual insights with others. As much as I longed for his affirmation, I also knew in my heart that he would never give it to me merely to appease my ego; and I berated myself for even thinking of such a thing.

I wrote a lot in those five days, and I meditated even more. I rose every morning around 5 a.m. and walked for miles before returning to the hotel. The short gap during those pre-dawn hours gave the city time to breathe. Nocturnal residents had retired, exhausted from their long hours of thumping nightlife, while the diurnal visitors wouldn't be seen in the streets until the shops opened. The multitude of worshippers of Ra were still in bed, waiting for the resurrection of their god, before resuming their daily prostrations on the Waikiki beaches.

Every day after my walk, I made myself comfortable near the pool, ate a breakfast of tropical fruit, and wrote in my journal, returning to the room only after midday to meditate over the insights of the morning. It became a wonderful time of simplicity and solitude during which I seemed to consolidate and resolve most of my issues, which left me wondering what the next five days with Ram Dass would bring as there wasn't much more that I needed from him.

---oooOooo---

It was a quick 160km noonday commuter flight from Honolulu on Hawaiian Airlines in a southeasterly direction to Maui's Kahului airport and it took no time for me to find my way to the kerbside at Kahului for Kathleen Murphy (Dassi Ma) to fetch me.

Kathleen is bubbly, friendly and superefficient. She takes no nonsense. Originally from Philadelphia, Dassi Ma has been Ram Dass's private secretary and companion for a long time, taking care of his health, his visitors, his organic meals, his bodily needs, his internet and his diary. Her constant presence enables him to continue his work in selfless service despite his stroke in 1997, and his age, for he was born on 6 April 1931 in Massachusetts. I met her before, during my retreat in 2007, so I was familiar with her appearance and kept an eye on everyone pulling up at the kerbside to see if it was she.

While I waited, I watched a solitary cop who, like a lone ranger, paced up and down the pavement, keeping chancers from abandoning their wrongly-parked cars in search of the people they were meeting. It amused me no end, for he took his job very seriously and some mighty arguments ensued as he enforced the traffic rules that angry drivers challenged. Entirely engrossed in one such altercation, I lost concentration for a moment and was quite surprised to receive a sudden humungous warm hug.

'Aloha! Welcome to Maui. Namasté, Tom,' Kathleen said, beaming with excitement and enthusiasm. 'It's good to have you with us!' She hung a polished nut necklace around my neck, thus completing her greeting in traditional Hawaiian style. Kukui nuts, placed on a dry palm leaf and burned one at a time for light in ancient Hawaiian times, became a primitive timekeeper, since it took about fifteen minutes for a nut to burn. They are also versatile in cuisine, medicine, as tattoo ink, varnish and have many other practical applications and uses. I returned her greeting as she pointed across the parking lot, indicating the direction we should take to the car.

I slung my bag over my shoulder and trotted after her at a quick pace. She carried her short, stocky frame in a matronly manner but that's where the matronly image ended. She was dressed in beach shorts, a summer blouse, sandals and a large corrugated brimmed sunhat that almost flopped down to her shoulders – all in purple hues and, as I later learned, purple is the only colour that she wears.

We approached a little metallic blue Chrysler Sebring convertible with its roof retracted, and I remarked that 'I wouldn't leave a car open like that in Africa!' Dassi Ma just looked at me with a quick sideways glance, a flash of incredulity, as I dumped my bag onto its back seat. She walked around to the other side as I hopped in to the passenger seat. Everything I saw quickly forced me to recalibrate my rather austere and serious mental image of what I expected of this moment. It was all so incongruent, her outfit, the car and especially the plastic effigy of Barak Obama standing ankle-deep in a blob of white poster-tack on the dashboard, his head attached to a spring, nodding incessantly and persuasively with the movement of the car, each nod in full agreement with the sign behind him that read 'Yes we can!' My mental image was quite different: I'd expected a Hanuman *murthi* or a picture of Maharaj-ji in the car, and not Obama. I expected her to be calm, serious and serene, not effervescent, buoyant, beach-like and light-hearted.

Dassi Ma paid the parking fee and we zoomed around the south side of the airport, heading off east. The sun was directly overhead and I squirmed and fidgeted, trying to lift my small shirt collar to shade my neck against its blistering rays.

'Dassi Ma,' I asked, rather sheepishly, 'could we raise the roof as my skin is very sensitive and the sun is too strong?' She never slowed down or acknowledged my request but rummaged behind my seat as she drove and soon presented her trophy – a tiny summer peaked hat, in the brightest pink I've ever seen. Designed for the female skull, it perched precariously on my big head like a cherry on a cupcake. I wanted to say, 'You must be joking! Me, wear that!' but I didn't know her well enough yet and didn't want to offend, so I placed the silly thing on my head, knowing that my blush was orders of magnitude brighter than the hat. Speeding along in a shiny little blue car, sitting next to the sunshine woman in purple, wearing a necklace of rather large polished nuts, I held onto the pink hat to stop it from flying away, and I kept thinking, 'I must look like a real twit!' I tried ever so hard to bring my reeling mind into a calm and egoless state, in tune with the spiritual theme of my pilgrimage, but everything was surreal and it felt like an out-of-body experience as we drove away from the city into the countryside, chatting about my adventures thus far.

'May I treat you to some frozen yoghurt?' she asked, as we pulled into the parking lot of a little cluster of shops very near the Paia Inn Hotel, almost wiping out a solitary cyclist. Paia is a small wedge-shaped coastal town located on the foothills of Haleakalā, the taller of two volcanoes that rises some three kilometres out of the sea and which helped to shape the island. Nobody seemed to notice my pink hat and beaded necklace because the town is a haven for retired sixties-hippies who came from the mainland to live here in the gentler tropical climate of Maui. Dressed predominantly in surfer's trousers, sandals and sarongs, none of them seemed to care much about my bizarre garb and I felt a lot safer and far less conspicuous. I also realised that Dassi Ma couldn't have been more appropriately dressed.

The frozen yoghurt was delicious and Dassi Ma gently set the terms of my stay at the house as we spooned it from our typically American disposable cups: 'You will be staying in the guest suite where you have a private kitchen. We will now go to Mana Foods where you can buy breakfast and lunch supplies. Two professional vegetarian chefs, Kelly and Pip, take turns making our supper. Ram Dass will see you tomorrow morning at 10 a.m.'

I nodded obediently, thinking of Obama on the dashboard, while my past ego found momentary resurrection and boorishly bristled at her telling me what to do. Despite her gentle manner, I reacted in a defensive way. It harks from my youth when, at the age of eighteen, I was imprisoned by the South African Defence Force in their detention barracks in Pretoria for two years for refusing conscription. Ever since then, anything that smacks of officiousness quickly rubs me up the wrong way. It is an Achilles heel that took a long time to alter yet still rises up unexpectedly. I consoled myself that her set of rules might be vital in dealing with visitors to the house who could be brash, pushy or invasive, disrespecting Ram Dass's need for privacy and space.

Laden with an armful of provisions in brown paper packets, we left Mana Foods, an impressive whole food organic emporium that supplies residents with local products; and we set off on our forty-minute journey east along the twisting, turning northern Hana coastal highway to Ram Dass's house in the Manawai Estate at Haiku-Pauwela.

It was a beautiful autumn afternoon as we drove through the gates and up to the main entrance of the house, and I had a strange feeling come over me, knowing that somewhere inside was Ram Dass. It added to the surrealism of the day's experience. At some level, it felt as though I had come home – and yet I was a total stranger here.

I quickly shed my hat and returned it to its place behind the seat before anyone could spot me from inside the house. I then scooped up my bag and parcels and followed Dassi Ma to the annex that would be my home for the next week. Unlike our African suburban homes, the door was unlocked and there were no keys. No burglar bars covered the windows or trellis gates to secure the doors.

She gestured for me to enter and I stepped into a large, richly decorated room, about the size of a double garage, furnished in rich Indian colours and fabrics. In front of me, an invitingly comfortable double bed, piled with soft cushions and covered with a deep red silky duvet. To my left a picture window, facing into the driveway and garden. In front of the window was a small shrine with a copious supply of incense, a few candles and a statue of the Buddha. Two upright wooden chairs flanked the low table, while placed on the floor in front of it where one could sit and meditate was a small carpet and a firm cushion. To the right of the bed was a tall and narrow bookcase filled with many, many spiritual books; and I had the distinct feeling that each one had been personally read by Ram Dass.

Pictures of Ram Dass, Maharaj-ji, Hanuman and other Hindu sacred figures hung on the walls and all the counter surfaces contained personal trinkets given to or collected by Ram Dass. An abundance of freshly picked tropical flowers adorned the room, some in vases, others lovingly placed amongst the ornaments. I felt immediately at home and knew I'd be happy staying there.

'Come right in,' said Dassi Ma, gesturing for me to step into the room properly. There, behind the door, was an attractive small wooden desk up against the wall, beneath a window, with a tranquil, unbroken view of the Pacific Ocean. Further to my right, beyond the desk and at right angles to the front entrance, was the door to the toilet.

'Follow me through this strange bit of architecture,' she commanded, as she disappeared into the toilet. Still clutching my bag and parcels, I followed her curiously into the confined space as she opened up a second door on the back wall that revealed a lovely open-plan kitchen and a simply furnished, compact lounge. I dumped my parcels on the kitchen counter, shed my bag on the sofa and complemented her on the welcoming comfort and charm of the space and its incredible energy.

The back door led from the lounge onto a small private wooden deck, furnished with an aluminium table and chairs. Dassi Ma showed me an aluminium collapsible ramp stowed next to the door and taught me how to assemble it so that Ram Dass could enter easily when he visited. My mind became quite numb with information and my heart burst with excitement. I loved being in this very special place.

'I'll give you a little while to unpack and settle in, and then I'll return to take you on a tour, a short way down the road, to a waterfall where we can swim. Later on, after we get back, we'll walk to the rock overlooking the sea,' she said, and quickly exited through the lavatory. I stood alone in the living room looking at the countertop-shrine that spanned the entire length of the wall. Adorned with hibiscus flowers, many photographs and a fascinating collection of trinkets, it honoured Maharaj-ji. A large framed photographic portrait of him hung on the wall above the shrine. It showed him in his typical sitting posture, one leg folded over the other with his foot poking out from his blanket, his innocent, benevolent, toothless grin beaming across his face. It reminded me of a bygone time when Ram Dass sat at the feet of his guru and I was humbled, honoured and respectful of the sense that I now stood, second-generation in line, to carry Maharaj-ji's message of love and selfless service to others. Never before had I felt more prepared to do just that.

I lit some candles and a few sticks of incense that came from a packet originating somewhere in India, that proclaimed 'Packed Lovingly for Ram Dass'. The room filled with twirls of white perfumed smoke as I brewed a pot of strong tea. I felt Maharaj-ji's presence throughout the house.

Unpacking what little I had was easy and, as I sipped my tea, I had plenty of time to add a few more pages to Volume 21 of my ten-year series of journals in which I documented my spiritual awakening. My fountain pen slid effortlessly across the paper, leaving its squiggly record of thoughts that flowed freely in this heady, aromatic, spiritual atmosphere. Dassi Ma's 'little while' was a lot longer than that, which didn't bother me at all as it's a common phenomenon back home (we call it 'African Time'), and besides which, I enjoyed writing in my journal.

The sun's sting had subsided by the time we collected our towels and cameras and hopped into the little blue car to take our afternoon tour. Flanked by enormous homesteads each on acres of land, the suburban byroad from Ram Dass's house leads away from the ocean for a kilometre, up towards the Hana highway. This stretch of road is beautiful and tranquil with paddocks of horses, orchards, trimmed hedges and splashes of colourful tropical shrubs. The simple picket or wire fences that enclose these homes enhance the feeling of spaciousness. Crime seems almost non-existent here but, on closer observation, one notices a different kind of problem. Boarded up, many homes stand unoccupied. 'It's the result of the recession,' explained Dassi Ma, referring to the big financial crunch that began in late 2007, caused by indiscriminate and unscrupulous sub-prime bank loans that, like a badly made soufflé, deflated, causing a worldwide monetary meltdown. A lot of these were holiday homes owned by mainland residents who could no longer afford their upkeep and the banks had to foreclose on them.

Instead of turning right onto the highway leading towards Paia, we turned the opposite way and drove along the convoluted road towards Hana. Just seven kilometres from the house, Dassi Ma turned into a small kerbside parking lot at Twin Falls Farmstand. We collected our towels and cameras and walked down through the forest thicket on a short stroll to a clear pool where we swam in the chilly water. I stood under the lip of a unique waterfall formed from strata of horizontal volcanic rock. Reduced to smaller, softer droplets as it splashed from ledge to ledge, the clear mountain water seemed to energise me as it touched my bare skin. It was a nice time to get to know her and it gave me chance to tell her a bit more about myself and to glean more information that might help me to prepare for my time with Ram Dass.

It was late afternoon and a bit cold so we dried off quickly and returned to the house where we dumped our wet gear, leaving us enough time for an afternoon walk to the nearby rock before the sun had chance to set. It was an easy walk to the flat, rocky perch overlooking the small cove of Uaoa Bay, where the restless waves pounded and churned at the dark volcanic rock face that sloped abruptly downwards, some fifty or sixty meters into the sea. 'This is a good place to come to for one's sunrise meditation,' said Dassi Ma, as we sat bum-to-bum, sharing this narrow natural bench. I set my mental clock to remind me to rise early the next morning so that I could return to Meditation Rock at sunrise. The light faded fast after the sun disappeared behind the ridge and Dassi Ma said, 'Come! We need to get back because supper will soon be ready. One of the chefs will bring it around to your apartment and when you're done, you can return the tray to the main house'. I had secretly hoped that we'd eat together but Dassi Ma's plans were different, and I respected their need for privacy.

Upon our return, she introduced Ken, a long-term houseguest who helped with the heavier chores around the property in exchange for board and lodging with Ram Dass.

I thanked her for her kindness and generosity and as we parted for the evening she said, 'You're very welcome to move freely about the property at all times so please make use of the heated pool and hot-tub out front'. I ate an excellent organic, wholesome supper silently in front of Maharaj-ji's shrine, in a state of total peace and bliss. It was early when I went to bed and sleep came easily.

It was still a bit dark when I set off for my walk to Meditation Rock the next morning but the autumn sea air was warm and wrapped itself like a dressing gown around me and I felt safe and loved. The walk took me away from the house, along a narrow tar road for about three hundred meters. To the left lay an unoccupied house with magnificent unbroken vistas northwards out over the Pacific and I fantasised about living there. I wasn't sure that I could readily settle into the brash, competitive and materialistic American way of life that set the tone in Honolulu, yet this part of Maui did seem quite different from the mainland culture and the people here appeared gentler and softer.

A couple of dogs, huddled together on the veranda of the house to my right, bounded across the paddock towards the wire fence with the conflicting intention of protecting their territory and satisfying their curiosity. The horses didn't flinch as the dogs dashed past them to meet me. Wagging their tails and barking, they followed me all the way to the end of the road and

I'm sure, given the opportunity, they would have readily accompanied me on the last leg of my walk down towards the sea.

A huge stone Chinese Shishi Guardian Lion, ball in mouth, marked the path. They're believed to have powerful mythic protective powers and traditionally they stood guard over imperial palaces, but this one had the more modest task of standing sentry over a cluster of flagged residential letter boxes.

The walk is easy and relatively flat, the last fifty meters running beside a well-tended orchard before reaching the steep slope down to the sea. The little rock bench, where Dassi Ma and I sat the evening before, marks the end of the path like a full stop at the end of a sentence. As I reached the gentle ridge on the orchard pathway, I saw somebody else had beaten me to Meditation Rock and, not wanting to disturb, I slowed down and padded softly forward. It was Kenneth, in deep meditation. I found an outlook slightly behind him and settled in to watch the sun split the horizon with brilliant rays of golden light.

He sat there for quite some time until a faraway mechanical drone penetrated the silence. Two guys on jet skis hugged the black rocky coastline on their morning ride towards Hana. We were miles from nowhere and I wondered how far they had already travelled and how far they intended going. Their arrival interrupted Ken's meditation and he realised that I was there. We greeted, and I moved forward to join him on the bench. He told me he came from Seattle and his parents thought he should have followed his younger brother's lead and studied instead of hanging out with the 'Old Man in Maui'. He didn't stay long as it was his turn to make Ram Dass's breakfast because Dassi Ma had left early to attend to other business. I stayed a while longer until the idea of breakfast could no longer be quelled, returned to the house and prepared a bowlful of Old Fashioned Oats Porridge, which I ate with a splash of soya milk and a sprinkling of brown sugar.

At ten, Ken popped in and said, 'Ram Dass would like to come around and meet you in about an hour. Would that be okay?' I was delighted and a little nervous too and the hour seemed to pass incredibly slowly even though I tried everything to distract my mind, which was on a mission of its own and refused to be still. I tried to write, but no words came. I tried to meditate but I couldn't. I made tea and paced about instead. Eventually, muffled voices indicated Ram Dass's arrival as Ken helped him negotiate the corners of the narrow cement skirting outside the apartment.

I had already placed the aluminium ramp against the small step, the door was open and I went outside to greet them. 'Hello Tom,' said Ram Dass in his warm, calm tone. I let Ken do the real work of negotiating the wheelchair up the ramp. I wanted to help but didn't want to interfere. Once inside, Ken asked if I could make a few small adjustments to the layout of the room and I moved a chair and display table to the other side to make space for Ram Dass' wheelchair. Ram Dass made the final adjustments himself, positioning himself closer to the sofa and unhitching his feet from the footrests. Ken quickly bade us farewell and left.

Ram Dass carefully placed a small analogue bedside clock on the table next to him to keep track of time. I smiled a little as it reminded me of some psychotherapy sessions I'd attended many years before. The counsellor'd began every session in the same way, touching and repositioned his clock ever so slightly, thereby implying in a non-verbal way that the clock had started counting the limited time I had with him and that I should use it wisely. I secretly wondered if Ram Dass was implying the same thing.

I adore Ram Dass's simple, casual style. He arrived barefooted, dressed in floppy blue cotton shorts and a well-worn beige tee shirt. I was a bit more reserved and dressed in a white cotton short-sleeved collared shirt, blue jeans and sandals; but formalities weren't important here.

I opened our conversation by telling him an abbreviated version of what I've written here and my motives for coming to Hawaii for the second time. I told him of my Jehovah's Witness past, my expulsion and the resulting estrangement from my family. I described how I'd been asked by my mother to come and help her attend to dad during the final weeks of his life and how, even at times like that, there was a distinct gap between us, dad and his beliefs and me and mine. I also emphasised to Ram Dass that I wanted to meet him as a spiritual friend, a co-worker carrying his, and of course Maharaj-ji's, message to receptive minds wherever I encountered them. I explained that I thought I needed some validation and authentication but that I had resolved most of those issues en-route and had arrived without an agenda and just a desire to hang out with him.

We spoke as though we were lifelong friends and I guess in some realm we always have been. It was a strangely comfortable feeling. Everything had pointed to a stiff and formal encounter but it wasn't anything like that at all. An hour passed, and then another. I made tea and it felt as though I knew Ram Dass personally, had a deep connection with him, and I sensed he saw me in much the same way.

We finished our tea. I collected the cups, stacked them in the sink, and returned to my spot on the sofa where Ram Dass picked up the conversation by asking, 'What is your spiritual purpose, Tom?'

It was an easy question to answer because I had given it plenty of prior thought. I quickly replied with a statement that I knew by heart: '*My spiritual purpose is to use the resources at my disposal, in order to reach the hearts and minds of many, that I may bring them a message of hope, truth and purpose, so they might find themselves'.* I had distilled this spiritual mission statement from reading and rereading the original texts that inspired me. I found purpose from the teacher/student relationship described in the *Course* and from a passage in *Conversations with God*. The *Course* says, 'A teacher of God is anyone who chooses to be one [...]. A light has entered the darkness. It may be a single light, but that is enough [...]. It calls for teachers to speak for It and redeem the world. Many hear It, but few will answer'.[124] *Conversations with God* says, 'Behold the darkness yet curse it not. Rather, be a light unto the darkness, and so transform it. Let your light shine before men, that those who stand in the darkness will be illuminated by the light of your being and all of you will see, at last, Who You Really Are'.[125]

Ram Dass let me speak for quite a while before drawing the conversation back to his question. He asked: 'You say your spiritual purpose is to help others find themselves?'

'Yes, Ram Dass,' I replied.

'But, *what is your spirit's purpose*?' It took him a little while to formulate and articulate these words and they had a surprising effect on me. His question caught me completely off-guard for it carried a very astute twist and I didn't have a glib answer to give him.

Ram Dass noted my awkwardness and continued, 'The *work* you do is to help others ...' he paused for a long while, his deeply-set watery eyes glazed as if he'd entered into a trance to fetch the remainder of the question from another realm, '... but what do *you* get out of it? What returns to your spirit?'

---

[124] *A Course in Miracles*, M-1.1.1-1.2.7, Combined Volume (Third Edition) Copyright© 2007 by the Foundation for A Course in Miracles.
[125] *Conversations with God, Book Three*, Neale Donald Walsch, Hodder and Stoughton, 1998.

Although I had never before applied myself to this line of reasoning, I thought I knew the answer to his question: tainted by dogma and having performed rituals for the sake of ritual, having witnessed much hypocrisy, my faith had for a time dispersed but Spirit had no urgency and waited patiently for Mind to orientate itself back towards Truth. Where I once chose to feel worthless and sinful, I now honoured all my experiences and saw each as a stepping-stone that would ultimately lead to *samadhi*.[126] Through my experiences, I want others to realise that no matter how difficult life is, one can transcend one's suffering and emerge in a new headspace of bliss, ready to embrace life from a different perspective. In response to a journalist's question regarding his message to the world, Gandhi replied, 'my life is my message' and I hoped that I could inspire others by sharing my story, with all its highs and lows, as an encouragement to those who feel as lost I once was. Ironically, though, as altruistic as this is, Ram Dass revealed that it isn't Spirit's real purpose either.

Ram Dass was in no haste for me to discover the answer. He masterfully yet simply challenged my ideas and demolished the foundations upon which they were built. Everyday conversation expects a flow of constant banter. Silence is awkward and compels us to speak. This was not the case now. Ram Dass drifted off into the cosmos on an inner journey of his own, giving me ample time to reflect.

I sought clarity of thought about the relationship between spirit, mind and body. I needed to consolidate my understanding of these aspects of my being before I could answer Ram Dass's question regarding spirit's purpose and what, if anything, returns to it. Many concepts came to mind in those fifteen minutes of stillness.

To know whether spirit has purpose, one ought to know first what spirit is. Here's my best guess: spirit is an individual and yet ubiquitous superset of incorporeal non-quantifiable essence, which bestows life to its distinctly separate subset of corporeal energy, substance or form. Whenever I'm in doubt about something I always refer to an authority in the field. Who better to ask about spirit than an entity living outside the realms of human form? Emmanuel, the disembodied being who spoke through Pat Rodegast, says, 'Soul, Spirit, Consciousness: these terms might be seen as synonymous. As I use them, a being is eternal consciousness and

---

[126] *Samadhi* has been described as a non-dualistic state of consciousness in which the consciousness of the experiencing subject becomes one with the experienced object, and in which the mind becomes still, one-pointed or concentrated while the person remains conscious – *Wikipedia*.

this is housed in what humanity considers a soul, which is, of course, the realm of spirit. Their absolute definition is impossible'.[127]

According to the laws of physics, energy is conserved in a closed system, which means it can never be created or destroyed although it may frequently change form. I feel that spirit shares these attributes. Spirit came into being through a higher creative process and has no choice over its existence. It never created itself and it certainly cannot terminate itself, it cannot commit spiritual suicide. Only the power that created it has the power to void it.

To me, spirit contains all of one's infinite potential. Microseconds before the Big Bang, in the infinite curvature of space and time, there existed a single point of pure potential, known in cosmology as *singularity*. Contained in this infinitesimally small and thus non-existent capsule was an impending universe. Enclosed therein was every possible thought, idea, word, action and form, not in compressed physicality but as opportunity, waiting expectantly to take shape. Science still debates whether our universe is an open or closed system, meaning that it could ultimately collapse in on itself in repeating cycles of Big Bang followed by Big Crunch (a closed system) or else it might eventually just fizzle away to nothingness (an open system)[128]. Whichever the case, there will come a time when singularity, the pure potential of an imminent universe, eventually reaches its fullest realised extent possible. All possibility then becomes fully realised. That moment is a time when all thoughts have been thought, all ideas are exhausted, all words are spoken, all actions are enacted and after all forms are created. The laws of cosmology and nature let the universe unfold as effortlessly as a rosebud coming to full bloom. So too is my idea of spirit. It's an intangible field of infinite possibilities, some realised, others yet to be realised. In time, Mind will successfully exploit all of Spirit's potential in the same way that the laws of nature utilise all of singularity's possibility to create the universe. The potential that drives the universe has no expectation of what it will become. It leaves the creation to the laws of nature that govern it. I suspect that our spirit, the field of all possibilities of who or what we will be, also has no expectations or attachment to its outcome. It remains wholly indifferent and leaves the manifestation to the creative forces of Mind.

Every experience of ours is simultaneously experienced by God. Every bit of wisdom gleaned from our experiences accretes through us to God. The moment in time, somewhere infinitely far into the future, when every possibility is fully and finally realised, Spirit will know Who It

---

[127] *Emmanuel's Book*, compiled by Pat Rodegast and Judith Stanton, Bantam Books, 1987.
[128] The Illustrated *A Brief History of Time*, Stephen Hawkins, Bantam Press, 1996.

Really Is. Simultaneously, as this wisdom reaches the godhead then he *fully experiences* Who He Really Is. To some extent, this implies a finite beginning and end to God but I know that that's an impossible notion given that he has no beginning and no end but then remember, our universe is not the only one but one of many in a system of parallel universes, a gigantic, enormous, unfathomably large meta-universe.

Spirit has presence in the universe. It has an awareness of being at the highest levels of consciousness. But does Spirit have purpose? Because, in order to have purpose, it must have a goal, a target, an aim, or at least a desire or intention. Purpose is possible only in situations of action or intent. However, as a field of limitless possibility providing only source potential, spirit might not therefore indulge in action. Spirit is in a pure state of *being* and not in a state of *doing*. But it is not just inert submissive potential, it has consciousness too – *Spirit Is*. Karma is the natural law of causation – every thought or action has a consequence. Since spirit is merely a non-attached observer and not a doer, karma is meaningless in the context of spirit. The word *culpability* derives from the Latin word *culpa* meaning fault or guilt. Culpability in law stems from *actions* in commission of a crime or offence caused purposefully, knowingly, negligently or recklessly. Inert as it is, it is impossible to hold spirit accountable; there is no culpability in *being*. What a refreshing thought to realise that spirit (our ultimate state of being) is untarnished, blameless and perpetually sinless.

If spirit was just submissive potential *without consciousness*, the universe would not have 'existed'. *Observed* by Spirit's awareness the unfolding universe is thereby imbued with meaning. A question posed in an old 1910 physics book regarding sound, asks, 'If a tree falls in a forest and no one is around to hear it, does it make a sound?'[129] William Fossett extended that idea nicely:

> Tease apart the threads [of the natural world] and the pattern vanishes. The design is in how the cloth-maker arranges the threads: this way and that, as fashion dictates [...]. To say something is meaningful is to say that that is how we arrange it so; how we comprehend it to be, and what is comprehended by you or I may not be by a cat, for example. If a tree falls in a park and there is no-one to hand, it is silent and invisible and nameless. And if we were to vanish, there would be no tree at all; any meaning would vanish along with us. Other than what the cats make of it all, of course.

---

[129] *Physics*, Charles Riborg Mann, George Ransom Twiss, 1910.

I began to find answers to Ram Dass's astute question. Spirit, as conscious inert submissive potential, is incapable of having purpose. The answer to his question: 'What is your spiritual purpose, Tom' became obvious: 'None, I have no spiritual purpose.' What returns to Spirit from every one of our experiences is wisdom that helps us know ourselves better. Imagine a point of consciousness out in the blackness of space. If it had no form and nothing around it as reference, it would know of its presence but nothing else. It wouldn't know if it filled all of space or only a minute part of it. It would need further references to know more. By manifesting in some shape, it could discover more about itself. 'Ah, I'm a green cube!' It could then learn the concepts of form versus formlessness, inside versus outside, edges, corners, colour, top and bottom, left and right, and so on. But it still wouldn't know about its size unless another point of consciousness manifest nearby. 'Hi, I'm a red ball!' Both entities would then learn something new: you and me, shape, size, position relative to each other, and so on. Every new trick in the manifestation game, every action, every experience brings wisdom to the entities playing the game.

Precisely what Mind is, is a hotly debated topic but most theorists concur that *conscious experience* and *intellectual thought* constitute it. Metaphysically, mind is a constituent of the greater entity composed of Spirit, Mind and Body. Mind serves spirit as its activating, creative agent. Where spirit is in a continuous, infinite state of *being*, mind is in a constant state of *doing*. Spirit consciously provides limitless inert submissive source potential. Mind utilises this source energy as the crucial element for its creative manifestations. Spirit inspires; mind creates. Mind takes advantage of passing opportunities abundantly supplied by spirit, and through its creativity, influences the behaviour of space-time. Mind, some believe, cannot decline when the body dies.

I once visualised the interactions between spirit and mind as a taut and perfectly flat trampoline. Suppose we flick a marble, representing an arbitrary opportunity of some sort, across its rubber surface. With nothing to block its path, the marble travels straight across the rubber mat and falls off the other side. Spirit constantly offers us opportunities in abundance but without anything on the trampoline to interrupt it, opportunities pass by without being realised. A creative presence must exist if opportunities are to be exploited. Place a heavy metal ball on the trampoline and it will stretch and distort the mat, creating a valley with the ball at its centre. Flick a marble across the trampoline and there's now a high probability that the mat's curvature will capture it and spiral it in to join the ball. Mind is the metal ball in this analogy and it has influence over the opportunities, the marbles, that spirit presents. The energy tapped from every marble that the ball attracts shifts the ball slightly on the mat, just as every opportunity exploited by mind alters it a little – karma – the laws of cause and effect. As the ball slowly drifts from one spot to the next across the trampoline, it begins to attract different kinds of opportunities that were hitherto unavailable. Because mind has free will, it could attract opportunities in one of two ways: naturally without effort, non-attached to outcome and completely non-judgementally; or it could strive, tug, push, manipulate and cajole its way across the mat. Eventually, at the end of eternity, the ball will have moved across the entire surface of the infinitely large mat and every opportunity that could come from the field of infinite possibility will have been realised. I've often wondered why I'm not engaged in the activities of murder and rape, especially after having suspended my judgement of them, and the answer is: my mind is not on the spot on the rubber mat where it is likely to attract experiences of that kind.

The Akashic Record is believed to be a compendium of all cosmic knowledge, including all human experience, and it is seen as The Mind of God[130] or Universal Consciousness. Think of it as paint-trails left by the ball as it moves across the rubber mat. Deep hypnosis, astral projection and certain forms of mysticism may give one access to these records.

This proposition about mind and spirit may seem a bit theoretical until we peek at some contemporary scientific thinking. The Superposition Principle comes from quantum physics and describes mind's influence over phenomena through the act of observation, which thereby alters its state. Once the observer knows its state, this stops it from being in any one of its other states. Using a double-slit apparatus, photons are fired through two parallel slits towards sensors on a plate where they are then measured. This experiment reliably proves that quantum particles (photons) create interference patterns on the sensor if they behave as waves, and as recoil pulses when they behave as particles. The observer can influence the experiment by locking the sensor with a pin to prevent any recoil detection. When the pin is in place, one cannot measure the recoil velocity, only the interference patterns. Experimenters found that interference patterns disappeared whenever they removed the pin. By removing the pin and thus allowing the measurement of recoil velocity, the experimenters had inadvertently set a mental intention to observe particles and not waves. To their surprise, the quantum particles fired at the apparatus behaved in the way that experimenters expected them to behave: no interference patterns occurred and only recoil velocity could be measured. The presence and intentions of the experimenters determined the outcome of the experiment.

---

[130] *Science and the Akashic Field*, Ervin Laszlo, Inner Traditions, 2004.

Mind had a direct influence on matter. For science to understand this principle further, in 1978 John Archibald Wheeler proposed a variation to the double-slit apparatus, whereby the locking and unlocking of the pin could occur *after* the quantum particle passed through the slits and in 2007, it was conclusively demonstrated that the act of observation definitely influences the behaviour of quantum phenomena. Science concurred that mind indeed manipulates matter.

We think our minds have original thoughts and ideas but that's an illusion. Ideas, contained in the field of infinite possibility (Spirit's conscious, limitless, inert, submissive, source potential) lie waiting expectantly to be realised. Mind's creative thinking draws ideas from the field. The Latin word *invenire*, from which we derive the word *invent*, means 'to come upon' and the Greek word *heuriskein*, which gives us the word *heuristic*, means 'to find out', both implying that an idea or thought existed at some realm before we came upon or found it. To dis*cover* it is to remove the covers from it. 'What has been will be again, what has been done will be done again; there is nothing new under the sun.'[131] Everything flows from the field of infinite possibility through mind's creative direction into form. Remember that God simultaneously experiences every experience of ours. The further we draw back towards our source, the closer we come to a conceptual point where everything merges. All my experiences become your experiences. There is a point where we surrender our notion of individuation, and merge with the godhead.

Ego is mind's conceptual identity, created as a sense of personal existence of self, distinct and separate from other egos. It is entirely illusory and the terms *maya* or *samsara* define one's entrapment in it. The ego causes mind to split from its source, spirit, believing that what it perceives through body's senses is its only reality.

'[T]he body is a learning device for the mind' is the *Course's* teaching. Body is like a spacesuit that bristles with sensors able to detect temperature, pressure, olfactory, auditory and visual stimuli. These signals travel along neural pathways to the brain, where they're interpreted and meaning is assigned to them. But, the world out there isn't actually out there – it's inside our head as a complex map of what we *perceive it to be*; how we've judged it so.

I tell the following story to illustrate by practical example how detached the mind can be from what's happening to the body. In my work as a hypnotherapist, I'm regularly asked to assist

---

[131] Ecclesiastes 1:9, New International Version.

people in the management of chronic discomfort. Pain is protective but sometimes it becomes rogue and 'an illness in itself'.[132] 'There has been a shift in thinking away from pain as only a sensory experience,' says Dr. Clifford Woolf, a neurologist at the Children's Hospital, Boston. 'Rather than targeting the suppression of pain as a symptom, the best treatment now has to be targeted at preventing pain as a disease. That insight really changes the way we understand pain.' In the field of hypnotherapy, one does this through *suggestion*, a term referring to a set of commands planted in the subconscious mind beyond one's critical judgement, the part of our cognitive process that regularly sabotages and rejects such statements. Without a brain, one cannot experience pain. When we interfere with the subconscious mind's focus on pain, we often can distract it enough to fuzz the feelings of pain and bring about relief from its debilitating effects.

Several years ago, I was discussing hypno-anaesthesia and analgesic techniques with a classroom of about twenty students. Amongst them were a husband and wife team of anaesthetists, a general medical practitioner, and a dentist. They challenged every assertion made and demanded endless practical proof. This added a fun element to the course, allowing us to experiment in ways we couldn't without licensed medical personnel on hand. Annelaine, the general practitioner, had her medical consulting bag with her and quickly produced a hypodermic needle and sterile swabs to test the power of suggestion on herself, as guinea pig, by stopping her bleeding and dulling her pain through hypnotic suggestion. She had one of the anaesthetists poke a needle through the skin on the back of both hands as a test. The hand that hadn't been prepared with hypnotic suggestions (the control in the experiment) bled freely and experienced pain. The other hand remained numb and didn't bleed at all. This abundant proof astounded and convinced everyone present.

Liesl, one of the students on the course, asked if one could undergo surgery without the use of chemical anaesthetics and I explained how it could be done. She then asked if I would officiate with hypno-anaesthetics during the removal of her tonsils. She explained how she had procrastinated, much to her doctor's concern, and said that she needed a tonsillectomy quite soon and was prepared to have it under hypnosis. How could a teacher of such techniques decline her request? So, I had no choice but to say 'yes,' gulped heavily and prayed that it would never occur. I felt quite safe, believing that she would never find a surgeon willing to slice out

---

[132] *Healing the Hurt*, article by Alice Park in *Time* Magazine, 4 March 2011.

a woman's tonsils while she sat fully conscious in the chair because, if things went wrong, the medical malpractice lawsuits would be endless and ruthless.

How wrong I was. We live in Africa where folk take risks and often cast caution into the wind. During the lunch break, the anaesthetists made phone calls to a few surgeons and by the time we reconvened for our afternoon sessions, they had scheduled Liesl's tonsillectomy in three weeks' time. I was now truly on the spot, couldn't back down, and skilfully hid my inner terror of the thought of it.

'Why, Liesl? Why do you want to have this surgery done without anaesthetics?' Her choice was an elective one in terms of medical ethics, and there were no decisive reasons against the use of anaesthetics.

'I feel that if I can do this, I can accomplish anything in life. There are several other important things that I would love to resolve but I don't seem to have the bravery to work through them. You would be helping me enormously.'

Liesl was the most un-hypnotisable student on that course and I feared that I wouldn't get her into a suitable trance, deep enough to bypass her critical faculty in order to give her suggestions to disassociate her mind from the input stimuli from the surgery. We booked two ninety-minute preparatory sessions, spaced about a week apart, and rehearsed our strategy for surgery.

Friday 23 November, 2007 finally dawned and she presented herself for admission at the Milpark Hospital, one of the biggest and most established private hospitals in Johannesburg. Doctor Kishen Dayal, ENT Surgeon, agreed to conduct the operation on condition that Doctors Ian and Kantha Lander, the husband and wife anaesthetist team, were present and that Liesl was medically ready to receive an instant anaesthetic should the hypnosis fail.

Ian showed me around the hospital's theatre facilities and took me to visit Liesl in the ward to conclude plans for her surgery. Around seven o'clock in the morning, I was escorted down a corridor marked 'Theatre Personnel Only' to ready myself.

I received VIP treatment. My first task was to dress in theatre garb, comprising a blue sterile suit that had a red embroidered label 'Doctor' across the jacket pocket, a funny blue elasticised net hat that covered my hair and a pair of non-static over-boots that covered my shoes. I looked the part, but inside I was exceptionally nervous and feared making a mockery of us all. Ian introduced me to Doctor Dayal. 'Hi, I'm Kishen,' he said in a kind and friendly tone. 'I would like you to join my team in theatre from the beginning and we will operate on Liesl at midday.'

Most of his operations that morning involved children, several less than two years of age. The majority of the procedures were grommets inserted in their eardrums and Kishen allowed me to observe it all through a microscope eyepiece used by medical students. I was amazed at the delicate nature of this microsurgery. The grommet looks like a bobbin in a sewing machine, a bit like two steel buttons fused back-to-back with a hole in the middle. Essentially, the surgeon inserts the grommet into the eardrum in a manner similar to the way we fasten a shirt button. Using the tiniest surgical scalpel, Kishen cut a microscopic buttonhole in the child's eardrum and then with the tiniest tools, an ultra-steady hand and intense concentration, eased the microscopic grommet into the slit. Unwanted fluid behind the eardrum could now drain out through the hole in the grommet and into the child's ear canal, thus relieving their condition.

He'd completed about six of these procedures when a teenage girl arrived in theatre for her tonsillectomy, and I was once again invited to observe. Ian explained that the anaesthetics for this type of operation were much deeper than the ones administered to the previous children because, during a tonsillectomy, surgeon and anaesthetist must share a common passageway, the throat, which, to prevent blood and saliva running into the lungs and giving rise to serious infections, had to be completely sealed.

'The operation is somewhat brutal and quite messy,' he said, and those words haunted me for the remainder of the morning.

Ian was indeed correct. The partially sedated teenager was quickly transferred to the operating table where he skilfully induced a moderately light anaesthetic. The surgeon's assistants worked with Ian to pack the girl's throat with wads of surgical padding as he took her into a much deeper state of anaesthetics, to a point where she stopped breathing altogether. A respirator took over the responsibility of breathing and Ian stepped aside to let Doctor Dayal and his team perform the surgery. Kishen beckoned that I should stand next to him to watch. 'This is the same procedure that we'll perform on Liesl in a few hours,' he said, and I became increasingly nervous that the hypnosis might not succeed as planned – the operation seemed quite invasive and I feared that she might feel claustrophobic and, given the tender nature of the throat, she might gag or have pain enter her consciousness.

They deferred the operation to midday because it rendered the theatre unsterile and it had to be the last one scheduled for Doctor Dayal that day. Close to midday, theatre staff brought Liesl into theatre for her procedure. Unlike the other sedated patients that morning, she sat bolt upright in bed, completely conscious and alert. Attendants lifted the other patients onto the table but she hopped from one to the other by herself. As soon as her bed was wheeled from the ward to the theatre, a queue of twenty-five hospital dignitaries, including the General Manager, a publicity team, Pain Management staff and others filed in to witness this spectacle. I hadn't anticipated an audience and I felt like an impromptu performer on a stage. They stood in a long line along the back wall of the theatre and Ian led me past each person to introduce them to me individually, like the Queen receiving guests at Buckingham Palace. This operating theatre is spacious and easily accommodated everyone. I now realised why the theatre would become unsterile – because of so much breathing without surgical masks and no wearing of proper theatre garb.

My nervousness overwhelmed me and a funny kind of numbness replaced my conscious thoughts. Everything from then on became surreal and happened as though I ran on autopilot.

The operating table, instead of remaining flat as it was all morning, had the head section raised and the foot dropped, configuring it into an awkward chair. Liesl sat in her theatre gown smiling at the audience she now faced. Ian and Kantha attached sticky sensor pads on her chest to monitor her vital signs and inserted a flexible plastic *cannula* mounted on a metal *trocar* into a vein at the back of her left hand, just in case a general anaesthetic became necessary during surgery. The surgical packing in the back of the throat was absent on this occasion as Liesl was conscious enough to either swallow or spit out any blood and saliva.

The theatre team stood behind Liesl to her right and Doctor Dayal waited at his writing table behind her to her left. Ian and his wife Kantha finished their preparations and stood back as Doctor Dayal walked forward, shook my hand and patted my shoulder to reassure me as he said, 'She's yours, Tom'. Although I had no time restriction, I knew I couldn't waste a moment inducing trance. I required a sufficiently deep trance, enough to disassociate Lisle's mind from the input stimuli of her body. I looked at her and smiled broadly but I knew my smile was fake. I padded up to the reconfigured table in my soft over-boots, squatted and held her bare feet.

With programmed post-hypnotic suggestions, ones her subconscious mind instantly recognised, I led her quickly and irresistibly into the Esdaile State, a very deep trance associated with limb catalepsy. It worked! I then layered several other suggestions into her receptive subconscious and tested their efficacy to determine trance depth. The whole induction took six minutes to complete.

Liesl sat on the table, eyes closed and in deep trance, as I stood up. One could hear a pin drop as everyone drew in a slow deep breath and braced for what now lay ahead. I walked back to where to Doctor Dayal stood and relinquished control of the patient back to him: 'She's now yours again, Doctor'.

I took up my position directly behind her left shoulder and began to whisper in her ear. I kept a constant commentary throughout the procedure, reassuring her and holding her mind far away from the sensations her body produced. Kishen called for his first tool, a pair of locking forceps. He reached into her gaping mouth and I heard the forceps ratchet click tight with two or three rapid clicks followed by another and then, more slowly, another as the tips laboured under the flesh they grasped. I shuddered in horror knowing just how painful that would be under any circumstance and I hoped with all my might that Liesl's conscious mind would ignore it. He pinched the side of her right tonsil and pulled it firmly aside to give him space enough to excise it. The forceps dangled out of her mouth and rested on her cheek.

Liesl didn't flinch.

It took about fifteen minutes to remove her tonsil and I began to look about the room as my confidence grew. Against the bright light that Illuminated Liesl's throat, I could barely make out the shadowy figures standing against the wall. I remember seeing a row of dimly lit faces filled with incredulity and disbelief. Jaws were slightly ajar and eyes wide open as they witnessed the rising smoke and sizzles emanating from the electro-cauterisation. Doctor Dayal's theatre sister periodically probed Liesl's mouth with a plastic vacuum catheter to suck away blood and saliva, but there was none to remove. Specific hypnotic suggestions effectively shut down her blood vessels and stopped her salivary glands secreting.

As I became more aware of the room around me, I saw that it was Doctor Dayal who was sweating profusely and I realised that it must have been as radical for him to perform this operation on an awake patient as it was for me to assist.

One last dexterous manoeuvre freed the first tonsil and it dangled from the forceps on its way to the steel kidney dish. Still with her eyes closed, Liesl asked, 'Is that the first one out?' with a note of pride and relief in her voice.

'Yes, it is,' I said, 'We're already halfway done.'

The theatre sister broke the silence. 'She can talk!' she exclaimed, with a touch of panic in her voice. 'How can she talk but not feel the pain?' Nobody answered, and the surgeon called for the second forceps. With the second clamp now in place on the remaining tonsil, I resumed my hypnotic patter to keep her as detached as possible, while I watched people's reactions.

Quite a few had gathered around Ian's monitor and they took turns tapping on the equipment as they whispered quietly to each other. Some heads shook slowly from side to side in disbelief, others nodded knowingly. I couldn't see the graphs and charts from where I sat but I could hear the regular beep as Liesl's heartbeat was tracked, and I sensed that it had slowed down considerably. I wasn't worried because I kept a keen eye on Ian as my litmus test: if he became concerned, then so should I. But he seemed quite relaxed and appeared to be sharing some of his own hypnosis skills with the people who were clustered around the monitor. I later heard that Liesl's vital signs kept showing signs of sustained relaxation as Kishen worked with her, in stark contrast to the usual signs of distress displayed on the console even for a heavily anaesthetised patient.

A final clank in the kidney dish marked the end of the operation. Kishen stood up, mopped his brow and received an impromptu round of applause. I could sense the relief in the clapping as the thunderous sound dispersed the tension and silence that had been held throughout. Kishen meticulously recorded the details of the operation in the logbook and announced that the procedure had taken just thirty-one minutes, which included the six minutes that it took to induce trance.

He pulled off his latex gloves and a few assistants gathered around Liesl to tidy up. They detached the sensors and removed the intravenous cannula, after which a queue of spectators lined up to peer into her throat one by one as Liesl sat there and obligingly answered the barrage of questions that they threw at her. The room was abuzz with exaltation and exclamation: 'Wow! Incredible. I've never seen anything like this before. It all seems a bit spooky.'

Doctor Dayal took control once more. 'We have to get her to the recovery room,' he said.

'But I'm okay to walk,' replied Liesl, fully *compos mentis*, readying herself to stand up from the table to stroll back to the ward.

'No,' came the stern voice of authority from an otherwise gentle surgeon, 'we will follow procedure and transfer you to the recovery room on your bed.'

Nobody challenged his directive but I smiled thinking how bizarre it was in the light of all the non-procedural stuff we had been doing during that half hour. I knew that it was his way of gaining control and taking stock of the situation because I do much the same sort of thing whenever I feel overwhelmed and swamped in my world: I begin to tidy up and pack away. I rearrange the furniture; sweep floors; do some paper filing and anything else I can to bring structure and control to my outside world. Once I've gained outward control, I seem to recover inner control too. Kishen, I assumed, was doing much the same thing subconsciously.

Theatre staff helped Liesl back onto her bed and, followed by an entourage of well-wishers, wheeled her out of the theatre and into the adjacent recovery room. Her husband joined her there and she said that her throat was very dry and asked if he would get her something to drink. He scurried away and returned smartly with a giant-size can of Coca-Cola that he bought from a vending machine in the corridor. He prized open the tab and with its customary 'pshst,' the can announced the next significant moment to everyone watching this extraordinary sequence of events. The buzz of conversation halted instantly and all eyes turned to Liesl to look at her take a long sip of the chilly liquid. She swallowed it with ease and expressed her satisfaction. 'Ah, that's better!'

By two o'clock, she was back in the ward and had eaten her lunch of chicken and rice. When I called her on Monday morning, she said she was at her desk at the publishing company and that her throat felt a little raw, 'like a strep-throat'.

'I could kill you though,' she said in a half-teasing, half-jocular tone.

'Why? What have I done?'

'You didn't say anything to prepare my subconscious for the needle they inserted in the back of my hand. It is so sore! I don't know what to do with it.'

This story has spiritual relevance because it serves as a convincer that one can separate mind from body. After all, how do we know that we even have a body? The only possible way for mind to know there is a body, is for it to utilise the five bodily senses to see, feel, smell, touch and taste body's presence. Without them, there is no way of knowing whether the body exists or not. This is precisely how I helped Liesl through her tonsillectomy: I focused her mind away from the sensations produced by her body. We call this hypnotic disconnection or disassociation. Through the powers of suggestion and imagination, we dislocate mind from the world of the five senses and focus it on more pleasant and safer images, albeit in a world of fantasy. Under deep hypnotic trance, one's subconscious mind cannot tell whether an idea emanates from imagination or reality. By focusing her mind elsewhere, she couldn't hold two contexts concurrently – and she never noticed the input stimuli coming in from the operation.

The apparent world of reality reaching us through our five senses is thus no more real than the world we create inside our heads. We've trained our minds to believe that the outside world is solid and tangible but, in truth, mind processes our sensory input and gives it all the meaning it has.

We think the outside world shapes and moulds us through a never-ending series of random events that come our way, as if an unseen hand rolls the dice and moves us along the board in this game of life. It might seem as if God has a script specially prepared for us and we, as actors on the stage, have little choice but to enact it.

It reminds me of the little boy playing Monopoly with his friends on the lounge floor. The dice seem stacked against him and quickly his money reserves are lost paying rent for properties he didn't own and, all too often, he lands on the square that dispatches him off to jail. The boy, distraught, calls to his father sitting reading his newspaper near the fire, 'Daddy, daddy, please help me! I don't know what to do ... I have no money, no house and I keep going to jail! What should I do next?'

Getting up from his chair, dad walks up to the little boy, tousles his hair and smiles lovingly, 'It's only a game my boy, just keep playing the game because playing cannot harm you.'

The boy had lost perspective for a moment and thought he *was* the little locomotive on the Monopoly board. He identified so closely with the game that he lost sight of the truth of who he really was – the game player! Our minds can easily get lost in illusion, leaving us in the belief that we're fragile mortal beings swept along by life. Liesl's operation opened my eyes to a much more magnificent realisation because it proved to me beyond doubt, in a highly controlled environment, with sceptical witnesses, that a different inner world does indeed exist separate from the one we create through our senses.

Mind quickly loses track of the reality of Who I Really Am and gets lost in its fantasy creations of us as bodies, separate from one another in time and space. On a visit to New York City, I stumbled upon the Museum of Holography housed in a dingy building with street access through a single narrow doorway. Displayed inside was a spectacular array of holograms of various forms, but one stood out because of its simplicity. It wasn't actually a hologram at all, as they are three-dimensional images produced by the coincidence of laser beams or by properly illuminating a photograph of interference patterns. It was a faceless sculpture of a life-sized human head, similar to the polystyrene moulds displaying acrylic wigs in cheap salons. Projected onto this featureless face was a movie of a man speaking, and it mesmerised me. The trick was so simple yet so convincing, and it readily captivated my mind which interpreted it as a real talking person.

Everyone we know is a featureless form upon which we project our thoughts of *who we believe him/her to be*. We create caricatures in our minds, illusionary images and representations for each person we know, and then we project these images onto the blank sculptures of their form, believing that what we see is real. These ego-placeholders in our minds are montages, cut and pasted from our history and association with these people. The images are not static because we constantly change our mental collage whenever we glean new information about the people we know. Yet the people themselves are not those illusions that we hold of them in our minds. They are quite different.

I received a call some time ago from a man seeking a private consultation with me. He had a heavy Afrikaans accent and we agreed on a time for his visit a few days later. When I met him in reception, my heart sank because I wasn't sure whether there would be any rapport between him and me. He was a thickset man with a neck as wide as his head. He wore heavy-duty clothing splashed with paint, and shoes covered in cement. He could have easily been a macho rugby player and I wondered how my gentler brand of help could assist him. I ushered him in, sat him down and began to chat with him and, in no time at all, he unbundled his woes and wept profusely. Here I was, sitting to the side, holding his hand reassuringly and guiding him to a better understanding of what had happened. The shift was profound for both of us. He walked away empowered and I was humbled. Of all the unlikely connections, the universe decided to connect us. I returned to my rooms, sat quietly for a while, and promised that I would never judge anyone again as I had judged him. I had projected my prejudiced image onto his formless blank and read him amiss. From that moment, I decided to see everyone differently. If he wasn't the thickset Afrikaner I thought he was, who was he really?

Namasté is a greeting often accompanied by a gesture of bringing the palms of the hands together at the heart. The word literally translates as 'bow me you' or 'I bow to you,' but carries the much deeper meaning of 'I bow to the divine light in me that I also recognise in you'. We sadly fail to see others' magnificent potential and project our egoistic image and perceived identity upon their spiritual blank instead. The man's identity spanned a spectrum of identities from my 'thickset Afrikaner' to one of spirit being. His identity depended upon my choice of identities for him. After our meeting, I chose to forgo identifying him with his form and saw him and all others as divine spiritual beings, whole complete and content. How he chose to manifest became a compassionate curiosity instead of a misjudged threat.

Our identity occurs at many levels. At a material level, we have unique body shape, fingerprints and other biometric indicators that distinguish us. Yet, strip away the skin and lay the body next to one of similar shape, and one is hard-pressed to tell the two apart. However, much more of our identity comes from the abstract aspects of our personality: our unique thoughts, ideas, beliefs and emotions. Remove the abstract identity from a person and their body becomes a corpse and while it may still look like them, it clearly isn't.

René Descartes proposed, '*Cogito ergo sum*' [I think, therefore I am]. Meaning that someone pondering their existence is, from this perspective, seen as proof that something, the 'I' exists – and this opens up a philosophical challenge as to whom or what that 'I' happens to be.

Often, our projected self-image is an unhealthy composite of shifting identities as we move from one role in life to the next. We learn to project the identity of *child* at birth, someone's son or daughter; but we never retain that identity indefinitely. We allow new identities to supersede obsolete ones whenever our situation changes, and we adopt new personalities to maintain our congruency with life, our sense of coherence. Just as I had judged the thickset man amiss, so too do we often judge ourselves amiss. Our real identity is one of spirit, that constant stream of source potential flowing from the Divine through the creative agency of mind and into form. Once we come to realise that we are not our bodies but that our true nature is one of spirit, the illusion unravels, judgement ceases and unconditional love abounds. When we draw our self-awareness back towards our source, we see everyone as equals for then, we're all divine spirit beings. True, our manifestations are infinitely variable but our essence is always the same.

The distant echo of Terry Winchester's words at his presentation at the Maritz Brothers esoteric faire rebounded: 'All your problems are an illusion. If you want to change your life, you need to change your thoughts. Hell then instantly transforms into Heaven and we then experience Heaven on Earth'.

The traditional Hawaiian cleansing practise of *Ho'oponopono* has morphed, like many other spiritual practises. Regrettably, our capitalist world has diluted age-old and incredibly wise rituals to tiny commercially exploitable doses of syrupy cordial, palatable for western consumption. Nevertheless, the contemporary distillation of *Ho'oponopono* in the form of the chant 'I'm sorry. Please forgive me. I love you. Thank you' still has enough essence to change the way we see others. Let's take, by way of an example, a woman who was repeatedly abused as a child by a male member of her family. We could encourage her to use the mantra to seek reconciliation. But how could the four ideas of regret, forgiveness, love and gratitude help her reframe her past? It seems even more bizarre when we ask: 'Why, in the first place, should she, as the offended party, repent and seek forgiveness from him, the offender?' Surely, it should be the other way around.

However, *Ho'oponopono* works perfectly when we return to our notion that everyone is a blank template upon which we project our thoughts of who we think he or she is. When we say 'I'm sorry,' it's not that *she* seeks repentance, a feeling of remorse for doing wrong or sinning; it's that she regrets having projected onto his faceless form the image she holds of him in her head.

'All the world's a stage, and all the men and women merely players'.[133] Here we are, consummate actors playing our different roles, delivering a convincing performance involving love, hatred, rape, murder and every other experience known to mankind. The drama is intense, the performances convincing, but after the final curtain all the actors depart. They go backstage, take off their wigs, unbutton their costumes and wipe away their makeup. Over a glass or two of bubbly, they toast each other for a performance well played: 'Thank you for playing your role so convincingly, for if you hadn't, I could not have played mine as well as I did.' Backstage, there's no personal vendetta for what occurred during the performance. After death, I guess we might gather with our group of soulmates, pat each other on the back and applaud our convincing performances carried, on-stage, during life.

---

[133] *As You Like It*, William Shakespeare, Act 2, Scene 7, 139–143.

'I'm sorry' isn't a plea for clemency. Rather, it's an acknowledgement of spiritual blindness: 'I'm sorry that I believed that your character in the play was real. For a moment, I forgot that you were a fellow actor.' In another way, it is regret for having held an erroneous image in one's head, which we project outwards onto the formless face of the real person: 'I'm sorry' for having held you in that role until I could find sufficient wisdom to see you differently.' Forgiveness, love and gratitude expressed in the *Ho 'oponopono* mantra now make contextual sense, not as a sinner would seek repentance but as one great being acknowledging another, *Namasté*. It's a mantra that acknowledges that I am ultimately responsible for everything that occurs in my life, and this thought brings immense personal power, hence the mantra's ending: 'Thank you.'

How could the *Ho 'oponopono* mantra help the woman abused as a child? Instead of seeing the abuser as 'the abuser', what if she chose to see him differently? What if she saw him as another perfect spirit being, acting out his role with her on the worldly stage of life? It might give her courage to ask: 'What wisdom do I glean from my past experience that I could not have obtained any other way? Having gathered the wisdom from the event could I then see him as my teacher instead of my abuser?'

There's plenty of good advice in the saying, 'If you don't go within, you go without'. Most minds are mainly undisciplined, unruly and seek external gratification through the pleasures of the five senses. It is however far more enlightening to seek inner wisdom than it is to battle the external world. We can't manipulate others as if they were puppets in the hands of a puppet master, that's not where our power lies. We can however change our perception of them – we can choose to see them differently. Nobody can strip that immense power from us, nor can anyone stop us from using it.

My understanding of spirit, and whether it had a purpose or not, was incomplete until I explored body's place in the context of this holy tripartite relationship. Only then could I fully answer Ram Dass's question. The *Course* says: 'The body does not exist except as a learning device for the mind'.[134] This raises some interesting questions: could a body exist without a mind? What would happen to mind if it had no body? Could mind learn anything?

---

[134] *A Course in Miracles*, T-2.V.1.9, Combined Volume (Third Edition), the Foundation for A Course in Miracles, 2007.

I suppose we could say that a body without a mind would have no knowledge of its own existence. A body separated from mind would operate like an automaton, a zombie. Just as no sound occurs when a tree falls in a forest without an ear to hear it, so too, an animated, functional body cannot exist without consciousness at its core to direct its experiences.

An animated corpse would have no concept of time or place. It would have no memory (that mental faculty of retaining and recalling past experience) even though it might carry the physical scars of past events as cellular memory. Neither would it have any sense of past or future. It would have no desires. It would live solely in the present. It would be indifferent to being naked or clothed. It wouldn't know about wealth or poverty, fashion or drabness. It would have no worries or concerns. A mindless body, if such could exist, might be purely reactive to its world. There are perhaps examples of mindless bodies: a body kept alive after the person is clinically brain-dead is one such example; another is someone chemically anaesthetised. Through its autonomous nervous system it would breathe when its carbon dioxide levels reach unacceptably high limits, it would shiver if it felt cold, and it would eliminate its waste when necessary. It might repair itself automatically if injured. A body without a mind would have nowhere to go, nothing to do, no ambition, no purpose and it is debateable whether its instincts would cause it to wander in search of food, shelter or to reproduce as these functions may actually belong to mind and not to body. Body detached from mind would always be free of pain, just as Liesl was, when I disassociated her mind hypnotically from her body. What the *Course* says seems very plausible after all, that a body cannot exist apart from mind. Body is present entirely for the sake of the mind.

What then about a mind without a body? The *Course* speaks boldly on these matters: 'There is nothing outside you [...]. Heaven is not a place nor a condition. It is merely an awareness of perfect Oneness, and the knowledge that there is nothing else; nothing outside this Oneness, and nothing else within.' It adds: 'And you have done a stranger thing than you yet realize. You have displaced your guilt to your body from your mind. Yet a body cannot be guilty, for it can do nothing of itself. You who think you hate your body deceive yourself. You hate your mind, for guilt has entered into it [...]. Mind cannot attack, but it can make fantasies and directs the body to act them out.' [135] A mind without a body is capable only of fantasy; it has no way of

---

[135] *A Course in Miracles*, T-18.VI ff, Combined Volume (Third Edition), the Foundation for A Course in Miracles, 2007.

enacting the fantasies unless it does so through the body. Body gives mind an illusory vehicle to let it believe that mind is real and physical.

---oooOooo---

I gently cleared my throat to signal that I was ready to continue my discussion. Ram Dass emerged from his trance on cue. He looked at me expectantly and I began to explain my answer to his question: 'Ram Dass, spirit has no purpose because it is wholly indifferent, sinless, conscious potential. The body is of itself guiltless. The mind is the only constituent in this holy tripartite capable of being split. It has the choice to either align itself with spirit to bring about a sense of grace or it could identify itself with the body and let ego wander about lost in the material world of its creation.'

Ram Dass smiled sweetly, nodded affirmatively and I noted a boyish glint in his eye, as if he was playing an intellectual game with me. I wondered how he next planned to undermine my belief system in order to help me rebuild it more robustly. He asked: 'Why then, Tom, do you need authority to teach? And anyway, who gives you this authority?'

I knew he'd probe deeper into the reason I'd come to visit him – my churning self-doubt and its resultant feelings that I let invalidate me. 'Spirit gives me authority, Ram Dass,' I said as he nodded his approval. 'It provides the potential, the opportunity for me to teach. I suppose I could say that it gives me the authority to work with others.'

My reply reminded me of the *Course's* words about teachers: 'A teacher of God is anyone who chooses to be one. His qualifications consist solely in this: somehow, somewhere he has made a deliberate choice in which he did not see his interests as apart from someone else's. Once he has done that, his road is established and his direction is sure.'[136]

Ram Dass smiled for a while, and his eyes gleamed with excitement, as if anxious to share a big secret. 'I give you authority,' he said, slightly teasingly, and my ego immediately latched onto his words and proudly leaped for joy. He paused to observe my reaction and, as if noting my ego's involvement, added: 'However, Tom, you are only looking at individualised souls but look beyond that and you will then see who really authenticates you.'

---

[136] *A Course in Miracles*, M-1.1.1-1.2.7, Combined Volume (Third Edition), the Foundation for A Course in Miracles, 2007.

I thought for a moment and replied: 'I authenticate myself. You authenticate me Ram Dass, Maharaj-ji does, so does God, for we are one and therefore we are him. Any authentication, at any level is ultimately God's authority, his potential in us.'

'Precisely!' he said, satisfied with my line of reasoning. 'What value is there in paper qualifications when you are validated by God?'

Again, he vanished into trance, floated off somewhere in the cosmos and stayed there silently for a long, long time. I absorbed the profundity and astuteness of his argument. I sat basking in the warmth and love of his presence and this time I was in no haste for his return. Slowly, his eyes flickered and opened and with a slight trace of a lisp as he battled the effects of his stroke, he asked, 'What do you understand by *surrender* and *faith*?'

I pondered for a while before answering: '*Surrender* is about trust, trusting enough to give oneself up completely into the arms of another.' After a further pause I added, '*Faith* is a conviction that something is true without needing proof. I remember from my Bible studies as a youth that "faith is the assured expectation of things hoped for." It's also an act of good faith. I suppose one could add that it's an obligation of loyalty and fidelity as in the context of the word "faithful". However, in spiritual terms, it might represent one's devotion to God and his reciprocated assurance to be loyal to us.'

'What I feel, I om,' he said, scrunching up his eyebrows and looking at me very knowingly and sternly, 'is that *you lack surrender and faith*!'

'I lack surrender and faith?!'

I was perplexed and dismayed at what he said and my first reaction was to reject it and go on the defensive. His words popped the ego bubble that I inflated moments earlier. In my heart, I knew that I'd tried hard to embrace every facet of life without judgement and to accept it all as schooling for greater wisdom. I believed I *had* surrendered and truly hoped I demonstrated faith. My mind whirled and I sat quietly without anything to add for quite some time but I could feel a slight tremor in my top lip that betrayed my emotions. Then, a hot flush of embarrassment rose up inside which made me blush for I remembered that it was I who first doubted Ram Dass's authority and validity. That entrenched doubt drove me all the way to Hawaii to meet him for myself, to know firsthand whether he was a fake or not. It was I that judged him amiss, yet here he was accepting me without question as one of God's teachers.

Was my teacher able see what I kept inside my transparent heart? He impeccably demonstrated at first hand the lessons he was teaching me about surrender and faith.

'I've got it, Ram Dass,' I smiled joyfully. 'You're showing me the contradictions inherent in my self-doubt, that I haven't surrendered to my godhead and neither have I had faith in my own validity. The purpose of this second trip to Maui is for me to learn to dissolve doubt about my higher-self and give myself up completely to the real me without needing someone else's accreditation, even though I might once have held contradictory beliefs about myself.'

'If you surrender completely to God, do you think your ego could ever take hold of the recognition for the importance of your work?' A flush of embarrassment washed over me. Was he reading me again? How did he know I had just fought off my ego?

'No, Ram Dass. If I surrendered completely, ego could not take recognition. It would be impossible, for the work would then be God's work and not ego's.'

'Do you think that you could ever take the blame for things that went wrong if you put all your faith in God?'

'No Ram Dass, I can't be blamed for someone else's mistakes. If I surrendered completely and put all my faith in God, he would have to take the blame for what went wrong. But, I know that God is perfect and doesn't make mistakes and I guess, that means there is never anyone to blame because nothing can possibly go wrong.' I remembered my earlier internal dialogue and remembered that at the source of my being, God and I are one. Talking about God was synonymous with talking about my higher self, spirit.

I understood where he was leading me gently and kindly. I added, 'When I surrender fully to my higher self, to my godhead, having faith that it, the only authentic part of me, knows only perfection, ego dies and I can no longer fall into trappings of fame and pride, nor can I castigate myself for failure, for there never is any.'

Ram Dass added, 'When you have faith to fully surrender, all thoughts stop and only God's thoughts continue, and that marks the end of karma.' When mind identifies with spirit and not with body, our existence becomes sinless and we are set free from guilt. That's our atonement, our *at-onement* with the divine.'

'And the end of karma, Ram Dass, is our moment of enlightenment!'

Chinese Zen master, Lin-chi I-hsuan who died in 866 observed:

> Students of today can't get anywhere: what ails you? Lack of faith in yourself is what ails you. If you lack faith in yourself, you'll keep on tumbling along, bewilderedly following after all kinds of circumstances, be taken by these myriad circumstances through transformation after transformation, and never be yourself. Bring to rest the thoughts of the ceaselessly seeking mind, and you'll not differ from the Patriarch-Buddha. Do you want to know the Buddha? He is none other than you who stand before me listening to my discourse. Since you students lack faith in yourselves, you run around seeking something outside. Even if through seeking you find something, that something will be nothing more than elaborate descriptions in written words; in the end you will fail to gain the mind of the Living Patriarch.

We laughed together, teased and joked a bit more before I wheeled him back to the main house where I made sure his chair was properly secured to the elevator.

He took my hand in his, drew it to his lips and kissed the back of my hand gently.

'You are so close,' he said tenderly, 'so very close.'

He pressed the button and rose up before me. Looking back, his eyes showed signs of age; his lower eyelids, outlined in pink, flopped forward a little. They were kind eyes, deep pools of pure love without a trace of malice. He said, over the drone of the motor that propelled his chair, 'There are so many parallels between us and I could easily spend many more hours talking with you, but Dassi Ma wouldn't let me.' There was a twinkle in his eye and I knew he was gently teasing her but I respected even more her firm stance and her need to shield him.

The elevator groaned to a halt and bounced up and down a little until it settled. He navigated his way inside the house and we smiled at each other one last time and as he turned to close the door, I walked the few meters back around to the cottage and pondered some of those similarities between us – and there were many. I felt serene and totally at peace with everything.

On the bookshelf in the bedroom, I found a copy of Ram Dass's classic square blue book, *Be Here Now*, containing amongst other articles a transcript of one of his famous speeches printed on brown wrapping paper and embellished with some awesome drawings. I read the passage on surrender: 'What are you giving up? A hollow little trip that's good for another forty years at best. You're giving it up for Eternal Union with pure energy and with pure light because surrender means you no longer die. It's as simple as that, that's what it means. Because: you that lives and dies is your ego and fear of death only comes through the ego. Total, total surrender. Surrender. There's no more you, no more life and death.'[137]

I filled the remainder of the day in and out of trance, long periods of meditation, punctuated by short breaks spent nibbling at pieces of fruit and sipping something light to drink. Incense filled the room with its heady aroma and I found myself giggling frivolously back at Maharaj-ji as he watched me knowingly from his portrait with his toothless grin.

---oooOooo---

I woke very early the next morning and felt disgruntled and tried to sleep some more but remained restless. It wasn't an ugly restlessness and I know the feelings well. It was subconscious dissonance – something had shifted and my mind was rebuilding a new belief structure. My mind was in a transitional phase where it needed time to process the new thoughts and ideas of the previous day, deciding what to keep, what to reframe and what to throw out. My mood felt like the oppressiveness before a storm, a pressure build-up preceding change. I lay in bed on my side looking at the gentle hues of the early morning light through the narrow vertical gap in the curtain, and I fidgeted with the pillow, straightening out the folds in the linen and trying to quiet my mind. Nothing helped so I eventually got out of bed, wrapped a *kikoy*[138] around my waist and went for a silent swim at first light, before anybody else woke up.

I came back to the apartment, made a bowl of fresh fruit salad, but didn't eat it. I charged my camera battery that didn't really need charging and tried to read but couldn't concentrate. I noticed an area of tiny red spots on my chest that extended all the way under my right armpit and discovered another area of them behind my ear. They were itchy and sharply sore to the

---

[137] *Be Here Now, Remember*, Ram Dass, Hanuman Foundation, 1971
[138] *Kikoy* – a simple garment originating in Kenya and worn like a kilt by men and a sarong by women that is about half the size of the lungi worn in India.

touch. I felt tired and emotional and realised it was more than just a mental shift: my body was detoxifying too.

I've often experienced times when part of my mind splits away and becomes a separate persona. The mind then becomes like a narrator keeping incessant running commentaries on the events of the day. This time, however, it took on an advisory role that was sometimes critical, often profoundly wise, but always caring and nurturing. I 'hear' this dialogue clearly in my head. The 'voice' advised that I should, 'Lie down and be with your emotions and surrender to your body's needs'. I had been fighting my feelings for hours, trying to control and ignore them via all manner and means of distraction, so I gave up fighting, lay on the sofa in the lounge and drifted into a deep, long, recuperative sleep.

A sharp metallic clack snapped me out of my sleep and I sat bolt upright and quite disorientated as Ken pushed Ram Dass in his chair up the aluminium ramp and into the living room. Somehow, Dassi Ma hadn't said anything about a chat with him and I hadn't expected his visit on a Sunday. I leapt up to rearrange the table and chair, clutching at my *kikoy* that began to unwrap and fall away half exposing my nakedness beneath. A sudden wave of embarrassment washed over me because I wasn't really properly dressed for the occasion and I felt disrespectful. Ram Dass clearly had no expectations regarding my dress sense and I began to settle down as the adrenalin subsided and my heart rate slowly returned to normal.

Since I didn't expect him, I hadn't prepared for his visit and had nothing relevant to say or ask and began to rattled off some inconsequential stuff to fill the conversational void. I've noticed this pattern in many of my clients when they're nervous. I continued my monologue, telling him of what I'd written in my journal and how my mind was undergoing a strange transformation that echoed in my body, causing some detoxification. Ram Dass did what I have often done in client sessions, he just sat listening attentively, never responding, until my voice dwindled away into silence and we sat looking at each other.

My eyes fixated on his. They were deep, serene pools of tranquillity and love. He closed his eyes and by inferred suggestion, so did I. It provoked the most magnificent state of deep trance. Feelings of swimming, swirling, dancing energy, twisting and turning in gentle wisps, ebb and flow of incredible waves of bliss and a sense of oneness, not just with Ram Dass, but with the whole room and into the infinity beyond. Tears of joy welled up, rolled down my cheeks and plopped down onto my *kikoy*. Time was no longer linear and collapsed into the infinitely present moment of *now*.

It wasn't the first time I'd had experiences of this kind. It was a returning friend, an intimate companion from my late teens when I spent night after night for two years, crouched in the corner of a cold prison cell with only a cotton waste blanket wrapped around my body.

The first time out of prison when I had an experience similar to the one with Ram Dass was about a year after meeting Terry Winchester, back in the 1990s. I attended a weekend event at his home, hosted by a Dutch woman, Greta, who hailed from the Endeavor Academy. This is a school founded in America in 1992 by a former real estate agent, the late Charles Buell Anderson, who was lauded as 'The Master Teacher'. In his Endeavor Academy, formerly known as the New Christian Church of Full Endeavor, he taught a mix of fundamental Christian doctrine and teachings from *A Course in Miracles*. I hold the teachings of the *Course* in high regard but I shuddered at the rigidity and complexities of his rendition of these teachings and I thought the message was overly complicated and obfuscated. The delivery was inflexible and scared me because it emanated from one man, The Master Teacher, who seemed to be the sole divinely appointed authority, a figure whom nobody dared challenge. It harked back to my Witness past, and all the warning sirens wailed loudly in my head, reminding me so much of the stories I was told over and over again of Charles Taze Russell, the founder of the Jehovah's Witnesses movement. It was said of him that God supposedly chose him above all others, to lead his sheep to greener pastures. The Witnesses view him as the 'faithful and wise servant, whom the master has put in charge of the servants in his household to give them their food at the proper time'. Be that as it may, this story isn't about Mr Anderson and his overly complex views, nor about Pastor Russell and his evangelical dreams. It's about an experience I had during the lunch break on the second day of Terry Winchester's workshop.

We sat out in the garden of Terry's Bryanston home eating a delicious yet simple vegetarian lunch. I sat at the pool staring into the water and listened to the conversation around me. I remained detached and somewhat antisocial, just hanging out with my own thoughts that drifted about like the refraction patterns the sun cast on the swimming pool floor.

Sunlight danced in the clear blue water and created arcs of light that changed as I touched the surface of the water with my bare feet. The images mesmerised me, and I soon lost all awareness of the conversations around me as I sank into a deep daydreaming state. Entirely engrossed by the light, I failed to realise that a call had gone out for us to reconvene despite friends having entreated me by name to return to the room.

The refracted arcs of light seemed to get brighter like sheet lightning on a dark stormy night, and appeared to move through the water with greater intensity and power. The light's energy enveloped me, suffused my body, and I felt as though my entire molecular structure began to vibrate faster and faster in ever increasing frequencies until its form vanished and ceased to be. All that remained was an incredible awareness of being. Nothing material existed around me while in all directions I seemed to be in the midst of the brightest, most intense light. It was as if I were in the centre of the noonday sun.

There were no sensations of any kind, no feelings of heat or cold, nothing tangible, no sounds, no form, no images – and yet I had this incredible feeling of peacefulness and tranquillity, and the colours swirled around me in wisps of gold and violet against a predominantly calm bright white background. My ears weren't registering external noises but I was aware of a serene and comforting background sound that was part of me, the melody of the universe and of all creation. I felt loved, embraced, welcomed. Concepts of time and space were foreign here and there was no reasoning, rational, analytical mind to question what, where or why I was having this experience. The best description I have for it, is one of pure 'isness'.

Friends later told me I sat outside for about two hours, which to me felt like an instantaneous lifetime (if that oxymoron makes any sense). Greta proclaimed my experience 'an awakening' and 'rapture.' I'm not sure what it was and I don't really want to label it but I remember it distinctly, for it changed forever my ideas of rituals. Their sacred purpose is to disconnect mind from body, to induce moments of spiritual epiphany, 'awakenings' and realisations of Who I Really Am – just like the one at the pool. If one can use rituals to achieve this holy state of mind but for an instant, one might realise how myopic, illusory and erroneous our identity as a physical person really is. When my awareness coincides with my incorporeal non-quantifiable essence, the experience becomes one of everlasting, blissful, non-threatened, perfect 'isness'. Rituals that do not induce states of oneness seem somewhat pointless and vain.

But, the intellectual mind latches onto its sensory experiences and craves them like an addict seeking their next fix. Ego tries hard to take ownership of one's spiritual experiences and seeks the importance and elevated states of righteousness they offer, anything that raises one's status beyond other mortals. Phoney holiness is as much an ego trip as ostentatious wealth and overt self-importance.

Ego tried everything on numerous occasions to recreate my spiritual experiences but the more it sought to induce them, the more elusive they became. Having learned and taught hypnosis techniques for many years, I came to realise that there is much truth in another of those hypnosis rules of the mind: *the more the conscious effort, the less the subconscious response*. Seeking reproducible steps to 'isness' calls upon the wrong part of the mind, the analytical, rational mind, to bring it into being; but one can't *do* meditation, one has to *be* meditation. One needs to let go, for only then does the other part, the subconscious mind, step forward and open the portal to spirit.

I remained in trance in the room with Ram Dass for perhaps ten or fifteen minutes before I slowly opened my eyes. Ram Dass already had his eyes open and looked at me, seeming to peer right into my soul. Only once before did I experience such an overwhelming feeling of pure connectedness with another being, like I enjoyed with him in that moment, and that was during the last few hours when dad and I sat hand-in-hand as he approached death and slowly left his body.

I started to tell Ram Dass my life story and we spoke as if we were brothers. The little analogue clock was absent and we talked freely over an aromatic pot of *chai*, until, many hours later, Dassi Ma popped her cheerful face around the door and said, 'Ram Dass, you have a Board Meeting conference call in seven minutes'. He looked at me disappointedly and both of us knew that we could have spoken for a lot longer.

I flopped back onto the sofa and stayed there for the rest of the afternoon in a state of tranquil bliss. I composed a pledge to Ram Dass, which really is a decree to me:

> Ram Dass, your passion and faithfulness in bringing Maharaj-ji's teachings to us, inspired generations of men and women to embrace spirit faithfully and fully, a legacy that cannot and will not end. I pledge to take my place humbly amongst truth's many flag-bearers, ready to take these universal teachings to future generations. I can only do so in my own way and in keeping with my unique character and style but I will always remember that behind the uniqueness of form, there is only one source to the message from whence we all speak.

My mind sank back into its peaceful state, the rash soon healed as I lay down on the sofa and slept.

In the late afternoon, I heard muffled voices and knew that Ken and Dassi Ma were taking their afternoon swim accompanying Ram Dass as he slowly waded across the width of pool at a comfortable depth. The water gives his body buoyancy that must be in stark contrast to its heaviness in the chair. It's also a time for him to meditate, gliding back and forth through the water nicely warmed by the Hawaiian sunshine.

I didn't join them, even though I knew I was welcome to, but chose to stay on the sofa in quiet solitude until Dassi Ma popped in with the dinner tray. 'I hope you will join Ram Dass for satsang[139] on the beach tomorrow,' she said, 'as this will be the last time I see you because I've planned a little trip for a few days with one of my friends to Hilo on the Big Island to swim with the dolphins.'

The Island of Hawai'i is some 10 000 square kilometres, an area more than all the other islands combined, and is a short hop of less than 50 kilometres by sea, southeast of Maui. Referring to the Island of Hawai'i as The Big Island prevents confusion with the State of Hawaii. Offset just to the north of its centre is Mauna Kea peak, towering more than four kilometres above sea level. Although Mount Everest holds the title of being the loftiest, Mauna Kea is actually the world's tallest mountain and volcano, rising about ten kilometres from the Pacific Ocean floor. It is home to one of the world's most renowned astronomical observatory sites. This 200 hectare precinct contains a collection of independent facilities that have sprung up since the late 1960s. NASA, the United Kingdom, France, Canada and the United States have huge investments in some very large telescopes and those interested in the subject will readily recognise famous names like the Keck Observatory and the James Clerk Maxwell Telescope. They'll also be aware of plans to complete a 30 metre segmented-mirror telescope on the site. Mauna Kea, chosen for its remote location and height, is ideal because the higher one's elevation above sea level, the better the seeing conditions become. Turbulent and perturbed air causes scintillation, the blurring and twinkling of celestial objects when viewed from Earth. At an altitude of four kilometres however, the air is very thin and the seeing very good. This new telescope boasts adaptive optics that compensate for the remaining atmospheric distortion even at such heights above the sea, making it one of the most precise earth-based instruments ever built.

I rose early on Monday morning, prepared my usual breakfast of oats porridge, and sat on the little wooden deck outside the living room. I wrote as I ate and watched the grey dawn change

---

[139] Satsang (Sanskrit sat = true, sanga = company) is a concept in Indian philosophy that involves (1) the company of the 'highest truth,' (2) the company of a guru, or (3) company with an assembly of persons who listen to, talk about, and assimilate the truth. 'The Satsang Network' *Nova Religio: The Journal of Alternative and Emergent Religions*, Volume 6, Issue 1.

as streaks of red and orange caught faint wispy clouds as though they had been gently tinted with a wash of watercolour from a soft brush. There was plenty of time before our excursion to the beach which Dassi Ma had scheduled for mid-morning – I had time enough to enjoy my solitude and the pleasure of unhurried contemplative writing. The initial exhilaration of being at the house subsided, giving space to new softer feelings of gentle peacefulness.

With only the colourful cotton kikoy wrapped around my waist, warm humid air tenderly touched and caressed my skin and I mused over how little I needed by way of material possessions. The bulk of my luggage remained in Auckland and I carried one small haversack of clothing and other articles to Maui as hand luggage. I had been away from Auckland for over a week and still barely used all the items in my bag. 'What little one really needs' I wrote in my journal, thinking of Maharaj-ji and his blanket, his only possession.

Every item we acquire requires further investments in time to clean and dust it, space to display and house it and additional expenses to maintain, insure and protect it. These demands create iterations of new demands and, before we know it, we're trapped in cycles of attending to our material belongings to the exclusion of living. I mentally tallied up the time I spent on inconsequential activities and compared it to the time I allocated for meditation and introspection and was horrified at how meagre the investment was. My infrequent meditations were glimpses of a magnificent view beyond the jostle of worldly errands and chores that obscured it.

I kept writing well into the morning, sipping tea that made a refreshing change from the watery coffee served in one-litre thermos flasks at the breakfast tables in Waikiki. I heard a car pull up outside around noon and peeked through the window to see if there was any urgency in getting ready and recognised Mike, Ram Dass' friend who drove him to and from the Maui retreat a few years earlier. Mike parked directly in front of the entrance and went inside the house. This gave me ample time to gather the few things I needed for the beach.

I don't really like the beach mainly because I have a fair skin that burns quickly. Noël Coward first performed his song *Mad Dogs and Englishmen* in 1931 and I adopted parts of it as my anthem regarding the sun's blistering effects. 'Only mad dogs and Englishmen go out in the noonday sun.' There are large Red Roman solifuges found in hot southern African sandy locations, known locally as Kalahari Ferraris. This spider-like arachnid has a golf-ball-size body covered in long ginger hair and emerges at dusk to hunt. They move fast and erratically, reaching speeds of up to sixteen kilometres per hour in short bursts and if found out of their boroughs during the heat of the day, they tend to find reprieve from the sun by running from one shady spot to the next. *Solifugae* is a Latin word meaning 'those that flee from the sun' and this strange idiosyncratic behaviour gives rise to a myth that spiders sometimes chase people. But Red Romans simply follow in the coolness provided by one's shadow. Wherever I go, I behave exactly like those solifuges, scuttling from one patch of dappled shade to the next. Whenever I venture into direct sunlight, I always cover my body with a long-sleeved shirt, long cotton pants and a hat and smear sunscreen lotion on all the exposed bits. On the beach I become a greasy magnet for sand, and in the slightest breeze, soon get grit in my ears, eyes, nostrils and teeth. I hate the daytime beach. When I packed my bags in Johannesburg, I didn't anticipate a day at the seaside and packed only a pair of bathing trunks and a few tee-shirts, definitely improper attire for a noonday blast of solar radiation. I asked Dassi Ma if she had sunscreen lotion, which she obligingly gave me but I must confess, I was too vain to ask for a hat because I was terrified of the bright pink one that lay beneath the passenger seat of her car and decided to use my kikoy as a makeshift turban instead.

The elevator drone and muffled voices signalled our imminent departure. I took my bag and strolled outside anxious to meet everyone. Mike helped Ram Dass and positioned him alongside the vehicle's passenger door. I stepped forward to help but didn't really know what to do. I was acutely aware that I was probably not needed as this routine had been executed hundreds of times before without my help. There's a fine line between helpfulness and interference.

I remember Tony, a former boss who stuttered terribly, telling me over a few drinks how disempowered he felt when others tried to finish his words and sentences. 'Th...ey mean well b...b...ut they s...s...strip away my d...d...dignity and p...p...ower.' I struggled with the conflict that arose between my desire to help Ram Dass and not wanting to be a nuisance and I'm sure Ram Dass sensed it. He looked at me, smiled gently and I took the cue to offer help. Mike, intuitively read the situation and sidestepped letting me step forward. I fumbled and heaved to help Ram Dass lift his heavy frame into position in the front seat of the car. Mike would have done it far slicker but I was deeply touched that he let me enjoy that special moment. Mike and Ram Dass sat up front. The engine sparked and roared to life and the large American sedan glided effortlessly around the oval perimeter of Dassi Ma's herb garden and gently accelerated and swished along the open stretch of road. The mood was jovial and light-hearted.

We turned right onto the Hana Highway and headed through Paia, south past Kahului airport and onto the Mokulele Highway, one of two that runs north/south across the land bridge joining the two volcanic mountains. Dassi Ma, dressed in her usual shades of purple, pointed out a farm of wind turbines on the slopes of the mountain behind Maalaea. Wind generates about a fifth of Maui's electrical needs[140]. Mike and Ram Dass chatted about business matters, plans for future events and shared opinions about other guests they expected to visit in coming months.

After a relatively short ride, we left the highway and headed through a small residential area to Kamaole Beach. The American system is very efficient. Wind turbines and a superb highway network support a relatively small community on Maui. One would be lucky to have gravel roads and diesel generators for a population of this size in Africa.

Our car pulled up and parked in a reserved bay parallel to the beach where Ravi Dass and Jeff waited to help. Ravi Dass already secured the use of a public beach buggy that looked like a product designed by a cartoon consortium from Disney. Its low-slung aluminium frame hugged the ground to give it stability, three large oversized bright yellow inflatable wheels prevented it from bogging down in the sand. Its economic army-webbing seat forced the occupant to recline thus eliminating any possibility of them falling out.

Mike and I supported Ram Dass under his knees and armpits, which caused his shirt to creep up under his arms and exposed his belly, and we carried him from the car to the cart. My heart filled with compassion and empathy for him but he didn't seem to notice or mind the indignant clumsiness of his body and welcomed our tender care as we readjusted his clothing and made him comfortable. I had drawn so close to him in such a short time.

The cart, perfectly suited to the beach, glided effortlessly across the sand on its balloon tyres. Ram Dass, barely visible beneath a pile of beach gear that we'd dumped on him, was pushed to special spot on the beach just above the waves' upper reach. Relatively few people were on the beach that day. The concave curve seemed to reduce the beach's length and accentuate the illusion of seclusion. People strolled past, intrigued by all the fuss as we hoisted Ram Dass out of the cart and onto a deckchair. Some folks sauntering by stopped for a moment to greet: 'How are you today Ram Dass?' before wending their way.

Slowly, a core gathered for *satsang*: Ravi Dass, skinny, well tanned with gentle hippie-like qualities. Jeff, wiry, heavily tanned with divinely serene and mesmerising eyes. I liked them

---

[140] *Lonely Planet Maui: Includes Moloka'i and Lana'i* by Glenda Bendure, Ned Friary

both instantly and quickly connected with them. Dassi Ma bustled around quietly, sometimes motherly and often matronly. Mary pulled up later in her plum-coloured Jaguar convertible with its fawn seats and snazzy 'ONE NOW' number plate. She's a warm gentle woman, a retired Pastor from a New Age Church, who wears a typically Christian face, like so many in the business of piousness.

I also liked Orion Kopelman, Candidate Mayor and creative thinker behind Mauitopia[141], a new holistic government ideology intended to turn Maui into 'a real paradise'. Ori's tenacity and *chutzpah* motivated me because he seemed able to set aside the hindering effects of Multiple Sclerosis that impeded his mobility. Ed Elkim, Ori's Campaign Manager and Consulting Synergist at the Universal Temple for Higher Consciousness, helped him onto the beach. Despite his difficulties, Ori passionately pursued his dreams and I cringed, slightly horrified and embarrassed at my timidity and ineffectual ability to manifest what lay waiting in my heart.

The group chatted easily about ideas to promote and facilitate changes in consciousness. Some shared bold ideas of new retreats and spiritual workshops while others drifted off and swam in the unpolluted, warm Pacific waters. Everybody made a point of spending time talking with me, asking what I did and where I came from. When I said 'I'm from South Africa', it usually drew a slightly blank expression. From previous trips to the United States, I discovered that everyday Americans generally have a distorted mental map of the word with continental USA dominating it and all other continents, like bonsai trees, squished between the American coastline and the map's decorative border. I gently scoff at the Americans because they take themselves far too seriously, unlike the Brits who have a long history of poking fun at themselves.

I made a mental note to ask Ram Dass why many of his friends dropped their birth names in favour of Indian spiritual ones. I assumed it was symbolic, discarding part of their 'somebodiness' as Ram Dass termed it. It might be metaphoric: peeling away a product label that brands and categorises us, chiefly the nametag that our parents attached to us at birth. We symbolically wear many labels, like parent, entrepreneur, housewife, student, clever, fat, etc. I despised my idiosyncratic labels and began to remove them ages ago. They tend to separate and lock us into compartments of belief and identity, pressurising us to conform to

---

[141] www.mauitopia.org

their ideologies. *What is expected tends to be realised*[142]. Perhaps, all Aquarians show typically Aquarian traits and characteristics because we're convinced we should behave the way astrology predicts. Is it a self-fulfilling prophecy and an inherent need to conform?

Labels, and there are many, contribute to our erroneous belief that we are *a body*. Without labels, we might sooner recognise that our true nature is one of spirit and not one of form. Spike Milligan, co-creator, main writer and a principal cast member of *The Goon Show*, also appeared in the BBC TV series *Q5*. In the series he performed the role of an inmate in a mental asylum wearing a strait jacket. Many parcel labels were pinned to his jacket with safety pins and bits of string. The satirical look at life appeals to me. I imagine myself fastidiously unpinning each label, reading its identification, tossing the tag into the air and letting it flutter to the ground as I abandoned the belief the label conveys. Every label detached brings a measure of freedom. The more of them lying on the ground; the closer I would get to source. Since we are all magnificent beings of infinite possibility, why should we wear labels to differentiate and separate us?

The motto on the Budge family coat of arms is from Virgil's Aenead: 'Stricta parata neci.' and literally means 'weapons drawn for killing', a phrase that morphed into 'I am prepared to destroy all that is evil' on ancient family heraldry. I suppose that's who I once was, a crusader for goodness. But I like the subtle irony of my name. There's my first name, *Thomas*. Although meaning *twin* in the Aramaic language, given to Thomas Judas, the second Judas of the Apostles, the name differentiates these two of Jesus followers. Thomas questioned Jesus and needed 'seeing is believing' proof of his resurrection. A *Doubting Thomas* is a term describing a sceptic who steadfastly remains such until confronted with good, hard evidence. I'm far from being gullible myself and, like the biblical Thomas, need some sort of evidence before accepting any belief. My surname, *Budge* is a verb meaning *to move*. That's also quite characteristic of me. I'm not a stubborn adherent to my opinions and will readily change them whenever I receive new insight. I don't believe I would be where I am today if I hadn't had two very important virtues: a healthy dose of scepticism (*Thomas*), and the flexibility to move forward easily (*Budge*).

After an hour or so on the beach, Dassi Ma pulled a greyish lifejacket from her bag and helped Ram Dass put it on. She slipped a neoprene webbed mitten over his strong left hand and

---

[142] This is one of *The Eight Rules of the Mind* often found in Hypnotherapy curricula, for which I cannot find a source to quote

secured its Velcro strap tightly at the wrist. A few strong men lifted Ram Dass onto the beach cart and pushed it slowly into the sea until he floated free. Ram Dass bobbed about on his back in the shallow water as others grouped around him.

'Wouldn't you like to join Ram Dass for a swim?' asked Dassi Ma. I was delighted at the prospect, quickly pulled off my shirt and sprinted the few metres into the water to take my place amongst his friends. He used his webbed mitten to ease his way through each incoming wave and in the backwash he drifted further from the beach. The ground soon dropped away beneath our feet, leaving us floating in the gentle, clear but restless turquoise water. Friends hovered around Ram Dass, without coming particularly close. None seemed overly concerned about his safety as he single-handedly paddled further and further away from the shore. Friends came and went, swimming up to him, sharing a word or two and then drifting away again.

At one point when I was the closest to him, a big wave tumbled over us. I dived under it, and as I emerged on the other side I saw that it had toppled him onto his belly with his face in the water. I watched for a while, waiting for him to turn over, but he didn't. Long seconds passed as he lay motionless and I looked to his friends for guidance, hoping that they would suggest my next move, but nobody looked our way. About a minute passed and I began to worry a little. I swam up to him and touched his shoulder. He sprang out of the water and sucked in a lung full of air. 'I had you worried!' he said, taunting me, mischief written all over his face. He again had that unique Ram-Dass glint in his eye. He smiled at me, sucked in a huge mouthful of seawater and spat it out boyishly in a long steady stream. I looked around at the others and realised that I'd been set up; the joke was on me. They were all giggling.

It took quite some time for us to swim out to an anchored buoy in the Maalaea Bay. Ram Dass grabbed hold of it first and hugged it firmly. Powered by the sea they bobbed up and down together.

I remember thinking that I have a far better sense of oneness in water. I feel part of the ocean but I never get the same feeling from the air that surrounds me. Water's density interacts with the skin differently from the way air does. We've become so accustomed to the feelings air produces on our skin, and soon after birth we forget that it envelopes us. Air connects us to everything else. Water's heavier density gives me a buoyancy that I don't have in air. I love floating in the sea as it carries me back and forth like a child rocked in its mother's arms. Sardine shoals respond as one organism in the ocean, as if driven by a common mind that belongs more to the water than it does to the fish in it. This got me thinking: are fish as oblivious of the water that envelops them as we are of the air that surrounds us? If we were sea mammals like dolphins, would we still think of ourselves as distinctly separate from one other in the same way we tend to do in air?

Out near the buoy, some 200 meters from the beach, the ocean force gently washed us back and forth and we could do nothing to resist it. The water had its agenda and incorporated us in its plan. It was futile to oppose it and the only course of action that remained was for us to *surrender*. I longed to fall into the arms of the divine in the same way that I surrendered to the ocean. I imagined how nice it would be to completely surrender to my inner godhead and be at one with everything around me in the same way we were with the ocean. We conserved our energy out there by yielding to the ocean forces, and I'm sure the metaphor remains consistent when we surrender to the ebb and flow of the divine within. I thought a lot about Ram Dass's advice about *faith* and *surrender* there with him hugging the buoy.

When I came within earshot, he held onto the buoy even tighter and exclaimed, 'Oh boy! Oh boy! Oh buoy!' He beckoned that I should come and do the same. 'It's our tradition,' he said, as I took my turn to hug the red and white barnacled marker and repeated his words aloud for all to hear. Ego squirmed, feeling a little stupid, bobbing out there with Baba on the buoy.

I was ravenous by the time we left the beach. We drove the short distance north to eat lunch on the shady wooden deck of a tiny, secluded seafood restaurant in the local neighbourhood. A small group of us sat around the wooden table chatting and eating. Sitting at the table behind me was a middle-aged couple. But the man couldn't contain his curiosity and eventually stood up to greet Ram Dass. He interjected politely: 'You are Ram Dass, are you not?' He told us that he and his wife were on vacation away from their hometown somewhere in a mid-American state and explained how Ram Dass's teachings had influenced them both so positively. Ram Dass graciously accepted their endorsement and, as the wife joined her husband in meeting him, Ram Dass kissed them both gently on the back of their hands.

On our drive back from the beach through Kihei's residential area, Ram Dass raised his arm and wiggled his finger urgently to catch my attention: 'Tom! Tom!' he said hastily. 'Here's something for you...' He pointed out to the right, giggling and drawing attention to the local Kingdom Hall of Jehovah's Witnesses.

'Thanks, Ram Dass! Who needs enemies when I have a friend like you?'

The next morning I watched the morning glow push away the darkness of night. In those twilight moments I heard Dassi Ma drive away to start her excursion to the Big Island. I settled down to my daily journaling. My perfectly tranquil mind opened the way to a quiet spaciousness inside that's impossible to describe. I had no agenda, no pressing need to do anything, and no issues jostling for mind's attention. Everything was perfectly serene – a splendid example of Eckhart Tolle's *Power of Now*[143].

By mid-morning Ram Dass was back for another chat, and I had my chance to ask: 'What is the importance of a spiritual name? Why have so many of your friends dropped their given names in favour of spiritual ones?'

'It's a process of rebirth.' He paused to think like searching for a missing piece in a jigsaw puzzle and struggled to articulate his words: 'By taking on a new name one drops the old identity in every respect and emerges anew.' He paused in one of his long trance moments: 'It's more than that for me; it is a remembering, every day a remembering.' We sat silently as I tried to digest what he'd just implied in so few words. Taking on a different name wasn't an ego trip, it was quite the opposite – it was a daily way of remembering that he had completely surrendered his former identity, favouring a new realisation of whom he is.

Ram Dass began to giggle boyishly. I raised an eyebrow and widened my eyes in expectation of what he was about to say. Slowly lifting his hand and pointing skywards, he asked, 'Do you want to know your spiritual name?'

I was naturally curious but I shunned my ego's immediate delight in having a spiritual name. I didn't really like the idea of a spiritual name because I thought of it as somewhat pretentious. I replied in a subdued and cautious tone, 'Sure I do!'

Ram Dass disappeared into the cosmos in trance, silently mouthing and repeating fragments of a name that slowly and magically took form. He tapped his third eye to encourage a deeper search for my sacred identity. I sat there trying to open my heart to the name in hopes that it might bring me closer to understanding my true nature, yet fearful of the consequences of knowing it. I doubted whether I truly wanted to know.

---

[143] *The Power of Now*, Eckhart Tolle, New World Library, 1999

His eyelids started to flutter like a butterfly dancing around a flower looking for nectar and then opened. One of the signs of deep trance is expressive aphasia and this, combined with the after-effects of his stroke, made saying the name that much more difficult.

'K... K... Kali...' he said, massaging the crease between his eyebrows, '*Kali Ram.*'

He sighed contentedly as if rewarding himself for a job well done. His posture froze in a motionless state of pure anticipation and expectation, waiting for my response, his finger pointing upwards, prompting, if not willing my next move.

Kali Ram. My ego wasn't happy with that. In fact, it wasn't amused at all.

Kali was the female goddess I'd encountered in Singapore.

> She has four arms, with a sword in one hand and the head of a demon in another. The other two hands bless her worshippers, and say, 'fear not!' She has two dead heads for her earrings, a string of skulls as necklace, and a girdle made of human hands as her clothing. Her tongue protrudes from her mouth, her eyes are red, and her face and breasts are sullied with blood. She stands with one foot on the thigh, and another on the chest of her husband, Shiva.[144]

Mmm, I really wasn't sure about this. I failed to find any enthusiasm for the name at all. I sat there quite numb looking at Ram Dass. My frown of incredulity and my bewildered state of mind betrayed my displeasure, but Ram Dass held his posture expectantly.

He broke the tension: 'You need to bring balance to the male energy in your life. In spirit there is neither male nor female. Both are the same. Honour both in you.'

This still didn't help me much and I don't believe I thanked him for giving me my spiritual name. I had plenty to work with, lots to research and much to contemplate before I could embrace it. I spent most of that day trying to discover parallels between my new name and me.

---

[144] http://hinduism.about.com/od/hindugoddesses/a/makali.htm

Ram, meaning 'pleasing', is a common Indian name for males. The name Ram originates from Rama the seventh incarnation of Lord Vishnu. Rama's life and journey is one of perfect adherence to dharma despite the harsh tests of life and time. He is the embodiment of chivalry and virtue. Rama is conceived as a model of reason, right action, and desirable virtues. Hanuman is his monkey devotee.

In Indian philosophy, *purusha* (male – the eternal, authentic self) is opposed to *prakriti* (female – material nature in its germinal state). The Encyclopaedia Britannica suggests, 'All animate and inanimate objects and all psychomental experiences are emanations of prakriti. It is confusion of purusha with prakriti that keeps the self in bondage; disassociation of purusha from prakriti is its liberation.'[145] Together purusha and prakriti constitute the two ontological realities of the phenomenal universe. *Kali* is highly symbolic. We see her standing on the body of her husband Shiva. He, the purusha, lies inactive below. Shiva's divine energy takes the form of Kali and does all the work. But they are not mutually exclusive. Together they represent two sides of the same reality of the cosmos and are inseparable – prakriti. Together they constitute the whole of existence. This single piece of Hindu symbolism neatly embraces everything I believe about mind, body and spirit and the tripartite relationship between them.

Why had Ram Dass connected Ram and Kali to form my spiritual name? I first thought that Kali, also known as 'the black one,' might have symbolised the darkness of my past. But I no longer judge my past as something dark. Kali is the goddess associated with eternal energy but is also 'she who destroys'. She conveys ideas of death, destruction, and the consuming aspects of reality. God is not just benevolent but also destructive.

Kali partly represents entropy, the transitory nature of matter that eventually falls into states of disintegration, the purely natural tendency of things to move toward chaos, not order. Batteries run down, machines break, buildings crumble, roads decay and living things die. One needs to lose one's fear of death, destruction and deterioration to find spiritual liberation. One should learn to embrace entropy as a holy function of form and not to fear it as a failure in the system. In a dualistic world, one cannot experience and appreciate birth without death, construction without destruction and conservation without consumption, just as one cannot fully comprehend heat without having experienced cold.

---

[145] http://www.britannica.com/EBchecked/topic/484231/purusha

Kali is the supreme mistress of the five elements in the universe[146] and holds the creative and destructive powers of time. Instead of being dark and devilish, she is actually the symbol of triumph over death. The *Course* says, 'Nothing real can be threatened. Nothing unreal exists. Herein lies the peace of God.'[147] What then is real? Spirit is. It can't be threatened; nothing exists beyond mind. What is unreal? Every*thing*; every aspect of form is unreal. It's a mere vibration of energy, a sensory experience registered in the grey matter of our brains. Form comes and goes. No*thing* is permanent. When we finally surrender to the highest constituent within, we heed Jesus' advice: 'Do not store up for yourselves treasures on earth, where moth and rust destroy, and where thieves break in and steal but store up for yourselves treasures in heaven, where neither moth nor rust destroys, and where thieves do not break in or steal.'[148]

Kali teaches us to move beyond form, to have faith to surrender fully to our godhead. Karma then disappears and therein lies the 'peace of God'.

---oooOooo---

As the sun's sting faded in the late afternoon, I slipped into my bathing trunks and headed quietly around the house to the pool. Not wanting to encroach on Ram Dass's privacy, I chose to swim at that moment, assuming that he wouldn't be swimming on Dassi Ma's day off with her friends.

Draping my towel over the wooden bench I took the leaf sieve and began to scoop out floating debris blown in by the high winds of the previous night. The house was quiet. Ken lives on the ground floor in the centre of the building, Dassi Ma on the east side and Ram Dass occupies the entire top floor suite. As I slowly worked my way around the pool's circumference, I kept a vigilant lookout to make sure that I hadn't disturbed anyone. Once finished, I quietly sank into the tepid water and swam back and forth using it as an opportunity for some serene meditation.

It wasn't too long before I caught a glimpse of Ram Dass sitting in a patch of late-afternoon sunlight on the upstairs wooden patio outside his quarters. I pretended not to notice him but

---

[146] Some say: earth, fire, water, air and ether; others say: wood, fire, earth, metal, and water.
[147] *A Course in Miracles*, T-Intro-2.2-4, Combined Volume (Third Edition) Copyright© 2007 by the Foundation for A Course in Miracles.
[148] Matthew 6:19-21, *New American Standard Bible*

he soon latched his chair in position on the outside elevator and descended into the garden. He started wheeling his way along the winding garden path and I met him, and helped him back to the pool. He had his towel and a little music system on his lap. We placed the music system on the bench where it played a soothing compilation of Hindu devotional songs.

I held Ram Dass securely and helped him out of his chair and into the pool. 'This is how I broke my hip,' he said. 'We forgot to latch the chair and it shot back sending me to the floor.'

Every step deeper into the pool altered his buoyancy and made helping him much easier. Ram Dass soon walked effortlessly from one side of the pool to the other, silently mouthing the words of the Hindu songs drifting on the gentle afternoon breeze. Ken joined us later and we swam until the sunlight faded.

'Guys,' I said, 'I don't think my stay at the house will be complete until I've experienced the hot tub.'

Ram Dass's eyes lit up instantly at the prospect. Matronly Dassi Ma was far away swimming with dolphins and I sensed he had a moment of freedom and intended using it.

'Now?' he asked, taunting me to say yes.

'Why not, Ram Dass,' I replied, 'why not!'

---oooOooo---

Tuesday was my last day at the house. I packed my bag early and placed it on the bed. Dassi Ma had organised a lift to take me to the airport later that afternoon. Ram Dass would also be away from the house in the afternoon for a medical appointment in Kahului. I walked the property in the morning, took a few snapshots and settled back onto the sofa in the living room for a mid-morning meditation in the presence of Maharaj-ji. Meditation had become effortless at the house, as though some invisible force influenced my mind to let go more fully than it would normally have done. The deeper I sank into trance, the more oblivious I became of time. Colours once again swirled and danced around me like playful companions. Greens, blues and hues of purple, like celestial beings, encouraged me to surrender as they took me on an excursion deep into the cosmos. Bodily sensations and mental thoughts subsided completely. Awareness drifted, floated and sank like a feather on the breeze, gliding through intangible realms of my subconscious mind. All was comforting and reassuring. The experience was intangible, without material content, and had no objective reference, which allowed it to be here and there simultaneously; everywhere yet nowhere, everything but nothing. All sense of personal identity disappeared as the outer boundaries of form dissolved. Emotions disappeared too and there was no great sense of joy or happiness. There was certainly no fear or anxiety, just an incredible sense of peacefulness and spaciousness. I was neither alone nor in company, limited neither by spatial reference nor by time, Awareness Was. I'd slowly become addicted to this state of connectedness.

As I slowly emerged from my morning meditation, a little disoriented, I looked up at Maharaj-ji and contemplated what the real purpose of my visit to the house had been.

I had no doubt that it was very important and brought my spirituality into sharp focus. There's a lot of energy in the sun's diffused rays, but when refracted and brought together through a lens they become a bright, blistering pinpoint of light and heat. I faced many personal demons on my way to the house. Taking the journey was the real work. Self-doubt, self-sabotage, a false sense of lack of authority and feelings of invalidity were the primary motivators to seek Ram Dass's advice. But one by one they were resolved before I had arrived. In the refracting presence of my teacher, spirit's magnificent rays were focused and the intensity of the energy within soon ignited a renewed enthusiasm and passion. I learned to surrender faithfully to the efforts of a higher force that propelled me forward.

Ken came across to the cottage: 'Ram Dass would like to see you over at the house to say goodbye.' I found my journal, slipped on my shoes and walked across the driveway. Ken showed me into the living room, bade goodbye, and left. Ram Dass was already there, sitting in his wheelchair in a patch of noonday light that shone down upon him like a beam of heavenly approval through the ceiling skylight. Our farewells were brief.

'My dearest Ram Dass!' I said, tears welling up in my eyes: 'I spent a lot of time distilling *Kali Ram*. I think it means *"A virtuous man of God who, despite the harsh tests of life, sees oneness beyond time and form and ably brings that message to others."* Ram is that man of God and Kali the goddess of time and change. She is associated with death and rebirth and is the redeemer of the universe through the destruction of the extremes of opposites. She really represents the oneness beyond time and form.'

'That's exactly right!' he said, overjoyed that I had finally comprehended the magnitude of my spiritual name.

I told him how my visit to the house had focused mind and how it had ignited new flames of enthusiasm.

'Right!' he said, waving his hand slightly and smiling with that all-too-familiar twinkle in his eye.

'I'm not too sad to leave,' I said bravely, 'But I'm overjoyed at having been here.'

'Two things, Tom' he said, putting on a sterner look by creasing the little furrow between his eyebrows, '*Surrender* and *faith*!'

'They're tied to my heart with an elastic bungee cord and each time I stray too far they gently tug me back.'

He hugged me.

'This has been good for both of us,' he said.

'We've shared a lot of very private stuff, Ram Dass '

'I know!' he replied, smiling sweetly as I left.

I returned to the apartment to wait for my ride to the airport, my heart bursting with a renewed zest for life.

At three o'clock, I heard a car pull up at the house and thought it was for me even though it was quite a bit earlier than I had expected. I hopped up to look outside. I was flabbergasted at what I saw. Parked in the driveway, directly in front of the house, was a hearse and the driver had already gone inside. This wasn't just some big American sedan. It was a real hearse with tinted windows and a black vinyl-upholstered roof, complete with all the decorative chrome swirls and twirls. Why was there a hearse parked outside Ram Dass's house? My mind ran miles ahead and I had flashbacks of the undertakers removing Dad's body from the house after he had died. Images of death flickered like a rapid slideshow through my mind. A flood of bizarre, macabre thoughts plagued my rational mind. But muffled voices brought me back into the moment and I realised I had been standing at the window for a long time in a state of utter bewilderment. I watched intently as Ken walked across to the vehicle and opened the door. Instead of wheeling Ram Dass out of the house feet first, Jeff, the person I'd met on the beach, pushed him in his chair and helped him into the passenger seat. Their conversation was lively and upbeat. Ken hopped in behind Ram Dass and they drove off.

The whole experience was quite surreal. It took some time for me to recalibrate the scene in my mind. Eventually, I shook my head to rearrange my thoughts as though they were a bag of loose marbles, and sat with a pot of tea pondering the ironical idea of driving a hearse as one's private vehicle. It's a lovely statement about one's comfort with death, bringing death and life together through the vehicle's symbolism. Every day, one would be aware that one's next journey could be feet first in the back of the hearse instead of upfront as passenger. That's a sobering thought and it reminded me of the wise saying, 'Learn to die during the day so that you don't have to die at night.' Meaning that one should be utterly comfortable with death so that it doesn't sneak up on one unexpectedly. Driving a hearse might not be such a repugnant thing after all. Simple actions like placing one's grocery bags instead of a human cadaver into the back of a hearse have a quirky twist to them – daily domestic use of a hearse continually mocks death.

My lift, Tom, arrived at four o'clock to drive me to the airport and slowly mind's serenity changed from spiritual bliss to hustle and bustle as we approached the busy airport. In stark contrast to the energy of the house, stress hung heavily in the air and fear loomed ominously, fuelled by the strong security presence at the airport. Rows of X-ray machines search for contraband and the sniffer machines hunt for malevolent and dangerous substances.

Inside the 'safe zone' many passengers gorged themselves on fizzy, sugary drinks and greasy, stodgy food. None appeared truly hungry but ate out of habit, perhaps to alleviate boredom and distract the attention away from their stress. I watched them and I thought of Africa. Not the wild Africa but the impoverished people of Africa, those masses living in corrugated-iron shanty houses in informal ghettos along the roadsides leading to the opulent shopping malls of the affluent. Some of these people might have to steal to feed their kids yet here was another group, quite oblivious and ignorant of the plight of others, burping and forcing down another mouthful at Kahului airport, distracting themselves from their pain of a very different kind.

I thought of the wastefulness in a world of material opulence, recalling Starbucks in America. No matter where I went, I never once saw them serve coffee in a china mug. Every coffee consumed in the store came in a heavy-duty, disposable, double-laminated container with its virtually indestructible plastic splash-proof lid and separate, thick, cardboard sleeve to prevent patrons from burning their fingers. I also remembered a lunch in a fine Indian restaurant in San Francisco. There, I ate from a disposable place setting made up of plastic plates, throwaway cutlery and a thick plastic beer mug. I cringed at tipping it all into the garbage after my meal. It appalled me because I understood the carbon footprint I created from just one meal. These were not flimsy utensils but as robust and stylish as any non-disposable item could be and I knew that poorer folk back home would cherish a set of them on their table. Here, in these bloated cities, refuse disposal teams clear the sidewalks of tons of similar items every night, all destined for the trash heap. Why would one do such a thing? For profit of course! With high rentals and soaring labour costs, discarding utensils is cheaper than storing, using and washing their reusable alternatives.

Despite the harsh realities of urban living, Ram Dass's teachings lingered exquisitely. Slowly, their profundity emerged like discovering layered flavours in a perfectly prepared meal. I cannot tell how and when my transformation occurred but it did. Unnoticeable, constant changes happened faithfully. Transformation directed me incrementally into finer states of grace. Fear dissolved into love. Peace descended leaving permanent feelings of blessedness.

I don't meditate formally much nowadays because I find myself in a constant state of connectedness. I still attract interesting challenges in life of course. But I'm more prepared now than ever before to surrender to my highest self and let His will be done.

---oooOooo---

I once saw life as a rollercoaster ride. Its track represented time from birth to death and the undulations were life's highs and lows. Ego revels in our ascent to success and it shrieks as we plummet from those highs. We take delight, watching the cart creep upwards to heights hitherto unattained. But the principle of 'more is never enough' keeps ego striving for more. Ego would like to see the cart reach higher and higher levels on the ride. Yet life has a habit of taking a dip from time to time and often plunges us into periods of despair.

Plummeting from the peak can be a frightening experience as ego takes stock of the losses. As we fall we begin to lose faith and hope. In states of panic we might lose self-respect, confidence, relationships and livelihood. Timidity and risk-aversion might turn us away from future opportunities of growth and recovery. Downturns in life are often as frightening as a long and treacherous ride on the downward slope of the rollercoaster ride. Nobody enjoys plummeting relentlessly downwards to the dip at the bottom of the tracks where we lose our elevated advantage.

Eventually the cart reaches the bottom, the dip at the end of the downward slope of the rollercoaster ride. It's the final spot before recovery is possible. At this point on the ride, one would not want to apply the brakes because it would bleed away the momentum and end the trip. Depression and a sense of giving up are not options when one finds oneself in a dip on the rollercoaster ride of life.

Consider this: would you pay for a rollercoaster ride that took you along a perfectly straight and level track? Probably not, as it would be too boring and wouldn't stimulate the senses at all. One seldom gains wisdom from the easy events in life. Tracking horizontally on our ride wouldn't yield much wisdom at all.

According to the laws of physics, energy in a closed system is never lost. The kinetic energy gained during the descent becomes the latent power that drives the cart up the other side. If we could only find a method to convert our value of loss (the accumulated energy of all our losses incurred during our fall) into a currency of gain (the kinetic energy), we might give ourselves impetus enough to reach greater heights. But how do we convert our value of loss into our currency of gain? We do so by taking wisdom from our tough experiences and applying them to future events. There's no future in our past.

I have lived most of my life in gold mining regions of the Witwatersrand. Here, the average gold yield is three to four grams of gold per metric tonne. That's about the weight of a small postage stamp redeemed from a cocopan-load of rock. But gold's high market value makes the whole exercise of mining it worthwhile. There is enough worth in a few grams of gold to fund mining it from deep inside Earth's crust. Gold's value pays for the people, equipment, processing and refinement. It yields profit for the mine's shareholders too. Wisdom is a bit like gold. There's a tiny yield of wisdom in every truckload of dirty experiences.

Knowledge is freely available, it is crammed into every bookshop and is freely downloadable off the internet. But wisdom is different. It is more precious than gold. Unlike gold however, it cannot be bought. We earn wisdom, taking it from life's experiences, converting the insights from our tough experiences into our currency of gain. Wisdom underpins our growth and helps erase karma. Wisdom is the scaffolding that supports our upward track.

Undulations in life are natural ebbs and flows of our creative energy. Spirit provides potential to a wide swathe of human experiences moulded by mind. I was once concerned about the amplitude of my experiences, the maximum absolute values of my periodically varying highs and lows. Like many others, I sought only frequent highs and fearfully shied away from any lows. However, now that I'm aware of the wisdom I glean from these waves of ups and downs, I'm more interested in their frequency and not their amplitude. It no longer matters how elevated the peaks are or how deep the troughs. I'm keen to recover as quickly as I can. The more undulating experiences I can undergo in life, the more opportunity I have to find wisdom. Where it once took me a period of years to cycle through one of these curves, I can now drop from one peak and rise to the next in a matter of days and sometimes in only a few hours. A question that quickly helps me in such times of crisis is: 'What does this experience teach me that I could not learn any other way?'

There is of course a fundamental flaw in my metaphor of the rollercoaster ride. I presuppose that time is linear, implying that we as passengers in the cart move relentlessly forward through life, being tossed about by some force over which we have no control. That assumption comes from our paradigm of time. Because we plotted the complete ordered field of real numbers along a straight-line vector with all positive numbers appearing in ascending sequence to the right and all negative ones in descending order to the left, we similarly tend to comprehend time in much the same way. We visualise it as a timeline with past events appearing to the left and future ones to the right. In the Gregorian calendar, Jesus' birth marks the zero point. Events that occur before Christ sequentially decrement while all others increment. The term *Anno Domini* [after Christ] or its modern equivalent 'The Common Era' encompasses all positively numbered years and is the predominant international timekeeping standard in use today. But what if our concept of time was different?

There is another time paradigm hinted at in holy texts, that of the Everlasting Moment of Now. For many, a conundrum arises when we try to conceptualise Now, especially when trying to map it onto our straight-line time vector. Now becomes a moving cursor relentlessly marching forward towards the right, into the future. It cannot backtrack nor can it jump forwards. We perceive Now as a division, an imaginary junction between past and future and as such, it doesn't exist at all. Yet holy texts urge us to live in the Now. How is that possible?

Now takes on a richness of understanding only when we switch paradigms. We must drop our linear concept of time and adopt a very different one instead. George, a friend attending one of my Bhagavad Gita Easter weekend retreats, drew my attention to the existence of another paradigm. We were using the rollercoaster metaphor to describe life's undulations as described above, when he proposed: 'It might be possible that the cart remains stationary and the entire ride moves under mind's influence.' Mmm, food for thought! That would imply that we are always safe, unharmed, motionless and that all the supposed experiences of moving through space and time are nothing more than fantasies of the mind. Perhaps that's what living in the Now implies.

I had an unusual experience on a flight one day. Tired from the preparations for the trip, I flopped into my seat next to the window and slowly allowed myself to enter a deep, relaxing trance-state. The crew closed the aircraft doors, the pushback began and we followed slowly along the taxiway to the runway's threshold. In my trance, I had the distinct sensation of being still in my seat and that the whole world was moving past me. The feeling was weird and I decided to enhance it by giving my subconscious mind a few compounding suggestions in order to create a self-induced hypnotic hallucination in which I firmly believed that the world moved around me and I remained stationary. The engines quickly roared to life on the threshold and the aircraft sped down the runway easing its way into the sky. I was convinced I had stayed still in space. Yet here I was hundreds of feet in the air. I hadn't changed my body posture, but the world around me had altered considerably. When the cabin lights flickered on and I emerged from trance, it was a deeply incongruent sensation trying to recalibrate the outside view with the nothingness that I alleged.

George's proposition wasn't that preposterous after all. Spirit is permanently still, resting everlastingly in the infinite moment of now. Mind's projected world is in constant motion, moving back and forth, up and down in three-dimensional space and apparently moving inexorably forward in time.

In the everlasting stillness of now, spirit peacefully observes mind's playful creations. Where mind perceives suffering and loss, gain and happiness, Spirit receives wisdom. By aligning our awareness with mind and body, life seems to become a hectic, adrenaline-filled rollercoaster ride; by aligning it with spirit, time and space dissolve and suffering disappears forever.

Just an afterthought: if all that there is, is the eternal moment of now, what lies outside that moment? Not-now! Past and future lose their meaning. Not-now is a compendium of possibilities, some realised and many untapped – a field of all that is and all that will be.

Not all Help is Helpful

The dogs barked without let up so I went to investigate and found two strangers parked in a little white Volkswagen Golf at my gate. Now you have to understand that the gate is some three hundred meters from the house and there were nine little dogs anxious to defend their twenty-hectare property. To fill in the picture, the locked gates straddle the access road that follows the contours around a hill to the house but there are no fences either side of the gate, only sharp Pelindaba rocks native to the area, strewn among the elephant grass across the gentle slopes.

We once hosted a function at Protea Ranch and the caterer, a rotund man, arrived earlier than expected and came huffing and puffing up to the house, completely out of breath and peeved: 'I found your gates locked and had to climb them to come to the house.'

'You did what?' I asked in a teasing tone, smirking gently.

'I climbed the gate' he said acerbically.

'Why do that when there is no fence. You could easily have walked around the gate?'

He hadn't noticed the missing fences and, for him, gates and fences went together like gin and tonic.

The two guys causing the raucous barking were equally aware of the solitary gates and prudently waited in their car. I felt safe enough with a pack of yapping dogs at my heels to walk the distance and discover their purpose.

One of them got out of the car as I approached and when I was in earshot, greeted me politely. 'Hi, I'm Martin and I hope you don't mind us being here.' He kept chatting until I got close. 'My friend Michael and I are performing an environmental survey in this area and we'd like to get your permission to place a few bait traps in the trees.'

'What are you hoping to catch?'

'Fruit Chafers. They're a certain type of scarab beetle and we're hoping to find one called the Goliath Beetle. It's the biggest of them all in this area.'

Having established their credentials, I gave permission for them to come in and so began an interesting friendship with Martin over several visits during his systematic survey across the ranch. I learned of Martin's fine arts talents, saw photographs of his skilled artwork, examined his impeccable insect collection and marvelled at his array of live baboon spiders. He's a man blessed with some remarkable skills. He has abilities and knowledge that would be the envy of many. But he lacks the ability to utilise the system in order to capitalise on his talents and so lives alone and frugally.

Martin spent the entire summer collecting insect specimens and then faded from the ranch during the winter months. About a year later, I received a telephone call from him early one Saturday morning and he sounded desperate. 'Please help me!'

'What's the matter, Martin?'

'The owner of the flat I'm in gave me the rest of the day to move out. I'm horribly in arrears with my rent and if I'm not out by sunset, he is sending men across in the morning to put my belongings on the pavement. My spiders will surely die outside.'

'What are you going to do?'

'I have no options! There's nothing I can do and that's why I'm calling you for help.'

There's always an element of human drama in tragedies like this, which limits one's choices. If Martin said, 'I'm looking for a change of scenery and would like to live on the farm,' my response would have been much easier to make and I would have probably declined because I enjoy my solitude and independence. With the situation skewed by compassion for another person's plight, the decision wasn't quite so cut and dry. I often wonder what I would have done if it was I that was in Martin's predicament. Whilst I had deep empathy for him, I doubt that I would have ever mismanaged my affairs to the point where I would be on the verge of eviction. However, assuming that I was desperate for help, I'd probably be very grateful for any assistance and I'd do everything possible to limit any presumptuous need of my helper's resources. There was a time when I lived with Graham and Myrtle after my breakup with Johann and I believe I did my utmost to contribute in cash and kind to the running of their home in order to minimise the impact of my stay with them. I assumed Martin would do the same.

'Well, I have an empty cottage on the property where you can stay for a little while until you find your feet. I'll come across town and fetch your things now and we can bring them back to the farm.' And so Martin came to live on the ranch.

I live and work on the farm, conduct workshops in the auditorium on the property over weekends and consult with clients at other times. During Martin's first few weeks on the farm, I would retire to the main house in the evening after work, cook supper and invite him to eat with me. But that became awkward because of my vegetarian lifestyle and his different personal tastes and requirements. I soon stopped sharing meals with him but it became apparent that his financial predicament was far worse than I imagined. He didn't have enough money to feed himself. And so I gave him a small weekly allowance to provide for his basic needs.

It felt good because I had enough compassion and sufficient resources to help another person in their time of need.

However, as the weeks passed, a growing feeling of resentment slowly fomented deep inside me. I always enjoy my work even though the hours are often long and the responsibility of counselling heavy. But now I compared the inordinate amount of time I spent working against the endless days Martin spent swanning around the property, enjoying the ranch's facilities. Never once did he offer to contribute to the farm's running and upkeep in any way. On one occasion I sheepishly asked him to do some interior painting, for which I would pay him, but he refused, saying that it wasn't the kind of work he did.

I did some deep soul-searching to understand my umbrage to his presence. I quickly berated myself for being selfish. I certainly had the means to help so why should I not show generosity. Something was amiss in this equation.

It reminded me of a previous occasion when I travelled into Pretoria every Saturday morning to host my radio show on astronomy, anchored by a well-known broadcaster, Trevor. He and I worked together for about three years and grew to know each other quite well. He owned a sound studio and a company that provided background music and personalised advertising to numerous retail outlets. He lived with his wife and two sons in a spacious apartment near Pretoria's city centre. One Saturday close to Christmas, he asked if I'd join him for lunch as he had something he needed to talk about.

Sitting in the restaurant he asked, 'I'm so embarrassed to put this to you but I don't know who else to turn to. I have a lot tied up in my business but things aren't working out that well at the moment and I have some awful cash flow difficulties. Tom, I would like to borrow some money and I shall repay you at the end of January. If I don't get help, I'll have to let the apartment go and I don't know where else to live. I couldn't imagine putting the boys on the street.' This was quite an audacious request and certainly not the first time people have approached me for financial help. Like the situation with Martin, it's not always easy to say no because people's requests are often born out of a genuine need. One almost has to reciprocate their friendship and thus indebts oneself, obligating oneself to give them what they want. Saying no seems heartless. We feel that it could cause a rift in the relationship and collapse the friendship. One can of course be flippant, a little thick skinned, and ask, 'Have you approached a bank for a personal loan?' Invariably the answer is no. 'So if the bank won't give you a loan, and I'm sure they have far better ways of assessing risk than I do, why should I take the risk they won't incur? After all, I'm not a bank.' It's a way out of lending money to others but friendships are never run like businesses and that kind of attitude doesn't solve our friend's problem.

I asked Trevor, 'So how much do you need?'

'One hundred and eighty-five thousand.'

'That's an awful lot of money,' I responded. But he seemed so desperate and I'd known him to be a trustworthy person. I thought about it for a little while over lunch and agreed to help because it was only for a short period of some six weeks.

You already know of course what happened next …. He never repaid the money. He'd bought a plum coloured Rover within a month of securing my loan. It infuriated me. I was incensed at my stupidity and equally outraged at his audacity. Although we continued working together the relationship was strained and he absolutely avoided any conversation about repayment. Some six months later I received an invitation to one of his business marketing functions, and decided to go in order to get an inside view. His wife had set out a buffet spread of eats and drinks and we milled about until he called for our attention, hailing us to listen to his speech.

'Thanks everyone for being here,' he began. 'The Lord blessed us generously over the last few months. The Lord provided everything we needed and I'd like to start with a prayer to ask Him to bless our business too, so please close your eyes and join with me.'

The hair on my neck prickled and I clenched my jaws in rage, thinking, 'It's not the Lord that's been generous, it was me! I paid for this food, these drinks and for the Rover parked outside. This has bugger-all to do with the Lord.' I put down my drink and left during his lengthy and pious prayer. Fuming all the way home, I resolved that I would never help another person ever again. Dad said, 'Never lend anyone your money, your car or your wife'. Trevor's business promotion pushed me over the edge. With enough emotional energy coursing through my veins and my patience exhausted, I wrote him an email demanding the repayment of *my* money. But soon, I became the villain. He accused me of being too insensitive to his situation, too heartless. My radio contract came up for renewal and I declined another season and moved on but the anguish remained with me for many years.

Martin settled into a comfortable lifestyle on the farm and, while it wasn't opulent living, I provided him with a roof over his head, hot water and food. I kept enquiring whether he was seeking employment or not and the answer was always the same, 'I'm too busy'. He regarded collecting, cataloguing and pinning insects as his employment. In fact, it obsessed him. He enjoyed getting up whatever the time, walking about the surrounding hills and flopping into bed with a full tummy at his leisure. Three months passed and there was no sign of him moving on. His 'work' required my support and funding. I was caged; he was free. It dredged up old anguish I felt over Trevor that I thought I had processed but which I had clearly not. That incident settled inside me like silt in a river. It took another event, Martin's residence on the farm years later, for the anguish over Trevor to rise to the surface once more.

The situation dominated my meditations as I tried to figure out a strategy for dealing with Martin. Whatever I chose to do, I wanted to ensure I kept a compassionate open heart and avoid wallowing in my ego's umbrage. I had already replaced my former material values with more meaningful spiritual ones. Consequently, a theme arose repeatedly in meditation that I should simply let the situation be.

It seemed like a nice altruistic notion but there was still something nigglingly wrong with it and I couldn't identify what it was. A trace of favouritism and injustice bothered me. Three employees, that are like family to me, live on the property. Out of convenience, they took up residence in the staff quarters during the week. These quarters are basic brick structures with hot running water, proper sanitation and electricity, but they aren't nearly as spacious and well appointed as the main house and cottages on the ranch.

The staff contribute to the running of the property and live in their simpler quarters, yet Martin, who did not contribute to our communal living, was ensconced in one of the more luxurious cottages. What kind of message was I sending out to Martin and especially to my staff? It would have been fairer to let the senior staff member occupy the cottage and downgrade Martin to one of the staff quarters. Would Martin have accepted the swap without feeling insulted? I doubt it. This really bothered me as it might have been construed as low-grade racism as the staff are black folk and Martin is white. However, this was only one aspect of the situation and I was missing the real key to solving this dilemma. I had an inkling that it had to do with reciprocity. Martin and Trevor had given me friendship. It was the old story of give and take – and then, take some more. In his book on Influence, Robert Cialdini states it quite bluntly:

> A person who violates the reciprocity rule by accepting without attempting to return the good acts of others is actively disliked by the social group. [...] For the most part, however, there is a genuine distaste for individuals who fail to conform to the dictates of the reciprocity rule. Moocher and welsher are unsavory labels to be scrupulously shunned. So undesirable are they that we will sometimes agree to an unequal exchange in order to dodge them.[149]

At one of the Circle of Friends meetings during Martin's stay on the farm, I talked to the group about the personal pronoun *my* and its egoistic dangers. I drew a fifty-rand note from my wallet and gave it to one of the people there.

'Here, this is for you,' I said, genuinely parting with the money.

'No, I can't accept it,' was his reply.

'Why not?'

'Because it's not mine.'

---

[149] *Influence*, Robert Cialdini, HarperCollins, 2007.

'To whom does it belong?'

'You, it's your money. I didn't earn it; you did. I don't deserve it.'

'*My* money, you say. Look carefully at the note and tell me where you see my name giving me title to it?'

'Nowhere!'

'So, to whom does the note belong?'

'The government?'

'Exactly. It's a promissory note issued by the South African Reserve Bank and is signed by the Governor. The money isn't mine.'

'Yeah, but it's not mine either.'

'Ah, so it's just money, isn't it? It's *the* money and not *your* money or *my* money. What then is money?'

'I dunno ....' he said, unable to sense where the conversation was leading.

I stood up, walked across the room, picked up a large candle and offered it to him. 'What's this?'

'A candle?' he said sheepishly.

'Yeah, a candle. But what is it really?'

'I dunno ....' he repeated once again, shrugging his shoulders and bashfully looking around the room to solicit help from the others, but none was forthcoming.

'It's light and heat conveniently packaged, is it not? We couldn't carry light and heat in our pocket or purse but we can carry the candle and we could light it whenever we needed to convert its wax into light and heat. Correct?'

'Yeah, I suppose you're right.'

'So what then is money? It's solidified energy. It's common for energy to move between us when you and I interact in some way: it's part of the principle of reciprocity. In the past, one might have reciprocated with bartered goods and services. But the exchange of money is simpler.'

'Mmm.'

'Let's return to the candle for a moment. What is this candle?'

'Solidified light and heat!' he said confidently with a wry smile on his face.

'Wax!'

'Wait a bit ....'

'The candle is a lump of wax, nothing more, nothing less. It's only when we ignite it that it converts to light and heat. Therefore, what is money?'

'Paper?' he tendered gingerly.

'Exactly! It's a tiny worthless paper rectangle. It's only when it flows from one person to the next that it unlocks the energy that's inherent in it. I can swap its energy for food or deploy it in numerous other ways.'

I concluded the discussion by asking whether there was any merit in building a dam if one lived along the banks of a perennial river because one could draw water directly from it whenever one needed it. Since it was a guaranteed source of water, building an adjacent dam would seem pointless and somewhat neurotic.

We live in an abundant universe. Our source energy, spirit, flows endlessly from the godhead. It reminded me of one of those domed plasma lamps, a clear glass orb filled with a mixture of various noble gases. Inside, at its core, is a high-voltage electrode. Moving tendrils of coloured light radiate outwards from the central electrode to the glass on the outer encasement. The electrode represents the Divine, God, pure potential or whatever other terminology one

Not all Help is Helpful

chooses to use. The radiating plasma filaments symbolise spirit, our individual source energy flowing outwards from its central source, the Divine, God. Mind is the finger on the outside of the glass sphere that attracts and influences the path taken by the plasma tendrils. Spirit is a continuous conscious benign outflow of spiritual energy emanating from the Divine and manifesting in all of mind's creations.

We indeed live on the banks of a perennial river. Our energy flows from the electrode at the heart of the lamp. Our existence is permanent and our continuity assured. 'Are not five sparrows sold for two cents? Yet not one of them is forgotten before God. Indeed, the very hairs of your head are all numbered. Do not fear; you are more valuable than many sparrows.'[150]

If one lived next to the perennial river, there are only two reasons for building a dam: to climb the hill and see how big a dam your neighbour has; or to allay any nervous fear that the promise of a perennial river might fail. The former reason is egoistic and the latter lacks faith.

After coming to these realisations about money, I made a promise that I would never count it again. Money now flows into my wallet and from there back out into the world. If there is money in the wallet, I can spend it; if there isn't, I can't. Never once since making this promise has the wallet ever run dry but neither has it been stuffed with notes. It's always been just enough.

There is still a little experiment I'd like to conduct with money but I'm not sure that the subjects of my experiment would understand what it is that I'm trying to achieve. I would love to have a conveniently situated money jar. Clients could deposit my consulting fees into it and anybody needing money could take from it. I would tell the workers to help themselves to what they need at the end of each week. But there's a catch to it: I'm expecting them to take what they *need* and not what they *want*. Imagine if the staff could take enough to satisfy their needs for the week instead of accepting set wages. Their individual needs would naturally vary from week to week. However, if they took too much, others would go without or sacrifices would have to be made elsewhere. It would also be nice to let clients contribute whatever they felt was commensurate with the value they derived from our session together. I believe the

---

[150] Luke 12:6-7, *New American Standard Bible*

outcome of the experiment would ultimately find its natural balance and everyone would have a better sense of worth.

I returned to the man holding the fifty-rand note and proposed: 'Take the money and put it into your wallet.'

'Why, there's been no exchange of energy and I still don't feel I deserve it.'

'Why do you need a reason to take it? Just accept it and move on ....'

'Okay then. Thanks!' he exclaimed in a half-jocular, half-teasing tone.

'Thanks? Why do you say thanks?'

'Why not?'

'You've said it to create balance. It's a tiny exchange honouring the reciprocity rule. I've given you something and you feel obliged to reciprocate it, even if it is merely a polite word of gratitude. How do you think I would feel if you took the money and didn't say a word about it?'

'A bit pissed off?'

'It's nice to give without expecting a return. But how could I give you a gift that benefits you without impoverishing me?'

He thought about it for a moment and replied, 'I dunno ....'

'By giving you love, unconditional love. Love is the purest gift. Giving material things may easily create imbalance, which would invoke the reciprocity rule to bring the inequality back into balance. With unconditional love, however, the more I let it flow, the richer we both become.'

A few days after this, and after many years in which I'd had no contact with Trevor, I wrote him another email. I came to realise that I kept myself trapped in a cage of expectations of payback. I needed to learn that I had the power to set myself free. Until then, I believed they held me captive through their inconsiderate behaviour. What would happen in my heart if I turned

Trevor's loan into a gift of unconditional love, one that had no expectation of return? I explained this to him in my email. I also vowed that any other appropriate outflow of money to another person would always be a gift of unconditional love. I would never again lend money; I would henceforth give it away. What the other person did with the gift would be their issue. How they spent the money altered their karma; the way I gave it to them affected mine.

I now had a different framework in which to work with Martin but, after a year with him on the property, something was clearly still wrong. I still anguished over his residency. My unconditional monetary and material gifts weren't helpful to Martin, a point well proven when a once very close friend wrote to me after I had given her some assistance:

> I don't even know where to start apart from saying that I am so sorry I have not paid back your money. I don't know whom to turn to anymore and I am at rock bottom. My life has been an absolute nightmare the past year and I have lost everything. [My partner] brought me to my knees financially and emotionally. I am struggling to find work and am spending most of my days in my room. The only place I could find to stay for a while is with a friend of a friend and it is dreadful! I am desperate to get out of here, as the conditions are very bad. I just don't know what to do or how to do it anymore. I do not have any money for petrol and airtime, and sometimes I go days without food! I know it sounds dramatic but I can only be honest, put my pride in my pocket and try reach out to people I know. I am in a desperate situation, and if there is anything you can help me with, and please let me know if you know of any work and a decent safe place to stay. I have a few pieces of furniture that I am prepared to give in return for rent or money until I have a job. I am very embarrassed about my situation and having to ask for help but I have exhausted every avenue already.

These are not isolated pleas for help from desperate people and the problem arises as to how one can best help them – all of them. The ego's fear is that if one opens up one's wallet and allows people to take what they need, they will plunder our resources and we will eventually find ourselves huddled together with them in a dingy room without food. Surely, there is a limit to what we can give before jeopardising ourselves.

Shortly after the African National Congress [ANC] came to power, white South Africans were terrified of possible 'redistribution of wealth', transferring white assets into black hands. A journalist calculated that if all white-held wealth were redistributed to black people, there would be a once-off transaction of say five hundred rand per recipient, after which there would be nothing further to transfer and the economic system would collapse. The risk of helping too many people might therefore cause one's own financial demise.

This is true if one believes that money is the only form of help. It is often an easy way out, a quick way to fob off responsibility and avoid any personal effort. A quick buck passed through the car window to the beggar at the traffic light, and we're done. No further involvement is necessary; we appease our conscience and we are free to go.

Further meditation on the Martin matter yielded a surprising insight: 'Not all forms of help are helpful.' I thought I was helping Martin by letting him stay. I thought it was unconditional love by putting food on his table. What I suddenly realised was that my help was not at all helpful. Instead of enabling him, it stripped away his incentive to help himself.

Buddha could take a hollow grass straw, place it into a devotee's nostril and suck out the dark sooty cloud of karma. Christ too has the power to wash away the sins of the world. Then one begs an answer to the question, why don't they? What would happen if they sucked out our karma, if they instantly washed away our sins? We would most likely come to instant enlightenment; we would reach Buddhahood, Christhood or *Samadhi*. But if Buddha or Christ took away all karma, it would leave us with a life of permanent inconsequence. We would have nothing further to do, nothing further to learn. Human life is an intricate learning experience and one can never judge what profound wisdom may come from some of the darkest moments in one's life.

Imagine for a moment that you are enjoying a picnic with friends or family in the dappled shade under the big willow tree down by the river. The water flows by swiftly and silently until it cascades over the lip of the waterfall just a short distance downriver. There, meters below, you can hear the thunderous roar as the water crashes onto the rocks below. It's a tranquil and happy scene with laughter and frivolity as everyone enjoys the scrumptious meal laid out on the chequered tablecloth. Then you notice a stranger walking down to the river's bank, midway between you and the waterfall. He rolls up his trousers, takes off his shoes and begins to wade out into the river.

'What idiot is this?' you think, for if he makes one false step, one slip on a mossy rock, the current will sweep him over the edge and to his certain death. You now have quite a dilemma, so you tie a rope around your waist and around the willow tree and you hasten to wade out into the river, grabbing hold of the guy, saying, 'What do you think you're doing? Do you not realise the danger of your actions and the dilemma you have caused me?' and you haul the protesting man over your shoulder, like a sack of potatoes, and deposit him on the bank from whence he started.

'You don't understand,' he protests. 'I must get to the other side!'

'Why didn't you say so,' and lifting him again, you deposit him on the other bank, knowing that you are safely tethered to the tree and that you've just done him a huge favour; but the guy's still not content with your kindness.

'Getting to the other side,' he protests, 'isn't about reaching a destination. It's about having undertaken a journey. I need to prove that I can, against all odds, reach the other bank.'

Now, your dilemma deepens. What do you do? You can't return to your picnic and ignore him as though he doesn't exist. The picnic will never be the same again as everyone will stand there shocked and stunned by his solitary attempt to cross the dangerous river.

We've already explored the wisdom that comes from some of our most difficult experiences and came to the understanding that we can quickly transform apparent suffering into divine tutorship when we set aside ego's fear of dying and begin to identify ourselves with spirit. How then could we intercede and provide help that is truly helpful for this man crossing the river of life?

Anchored as we are, with the rope tied around our waist and the tree trunk, symbolising our spiritual security, we walk out next to him, hand outstretched, saying 'Here is my hand, take hold of it whenever you wish. I will not grab you but as soon as you reach out to me, I will reciprocate with equal force and, conversely, I will let go as soon as you do. I will walk ahead, to show you where to place your feet, pointing out the treacherous as well as the stable rocks so that you might find your passage across the river.'

Should the man slip and fall to his death and not reach out for help, the onus would rest upon him and not upon you; for you neither neglected him nor interfered with his crossing the river of life.

I realised that I had to help Martin differently and served him notice. After three months, he left angrily and hurt that I had sent him on his way. Nonetheless there was a lot of cushioning to soften the blow as I gave him extended notice and paid for his new accommodation for a finite period. Martin has come to the brink of the chasm on many occasion but he always seems to rescue his situation at the eleventh hour, just before disaster strikes.

I've spent further days with Ram Dass during a subsequent trip abroad and will perhaps do so repeatedly as often as conditions permit. I asked him about my actions regarding Martin and others. He reached out his left hand, placed it on the wall next to him, and began to stroke the surface gently, asking, 'Do you love my wall, Tom?'

'It's a nice wall, Ram Dass.'

'Love it,' he said with that idiosyncratic glint in his eye, 'Love it.'

He stroked the wall for a while, letting his message take root in my consciousness: 'Love everything .... Love everything,' he added, sighing contentedly as he waved his hand slowly through the air as if to equally bless everything, inside and outside the room.

I knew that it was spiritually acceptable for me to honour another's choices and the karma they accrued or disposed of during their lifetime of experiences. I knew that even if they died, all that would have occurred was the dropping of their body as they returned to their source. Mind might separate spirit, one's source energy, from form for a moment but like a snail that withdraws into its shell after being touched, mind's curiosity would soon direct source energy into new formations, each yielding further opportunities for wisdom.

This is of course a very delicate attitude to embrace because ego can quickly take ownership of this principle in a careless attempt to abdicate responsibility in order to avoid compassionately serving others. It's much more difficult at first to disown ego's futile attempts to shirk responsibility and to let one's spirituality hold the other in a gentle compassionate space, walking with them across the river. I'm now able to be Martin's friend, regardless of the karma he chooses to hold and the experiences he allows himself to draw into his sphere. I will always be there for him and others, to help shine the light of my being upon their footpath so that we might find our way together through the darkness.

After Johann and I ended our fourteen-year relationship, I moved out of the city to Protea Ranch and, some years later, around 1990, met Mark and we shared the next decade together. He's artistic, creative, and insightful. He has a flippant attitude toward other's opinions of him and, in that regard, he taught me a lot about living freely in a bigoted world. We had our difficulties. There were times when we lived together and others when we lived apart, especially over divergent views over the recreational use of drugs.

I was the fortunate one out of a close group of twenty-one friends of varying ages and gender, to come out of the experience of early to middle adulthood having gained spiritual insightfulness. Others weren't so fortunate: two died from drug overdoses, more than half lost jobs, relationships and, sadly, their dignity. Nobody emerged from their drug experiments unchanged. Why did we all do it? I believe that life seemed quite pointless at the time.

Dad took a job with Standard Bank at eighteen and slowly worked his way up the ranks until he reached Senior Manager at the bank's Stock Exchange Branch. It was a lifetime commitment to one company and our parents taught us to believe that this was common practice – to demonstrate loyalty, to hang in no matter the personal problems that might arise, and never to quit. Regrettably, after all those faithful years of service, dad's exit from the bank was far from the golden handshake he'd expected. Dad was an expert on South African Foreign Exchange regulations. During the course of his work, he had two different strategies to take in 1978 regarding an inheritance a client of his had received in London. South African monetary policies became very complicated in apartheid's final decades to cope with international sanctions, and local wealthy citizens sought every avenue (including dubious transactions) to stash money abroad. The country ran a dual currency, the Rand and the Blocked-Rand, and the legislation was full of loopholes due to its complexity. Somehow, dad's client had a financial advantage in one of the two possible strategies relating to the repatriation of his inheritance, something to do with repatriating it as Blocked-Rand instead of Rand. Anyway, bank inspectors, during their routine checks on branch adherence to policy and law, uncovered this transaction and brought my father's decision into question. The South African Reserve Bank, the country's central reserve, decided to put the matter before the courts to test the law and in order to close the loophole in the legislation, and dad was charged with fraud. Standard Bank immediately suspended him on full pay, pending the court's decision. The High Court acquitted him, on 6 June 1978, of all charges, whereupon Standard Bank dismissed him because they couldn't have senior staff under suspicion or with a tarnished reputation. No matter how much dad protested, Standard Bank refused to reinstate him and summarily withdrew his pension, medical aid and other benefits because they were 'discretionary privileges'. It devastated dad. How, after a lifetime of loyalty and commitment, could the bank be so heartless? Through some prudent property deals, he scraped together a small pension that lasted him through to his death in 2001.

His only letter to me, written by hand on a small sheet of white paper, reads:

> Tom, my son, you have no idea how it hurts me to put you to such a test – a test that I have imposed upon you – not of your choice but through my doings. Please forgive me. You are stifled but stick it out a little longer until you get financially on your feet and then express yourself. I understand now and will do then. I think I know you better than all and perhaps, you too know me more than others. I cannot speak so I write. Dad.[151]

The bank's dealings with dad popped my loyalty bubble and I took on a very different attitude towards life as what, in corporate jargon, might be called a Future Valued Prospect. Live for now, was my new lifestyle policy, for tomorrow one might die. Employment was no longer a dedication but a transaction around the supply of a service; I had something to trade and my employer could buy it from me at a given rate. Suddenly, it was about feathering my nest and not satisfying some shareholder's aims for better profits.

Our group of twenty-one was a microcosm of a larger population of people that had lost hope. Post-apartheid South Africa was a land of opportunity for a segment of the black population who found a bright future in a newly liberated land but, outside that rather limited range of people, the rest saw no future at all. The promise of future value was empty and the people were disillusioned. Heavy partying and the recreational use of drugs brought one into the now and lifted one's spirits for a while but it too was a hollow promise, a transient myth that pretended to offer something better. Mondays were awful, hung-over, dull days. Tuesdays were the worst with post-partying blues, lethargy and a deep sense of remorse, regret and feelings of pointlessness. Wednesdays were better as the prospect of the next Friday night's druggy dance floor abandon approached with its marvellous ability to let one escape the senselessness of it all.

I say I was the fortunate one to have come through the experience better off because my use of drugs never ventured further than Ecstasy, LSD and a little weed. Others in the group were more adventurous and tried Kat and Cocaine and the former became a real problem for many, including Mark. The hallucinogenic effects of LSD liberated my mind and let me see further than would have otherwise been possible. It became a significant contributor to my spiritual

---

[151] 10th May, 1978

awakening and I bless it for having done so. I know that as I write these words, others may read them and find licence to experiment but I've seen too much heartache to sanction them outright; but then, the little voice of sanity speaks quietly in my ear and reminds me not to judge. Who knows what wisdom comes from crossing the river at this place, even if one should slip and the river should sweep one away.

Mark lived in one of the cottages from time to time, coming and going as he found his way in life. Some of his darkest days were after his mother's death. She championed him and, in her neediness, for she was always a sickly woman having had brain surgery in her younger years that dulled her functions, she gave Mark purpose and he looked after her unselfishly. She lived with him up until her death, after which he found that he couldn't cope. Mark used Kat to support himself but the grief of losing his mother overwhelmed him and twice, in his townhouse apartment in Fourways, he attempted suicide. I lived in dread because I never knew when I would receive a call from him seeking help.

Life soon unravelled for Mark and he came to live at the ranch for a while and turned his attention to painting sacred glass artwork, thirty-six exquisite pieces in all, each with a Hindu or Buddhist theme and done on framed sheets of glass with liquid glass-paint. He tried to sell his art but it was too unusual for the average South African and he sat with his stock of paintings and became ever so pessimistic about life.

One morning during the week, Richard, the longest serving worker on the farm, came to me. 'Come quickly, Mark is calling you and I think he needs your help!' I urgently followed him across to the cottage where I knocked on the door and called, but I couldn't hear anything.

'Are you sure that Mark called for me, Richard?'

'Yes, I heard him. But he's very sick.'

'Run and fetch the spare set of keys, quickly now! Do it quickly!'

As Richard ran off, I called again, louder and more urgently than before, 'Markie, are you okay? Answer me!'

A faint, shallow voice replied from inside, 'Come quickly, I'm dying and I need you with me.'

My heart pounded and I expected the worst and the few short minutes it took Richard to bring the keys seemed endless. I shook so much that I couldn't get the key into the lock and I turned to Richard: 'Open up here for me; but do it quickly!'

Inside, lying on the cold kitchen floor tiles, lay Mark, his eyes sunken into dark pools. Their sparkle had gone; the dilated pupils stayed transfixed on some imaginary spot somewhere in the distance. His lips were parched and his skin was sebaceous oily, grey putty, cold and clammy to the touch. He lay on his back but his entire body had contracted such that only his shoulders, hips and heels touched the floor.

I squatted next to him, placed my hand on his forehead and, holding back an overwhelming urge to burst into tears, asked, 'What has happened?'

His soft, tired breath carried its barely audible message, 'I just want to die.'

'Why?'

'I can't go on any more. Will you be here with me while I die, because I don't want to do this on my own?'

'You know I will be here for you but I think there is more living to do. Let me help you by taking you to hospital right now.'

'No ... no ... please, no!'

Here I was having a picnic with my friends under the willow tree when a guy came along, rolled up his trousers and waded out into the river. Mark was inches from death and asked me to be with him as he died. I wanted to tether myself to the willow tree, rush out to save him and take him to hospital, but it was as though an arm reached out behind me and gently held me back, urging me to think spiritually instead of egoistically.

I sat flat on the floor, lifted his head onto my lap and held his cold and dying body. 'I can be with you if that's what you would like me to do. I can go through this experience with you but we're not going to do this here on the cold kitchen floor. Would it be okay if I helped you back upstairs to your bedroom where I can stay with you through this process?'

His motionless eyes moved for the first time and slowly rolled backwards as he looked at me. 'I love you,' he said. 'Thank you for doing this for me.'

Richard and I helped him back upstairs. The cottage was immaculate. He'd tidied up and cleaned everything. Fresh linen adorned the bed and there was a neatly written suicide note and CD, which the note requested be played at his funeral, on the coffee table in the upstairs space that served as combined bedroom and living room.

'I don't want to mess things up so please put me on the spare bed.'

I didn't quite understand his rationale but obliged and laid him on the single guest bed under the slope of the thatched roof, covered him with the white duvet, and asked, 'How did you find yourself on the kitchen floor? It doesn't make sense, everything is so perfect here. Why were you downstairs?'

'I wanted to die here on the sofa but I needed to go to the loo because my tummy began to cramp and I didn't want to make a mess but I collapsed on the way back through the kitchen and couldn't get back up.'

'When was this?'

'Around midnight.'

'You've been there all that time?'

'I called for you but you couldn't hear me ....'

'It's okay now. Everything is okay now ....'

I couldn't have had the courage to accede to Mark's request had it not been that I'd observed others dying, the most significant being with dad during his death.

I didn't see much of mom and dad after my excommunication from the Jehovah's Witnesses in my late twenties but, as he got older, he relaxed the shunning rules of the Witnesses and let me visit more regularly. Around 2000, he began to manifest horrendous eczema on his legs, buttocks, back and arms. Oozing, itchy weeping sores plagued him and he found little relief from the medicines he was prescribed. His eczema was a paradoxical parallel to the eczema I had as an infant. I was hospitalised in my second year and had it not been for my mother's strong will, determination and courage, I would have certainly died there.

'I'm taking my child home,' she said one Saturday afternoon to the doctor in the paediatric ward.

'No, Mrs Budge, you can't do that because he will die.'

'But he's dying anyway ....'

'What is there that you can do for this child that we can't do here?' he retorted authoritatively.

'I can give him his mother's love.'

So she signed an indemnity release form and brought me home to die, but of course I didn't. But I had a deep empathy for Dad's eczema and couldn't help wondering what the common connection was between him and me.

By early 2001, the doctors diagnosed prostate cancer, which soon spread into dad's bone marrow via his pelvic bone. It was painful and I reflected sadly on the emotional stuff he suppressed and the effects that it might have had on his core, literally. About ten days before Easter, mom asked if I would be willing to come and help her to nurse dad. By now, my spirituality had blossomed nicely and I was able to set aside my prejudices against the Witnesses and had, long before that, forgiven my family for the way they'd disowned me.

I slept on a makeshift bed behind the sofa in the lounge of their small one-bedroom cottage and, lying there night after night, listening for changes in dad's breathing throughout the night, had ample time to think of the injustice of how I was being treated even in those troubled times. There was a spare bed in the main house where Anne and Kenneth lived but I had to be content (and indeed I was) sleeping in the narrow space behind the sofa. Whenever Jehovah's Witness 'Brothers' and 'Sisters' came to visit, I was quickly despatched off the property where I had to wait until they had gone.

Dad's condition deteriorated rapidly and we chose to let him die at home in familiar surroundings and bathed in the love of his family. The family doctor offered hospitalisation but supported our wishes and popped in every day to monitor dad's condition.

On the Saturday of the Easter weekend, the doctor notified us that dad's death was imminent. We already knew that. Mom switched roles and took on her former nursing identity, running their bedroom according to impeccable hospital rules and standards. She had seen the same signs the doctor had, and we were ready to see him through his last few hours.

'Are you strong enough to do this with me, my boy?' she asked.

'Oh yes mom, I certainly am.'

We changed dad's linen late on Saturday evening and he never moved his body from its position again. By Sunday, we could see marked changes in his pallor and the room was filled with an odour associated with the dying. We separated their single beds and I sat on mom's bed, holding dad's hand, watching the fire-element slowly leave as his fingernails turned from their usual pink through shades of blue. As the fire-element faded, his body cooled and his hand became clammy. Mom summoned the family and one by one they arrived and took their seats around his bed.

Justin, Anne's eldest child, sat on my left. I hadn't seen him since he was a boy of six or seven and here he was, a grown young man. Anne came and left with mom who officiated in a matronly way. About six or seven of us had gathered around and the atmosphere was sombre, but that wasn't my personal experience. The closer dad came to leaving his body, the more I sensed the freedom of his spirit in the room. There was a luminosity that I cannot explain and a communication between him and me that occurred in a telepathic way. Around mid-morning I desperately needed the toilet and tried to let go dad's hand but, even though he was so close to leaving, he firmed his grip and I felt that he didn't want me to stray too far away.

'I'm coming right back,' I said.

Slowly, the air-element began to leave and his breath became shallower, until it was just a reflexive gurgle deep in his throat yet the room became more alive with the swirling, dancing energy of ours in a frivolous playfulness during which we annulled all offenses, found ultimate forgiveness and united the kindred spirits of father and son forever in love.

When dad died in the early afternoon, Justin responded first to dad's suffocating sigh that marked the end by leaping up, beseeching mom, 'Granny, do something for Poppy; do something!'

'There's nothing more to do, my darling,' she said, still holding onto her nurse's role for comfort and support. 'He's gone Justin, my sweetheart, he's gone.'

Pandemonium erupted in the room as everyone jumped up, hugging each other, sobbing uncontrollably. Justin's next response caught everyone by surprise, including me. He sat back down on the bed next to me as I sat quietly holding dad's lifeless hand, revelling in the passage his spirit had just taken and the love that engulfed us. Sitting beside me, Justin turned to me and hugged me very tightly, saying, 'Uncle Tom, I love you so much. I've always loved you ever since I was a little boy. I don't know why we've been so horrible to you and it hurts me but I still love you a lot.'

I held him tight and replied, 'My dearest Justin, I too never stopped loving you. I've never blamed you for anything you've done to me and I'm so glad to hear what you have just told me.'

The room fell silent and all attention left dad's lifeless corpse for a moment as everyone's eyes turned to us in stunned shock. A minute passed in which time nobody knew what to do until Kenneth, Justin's father, called him from the room to the main house where he chastised him for his improper behaviour. The atmosphere changed quickly to one of tension and awkwardness and soon everyone left to have tea at the main house – everyone, that is, but Mom and me.

'Help me to wash your dad and change his pyjamas.'

'Sure.'

I hadn't slept much during that week. Tired and smelly and in need of a change of clothes, I decided to go back home to freshen up as soon as the undertakers had fetched Dad's body. Various family members gathered on the pavement outside the house and I walked up to greet them on my way out but only one hugged me and gave condolences. The rest were so brainwashed by Witness dogma that they couldn't do so even at an occasion like this.

When I came to my senses, I was in my silver Jaguar speeding down the eastern highway out of Johannesburg at 220km per hour, tears streaming down my face, overwhelmed with grief, not at dad's death but because of the manner in which I was treated. I identified profoundly with the lyrics of the track that I was listening to: 'Too much love can kill you', on Queen's tribute record to Freddy Mercury, *Made in Heaven*.

I showered, changed and drove back to mom's house, entering through the garage to avoid meeting anyone inside the main residence as there appeared to be visitors. I knocked, opened the door and entered. Mom said, 'Not now my boy, the Elders are here to give me some support. Come back later.' I drove home, climbed the hill at the back of the property and sat on a rock with my two Doberman companions, Jock and Juno, sleeping at my feet. I stayed there well into the night because I couldn't move. It was a day filled with immense contrast.

A few days later, I gave mom a lift to the Kingdom Hall to attend dad's Memorial Service. Kenneth had announced to the congregation that a disfellowshipped person would attend – a protocol hitherto unheard of. I parked in the grounds, adjacent to the hall. Many of my colleagues and friends had gathered inside. I helped to support mom by her arm and led her to the side entrance. She stepped in and someone helped her to a reserved seat in the front row. I waved to those whom I recognised inside but the Witnesses barred me from entering. One of the attendants barricaded my pathway and I couldn't follow mom up front. Embarrassed, humiliated and infuriated I turned and walked back to my car, got in and began to reverse out of the parking when I saw Mercia running towards me. I've known her for years as she attended the congregation where I grew up.

'They're not going to do this to you! I won't let them,' she burst out, genuinely concerned. She opened the door, escorted me back into the hall and up to the front row, muttering to the attendants and forcing them to rearrange some of the seating so that I could sit next to my mother. Johann later said, 'It was the worst and most embarrassing situation I'd ever experienced inside a church.' Another friend, also with the name Johan, is a senior journalist for one of South Africa's leading Sunday Afrikaans newspapers and he was so disgusted by what occurred that he wrote a half-page article about it that appeared on the next weekend edition.[152] The official stance from the Witnesses was that it was standard practice, demanded by God.

---

[152] *Rapport*, publication date unknown

It takes a lot of reframing to get to the point Jesus did when, at the height of his abuse, he said, 'Father, forgive them, for they do not know what they're doing.'[153]

I sat with Mark through his mother's death and experienced death up close many times. Every human death I observed was an okay experience; source energy withdrawing from its manifestation in form. The cliché is to 'go home', soul returning to its maker, wiser, more qualified, and perhaps sanctified. I just don't see it that way. Spirit Is. It's always perfect and in a state of perpetual love awareness. Death is a mind game and has nothing to do with spirit. Mind, as spirit's creative agent, directs the flow of source energy into the manifestation it desires. When mind attaches to form, conception occurs; when mind detaches, death occurs but spirit remains unchanged throughout.

Sitting with dying Mark wasn't hard to do. I could cross the river with him without judgement. I was a little nervous about the legal ramifications of letting him die without seeking medical help and I imagined a criminal charge of manslaughter if a charge like that would stick, so I went downstairs and called Mark's doctor, and asked, 'What do I do? I'm a bit frightened of the legal consequences.'

'Is he lucid?'

'Yes, he's very weak but calm and lucid.'

'Well, Tom, it's quite simple then. He's refusing treatment and he's perfectly within his legal rights to do so. If his condition changes, however, and he slips into a coma, the rules change and you will then have to call me immediately. We will then have to intercede as his proxy. More importantly, are you able and willing to stay with him until the end?'

'Yes, I can do it for him.'

Mark had drawn up a full syringe of various household poisons and, around midnight, injected the lethal cocktail into the vein in his left arm. A little while later, when he hadn't died, he repeated the exercise with what remained in the jar. It was then that he became violently ill and, not wanting to mess things up, not wanting to cause me any inconvenience, went to the loo and collapsed. I found him the next morning and we sat together through the long hours

---

[153] Luke 23:34, *Holy Bible*, New International Version

of the day as he neared death. In the afternoon things changed somewhat. His left arm swelled out of proportion and began to turn a strange blue colour, but tiny pink patches came back to his cheeks as though applied with a rouge brush. In the late afternoon I asked Mark how he was doing.

'I don't think I'm going to die. Why do you think I can't die?'

'It's a tough thing for me to say, Markie, but I can only imagine that the Divine Goddess has more work for you to do. If you are not ready to die, there is certainly some other reason for living that you can't foresee right now.'

'But I really want to die and I'm so sad that I can't.'

'I understand that you came to the very edge and thought you couldn't go further, that you had to stop here. I was okay taking these last steps with you, setting aside my prejudice, my judgement, and having to stop myself from bringing you back to me, because I've not once wanted to let you go. However, it's now something in you that refuses to die, that wants to live, and again I will stand by you, without judgement, letting you discover what that yearning for life is all about.'

'How can I face life after this?' he asked, with tones of failure laced into his voice.

'You haven't failed. Quite to the contrary, you've given me an incredible gift today, you've taught me that my belief about life and death isn't just a theory; you've allowed me to test my faith to the fullest and, for that, I'm immensely grateful. You have also tested yourself to the edges of your ability and you've come back from that place. It might take a while longer for you to understand what you are supposed to do but I know that there is a part of you today, which seeks life and not death. Give that part space to discover and grow.'

He rested his head on the pillow and sighed, tears running freely from his eyes.

'My dearest friend,' I continued, 'what would you like me to do now? There is a chance that you could lose your arm or that your internal system might collapse. I'll do whatever you ask.'

'Take me to hospital.'

I called for an ambulance and the paramedics. Two young men and a woman in blue overalls arrived and rushed upstairs. They were out to save lives and completely missed the profundity of the occasion. They asked me to step aside as though I could offer no help. They swiftly inserted a drip and, without a scrap of emotion, transferred Mark to a stretcher, and took him outside to the ambulance. Red and white strobe lights swept across the garden in the fading winter light of late afternoon.

Mark is still one of my best friends. He's a deeply spiritual being who can't always see his own magnificence. He teaches me always without knowing that he's done it. Martin might not like my reluctance to give him money but he's yet to take hold of my hand that I keep outstretched, offering him stability to cross his part of the river that he chooses to challenge.

Conclusion

Writing this book has been one of the most cathartic experiences ever. When writing parts of it, tears poured from my eyes and the wastepaper basket filled with tissues. There were times when I couldn't write any more, exhausted and emotionally depleted. I had to give it a break, sometimes for days, sometimes months. I reflect upon those tears and realise that they aren't mourning what was lost, they're not despair at what occurred, but they're sadness for the things we do to one another; the way we abuse instead of nurturing; the corruption of love, twisting it into rusty metal sculptures of tangled steel and power. There's sadness for a lust to dominate, to rape and plunder. There's sadness for the fact that we can't seem to get it right to live harmoniously, to live alongside nature instead of over it.

The book, however, is not only a personal cathartic experience, choosing to share what I've never dared to share before, but also an opportunity, through writing, to organise my spiritual thinking. There were times during the writing where I glowed at the profundity of thought and blessed the source from whence it came. I truly believe that I have had many previous incarnations under careful tutorship. During my 2012 stay with Ram Dass, he said, 'You are only the second person I've said this to – you are Maharaj-ji's true teacher.' It's difficult not allowing ego to play with such an endorsement, but somehow I know that my experiences are the threads in a story that allow me to pass on what I know. I hope that I succeeded in keeping the storyline free of self-indulgence while yet true to the message I'm keen to convey.

www.ingramcontent.com/pod-product-compliance
Lightning Source LLC
Chambersburg PA
CBHW081510040426
42447CB00013B/3171